CRACK99

CRACK99

The Takedown of
a $100 Million Chinese
Software Pirate

DAVID LOCKE HALL

W. W. NORTON & COMPANY
Independent Publishers Since 1923
New York • London

For information about permission to reproduce selections from this book,
write to Permissions, W. W. Norton & Company, Inc.,
500 Fifth Avenue, New York, NY 10110

For information about special discounts for bulk purchases,
please contact W. W. Norton Special Sales
at specialsales@wwnorton.com or 800-233-4830

Manufacturing by RR Donnelley Harrisonburg
Book design by Dana Sloan
Production manager: Devon Zahn

Library of Congress Cataloging-in-Publication Data

Hall, David Locke, author.
CRACK99 : the takedown of a $100 million Chinese software pirate /
David Locke Hall. — First edition.
    pages cm
Includes bibliographical references.
ISBN 978-0-393-24954-5 (hardcover)
1. Computer crimes—United States—Case studies. 2. Hacking—
China—Case studies. 3. Software piracy—China—Case studies.
4. Criminal investigation—United States—Case studies. 5. National
security—United States—Case studies. I. Title.
HV6773.2.H355 2015
364.16'8—dc23
                        2015022463

W. W. Norton & Company, Inc.
500 Fifth Avenue, New York, N.Y. 10110
www.wwnorton.com

W. W. Norton & Company Ltd.
Castle House, 75/76 Wells Street, London W1T 3QT

1 2 3 4 5 6 7 8 9 0

For my family

There is a tide in the affairs of men,

Which taken at the flood, leads on to fortune.

Omitted, all the voyage of their life is bound in shallows and in miseries.

On such a full sea are we now afloat.

And we must take the current when it serves, or lose our ventures.

—WILLIAM SHAKESPEARE,
Julius Caesar, Act 4, Scene 3

No maze   all is surprised   True deal

—XIANG LI
www.crack99.com

Contents

Introduction

THE DAY AFTER TOMORROW.

The Chinese BZK-005 drone executes a slow leftward turn during its routine patrol of the airspace above a string of uninhabited islands in the East China Sea, northeast of Taiwan. The Chinese call them the Diaoyu Islands. The Japanese do not; they call them the Senkaku Islands, illustrating an important point: when it comes to this territory, the Chinese and the Japanese don't agree on anything. Each country claims ownership, and asserts exclusive sovereignty, no doubt because of the islands' rumored oil and gas reserves, which have yet to be exploited.

The BZK-005 is a long-range unmanned aerial vehicle used in multiple mission sets, including surveillance. When the data link from the BZK-005 to the People's Liberation Army base on the Chinese mainland fails, no one gets excited; this has happened before, and it will be corrected shortly. This time, however, things are different. Although a squad of technicians swarms into the control room, no one can identify a problem with the data link. It has simply ceased to exist. There is a reason for this: the BZK-005 has ceased to exist. This is what happens when a Chinese BZK-005 is hit by a Sidewinder from a Japanese F-15 fighter.

People's Liberation Army Air Force J-16 fighters launch in response and quickly engage with the Japanese F-15s. If there were a way to watch this from a safe distance, it would look something like an air show—only deadly. The dogfighting is intense, littering the East China Sea with burning aircraft and burning airmen. It lasts as long as the fuel does, ending in a draw.

The USS *George Washington*, CVN 73, and her battle group are on patrol in the Philippine Sea. The carrier receives a flash message directing her northwest toward the disputed island chain. Two F-18 Hornets launch as aviators fill the ready room. Awaiting the intel brief, they mill about speculating on the situation and spreading the latest scuttlebutt. The room smells of burnt coffee and aviation fuel. The Chinese government issues a stern warning to the United States: stay out of it, or suffer the consequences. The threat is ignored, and the *George Washington* continues steaming northwest. Chinese J-16 fighters intercept her and are escorted out of the operating area by U.S. Navy F-18s. All is well until a salvo of Chinese antisatellite missiles is launched against the U.S. Navy's Fleet Satellite Communications System, isolating the *George Washington*.

"WAR!" scream the headlines.

This would be a bad day by any measure. But it would be particularly galling to learn that the technology employed by the Chinese during this bad day—from the drones to the antisatellite missiles to the fighter radar—was produced in the United States, that the ability of the Chinese to neutralize the U.S. Navy was enabled by the crown jewels of U.S. enterprise stolen by Chinese cybercriminals.

The United States is the victim of the greatest transfer of wealth in history. Digital thieves overseas—particularly in China—are systematically stealing U.S. intellectual property, largely without adverse consequences. The value of the information and technology being stolen each year is staggering: hundreds of billions of dollars.

Xiang Li was part of this Chinese cybercrime collective and the most prolific Chinese cyber pirate ever caught. From his bastion in Chengdu, China, he operated CRACK99, a website that from 2008 until the time of his arrest in 2011 sold powerful advanced industrial-grade software, the access controls to which had been circumvented—or cracked. The stolen software was worth more than $100 million and covered a lot of technological ground: aerospace and aviation simulation and design, communications systems design, electromagnetic simulation, explosive simulation, intelligence analysis, precision tooling, oil field management, and manufacturing plant design.

Cyber pirates like Xiang Li complement the Chinese government's national strategy to steal U.S. technology. One of the thousands of software titles for sale on CRACK99 was Satellite Tool Kit (STK) 8.0, designed by Analytical Graphics Incorporated to enable the U.S. military and aerospace industry to simulate missile launches and flight trajectories—and to track objects in flight, such as missiles, aircraft (manned and unmanned), and satellites. Moreover, Chinese hackers have reportedly stolen radar software for the $1.4 trillion F-35 stealth joint strike fighter, a fifth-generation tactical fighter still in the testing phase, employing the most advanced U.S. stealth technology. These thefts call into question the ability of the F-35 to remain stealthy in a future conflict with China. Chinese hackers have also reportedly stolen software relating to other military platforms, such as the Global Hawk high-resolution surveillance drone, the UH-60 Black Hawk helicopter, and missile defense systems, including Patriot, Aegis, and Terminal High Altitude Area Defense (THAAD). Some of these digital crimes are sponsored directly by the Chinese government; others—like Xiang Li's—are motivated by money. Either way, the Chinese are stealing U.S. technology to their strategic advantage, shifting the balance of power away from the United States.

The potential consequences are epic. So what is the U.S. government doing about it?

CRACK99

1 | PERFECT SURE

SPECIAL AGENT MIKE RONAYNE AND I sat in a blacked-out Chevy Tahoe outside the arrivals terminal. It was four a.m. and dark as ebony, except for the sickly amber exterior lighting. The humidity was stifling, only occasionally relieved by a welcome puff of sea breeze. We would have been nursing cups of strong black coffee, except that we didn't have any. On the Pacific island of Saipan, there aren't a lot of options at four a.m., coffee-wise.

"If this guy doesn't show up—," Ronayne began.

"I know," I interrupted. We were all alone on this one.

Ronayne's cell phone rang. It was Brendan Cullen, another special agent from Homeland Security Investigations (HSI). He was posted in the immigration bay, watching passengers deplane the flight from Chengdu, China.

"Brendan has eyes on," said Ronayne.

We focused on the terminal, which had suddenly come to life with a swarm of activity. Abruptly, the doors opened and a flood of Chinese nationals poured out, flowing in an orderly stream to waiting buses— orderly except for one kid who got loose, running around behind the bus, pursued by a pudgy man in a Hawaiian shirt.

That's when we saw him: Xiang Li, the $100 million software pirate.

We had been waiting more than a year and a half for this moment ever since Brendan Cullen called me in late December 2009, when I was still in government service as a federal prosecutor. I was at home on leave when my cell phone rang.

"Something's wrong," said Cullen, sounding unusually tentative.

Cullen was a man's man. Tall and lean, he might have been cast as Clark Kent, except that he didn't wear glasses. He was a superb athlete, a star football player in high school and college. If your idea of former football players involves meatheads with big necks, you'd be right about one thing: the big neck. But Cullen was no meathead; he was not only street smart, as the best agents always are, but also a deep thinker who wasn't afraid to close the shades and silently ponder a problem. He didn't miss much; when he looked at you with his unblinking blue eyes, he seemed to be reading your mind.

On December 23, 2009, Cullen delivered a brief in Exton, Pennsylvania, at Analytical Graphics Incorporated (AGI), a company that developed modeling and analysis software for the space, defense, and intelligence communities. AGI did work directly for U.S. government agencies, such as the Defense Department and NASA, as well as major defense contractors. Among the many applications for their products was the ability to track satellites and missiles.

Cullen was somewhat anxious going into that briefing. He had no experience in weapons and technology smuggling and had just been transferred into the counter-proliferation squad led by Mike Ronayne. After the HSI academy, Cullen worked on the airport squad, for the most part catching drug smugglers in the act. He excelled in that job and was moved to the drug-smuggling squad, focusing on long-term investigations of drug-smuggling organizations. There, he supervised the wiretap of a gang—mostly Vietnamese American—that smuggled massive quantities of ecstasy from Canada into the United States. The gang members were violent and impulsive; Cullen's wiretap intercepted coconspirators planning murders, and even recorded shots being fired. On one occasion, Cullen and other agents were following one of the gang members in Upper Darby, just outside Philadelphia, when he suddenly opened fire on a man walking down the sidewalk. Diminished impulse control being a side effect of ecstasy use, this was not particularly surprising. Cullen arrested him, and eventually his group took down the organization.

AGI's pristine offices amid the cornfields outside Exton were a long way from ecstasy-smuggling punks in gritty Upper Darby. The purpose of Cullen's brief was to solicit industry support for HSI in identifying rogue arms dealers. HSI special agents like Cullen regularly visit U.S. companies, particularly those involved in high technology and munitions, encouraging them to share information relating to suspicious solicitations or acquisitions of goods and services. HSI's goal is to use this information to initiate investigations and arrest black-market arms traffickers and smugglers. Cullen had given a more or less standard brief, warning the company about red flags indicating trouble, such as cold calls in broken English from dealers representing companies no one has heard of, suggesting convoluted methods of payment, and requesting indirect shipping routes through transshipment hubs like Dubai. AGI generally appreciated that sort of advice because many of its products required Commerce or State Department licenses for export and the company did not want to find itself on the wrong end of an illegal export investigation.

But illegal exports to the Emirates were not AGI's immediate concern on December 23, 2009; company officials were focused on something even stranger. They had discovered a website—CRACK99.com—listing thousands of high-tech software products for sale at astonishing discounts. Among these products was AGI's premier software program: Satellite Tool Kit (STK), first developed to determine the position and orientation of satellites, and the spatial relationships among satellites and other objects in space. Over time, additional capabilities were added, enabling STK to perform calculations for communications systems, radar, interplanetary missions, and orbit collision avoidance. STK's three-dimensional perspective allowed it to be used beyond the space environment, for example, enabling military personnel to visualize forces on land, sea, and air.

The price being offered for STK on CRACK99 was $1,000, a steep discount from the roughly $150,000 price AGI normally charged. CRACK99 also offered thousands of other advanced, high-technology software products used for aerospace simulation and design, advanced electronics, explosive simulation, intelligence collection, and space exploration. AGI didn't do business in China, and whoever was operating CRACK99 was not authorized to sell their products. Surely, CRACK99 was not permitted to sell the other software products either. Cullen didn't know exactly what the offense was, but, as he later told me, he knew "this software doesn't belong in China." Something was definitely wrong.

The question was, what could we do about it? The list of unknowns was long: Where was CRACK99? Who was behind it? How did CRACK99 acquire the software it was selling?

In early January 2010, Cullen and Ronayne met with me at my office in the United States Attorney's Office in Wilmington, Delaware, to find a way forward. We sat around my desk, surrounded by the detritus of a long career in government service: a wall covered in plaques, shelves filled with alien gimcracks from strange lands, and a four-foot anti-tank missile body from a case involving technology exports to South Africa. Cullen and Ronayne had driven down from their office at the Custom House in Philadelphia. They came to see me for a reason: I had been an Assistant United States Attorney (AUSA) for twenty years, and I had worked with Ronayne for nearly half of them. We had covered a lot of territory together. It had been only weeks since the sentencing of Amir Ardebili, an Iranian arms dealer who procured military components for the Iranian government. Our hunt for Ardebili had begun in

2004 and culminated in his arrest in the Republic of Georgia in October 2008. We ended up with Ardebili's laptop, enabling us to identify his sources of supply. Ronayne, the agents in his Philadelphia-based counter-proliferation squad, and I were busy in January 2010 running down those leads. We were accustomed to operating as a team, and so it was only natural that we would sort out this latest mystery together.

Like Cullen, Ronayne was a powerfully built man. But in contrast to Cullen's choirboy innocence, Ronayne radiated menace. His head was shaved, revealing a network of elaborate scars from fights and youthful shenanigans in his native Boston. Both Cullen and Ronayne had the condition suffered by so many Bostonians: they view their hometown as an entity unto itself, a shining holy city against which all other cities pale, and both sought to return as soon as their career paths would permit it. But for now, they were in Philadelphia. Like Cullen, Ronayne was acutely aware of everything going on around him. His expressionless green eyes gave him the look of a predator alien who was not so much reading your mind as thinking about which part of you he was going to eat first. But what was actually going on inside Ronayne was something far different: Mike was a thinker, although I'm not sure anyone ever told him how smart he is. And more than that: Mike Ronayne was a worrier.

To understand the website Cullen and Ronayne were describing, I had to see it, so I spun in my chair toward my computer and started typing the name in the browser. Abruptly, I stopped as an alarm went off inside my head. Having a peek at the CRACK99 website from a government computer was not a smart idea; I would be leaving a record of U.S. government interest. I could hear Cullen breathe a sigh of relief as I drew back from the keyboard. I waited to look at CRACK99 until I got home that night. This, admittedly, is not the smartest move from an operational security perspective; by searching from home, I would be stamping my own name on the website. But it was the best option I had, and what I saw surprised me.

CRACK99 looked like any website offering bargains—much like

Craigslist—except that it was on acid. It was jammed with messages
with special offers in vivid colors and randomly varying fonts. At the
top was the heading "CRACK99," with "CRACK" in red and rainbow
coloring on the "99." Below that was a heartfelt pledge of achingly
earnest probity:

> Faced with so many customers friend said to me: **"Thank
> you very much!"** I feel that my duty and responsibility to
> all the friends Provide in an **accurate, fast and reliable service!**
> *We have already done, will prove that we will do better!*
> **Trust WWW.CRACK99.COM Professional site!**
>
> We Guarantee, absolutely not deceive!
>
> *Still expect you to tell for us:*—**"Thank you very
> much!"** Thank you for your trust and support!

As if this guarantee was not enough to earn my uncritical faith in
the mysterious operator of CRACK99, there was a flashing yellow box
immediately below stating the following:

> ### No maze   all is surprised   True deal

And below the flashing yellow box, just to make sure the central
thrust of the message was not lost on any member of the Internet
community, was an orange pop-up in which a pretty Asian girl said,

> *100% NO PROBLEM*
> *Security*

No Maze? No Problem! Needless to say, I was impressed. But
not in a good way. After learning about CRACK99 selling AGI's

satellite-tracking technology, I was expecting the sort of website a Bond villain would have designed in his lair deep within a dormant volcano in a Caribbean archipelago: something dark, sinister, and overtly threatening. But CRACK99 was just the opposite: a self-parody, amateurish, and even juvenile in its presentation. It was as if a group of overeager preadolescents hyped up on gummy bears had created their version of optimal visual marketing, featuring bright colors and randomly flashing objects. It made me wonder if we were starting off on the wrong track altogether.

I was reminded of such a false start at the very dawn of my career as a federal prosecutor. I was the duty AUSA in Philadelphia, where I served the first half of my government career. Being the duty AUSA meant I spent the day answering inquiries from agents and citizens. I had already had two calls about aliens—the kind from outer space—one of whom was alleged to be a senior official at City Hall (a proposition I did not immediately dismiss). Then a Secret Service agent called to tell me he had uncovered a currency counterfeiting ring. The conspirators, he said, had a contract to clean the premises of a printing company every night and had unsupervised access to the equipment. They took advantage of that situation to print counterfeit twenty-dollar bills. "The ringleader is a female from Pottstown," said the agent. "She was caught trying to pass the twenties at Sears."

"Let's bring her in," I said with authority.

The Secret Service brought her in, and we confronted the ringleader directly to let her know we had the goods on her. After summarizing the evidence against her, I said, "What I'd like to know now is whether you're prepared to tell us the truth about your counterfeiting ring."

"I . . . ," said the ringleader.

"Yes?"

"I . . . ," she repeated.

"Yes?"

"I . . . I'm going to be sick," said the ringleader, just before throwing up into my government-issued gray metal trashcan.

Further investigation revealed that the "ringleader" was a very nice, middle-aged woman who supported her family by working two jobs, including one overnight at the printing company. Her only connection to counterfeiting was the fact that she had paid for vacuum bags at Sears with a counterfeit twenty she received as change at the Acme supermarket. And my contribution to the common good was to make the nice lady vomit.

This was an important lesson, as are all lessons in humility. As a result, I learned to be careful at the intake stage of new investigations. But, even so, as I continued thinking about CRACK99, my initial skepticism gradually gave way to grave concern. The CRACK99 format might not be menacing, but the products being offered were top-of-the-line engineering software programs for the most sophisticated applications. Many of the manufacturers were eminent American technological innovators, including Altera, ANSYS, Mastercam, Autodesk, National Instruments, Agilent, and MathWorks. And the products were offered at absurdly low prices: $40, $50, $100. Something really was wrong. This was a lead worth pursuing.

The first step was to figure out where CRACK99 originated. AGI told us the CRACK99 website was hosted in Los Angeles, but websites can be hosted anywhere on servers that rent space to all comers. So, we could not infer from the server location that our offender would be found in Malibu, wearing wraparound shades while lounging by an infinity pool, waiting to be arrested. Another point of origin was more likely. On this important question, there was no shortage of clues, starting with the pretty Asian girl in the orange "100% NO PROBLEM Security" pop-up. An even better clue was this: the mysterious operator of CRACK99 invited initial contact at the e-mail address: china9981@ gmail.com. Of course, none of that was conclusive: the website could be made to look Chinese by someone in Belarus, for all we knew. But our preliminary assumption was that our target was in China.

This is the point where most investigations founder: the standard government response is that if the bad guy is in China, you'll never get him; it's best to close the file and move on to a target within reach. There is more to this negative response than sloth alone: going after someone overseas, and particularly in a totalitarian nation at odds with the United States, is no easy undertaking. There was no template for this case; we would make it up as we went along. If we failed, investigating CRACK99 would go down as a fool's errand, and we would be the fools. On the other hand, I had two hole cards: Cullen and Ronayne. Both were proven commodities—diligent, thorough, and tough-minded. They were two stars in the Homeland Security constellation, and national security was their sweet spot. They—and I—would not be walking away from CRACK99.

But that did not resolve all of my concerns. Cullen, Ronayne, and I might not be willing to walk away from the investigation, but would we get the support we needed from our respective agencies, particularly mine? You would think the answer to this question would be resoundingly affirmative. After all, the illegal sale of high-technology software presented a national security issue, and everyone is in favor of national security. Unfortunately, it's not quite as simple as that: everyone is for national security when national security is within easy reach. In federal law enforcement, you will find no shortage of people willing to take a courageous stand against national security crimes, until it comes to making sacrifices and taking risks.

There are ninety judicial districts across the nation, and each one has a United States Attorney, appointed by the President, to serve at the pleasure of the President. The United States Attorney is often called the chief federal law enforcement officer for the district, but this is not strictly true. Not one of the badge-carrying federal agents in the district works for the United States Attorney; only the AUSAs—federal prosecutors responsible for investigating and prosecuting federal crimes—do. I served as an AUSA for twenty-three years, watching United States Attorneys come and go, depending on which way the political winds were blowing.

F. Scott Fitzgerald wrote, "Let me tell you about the very rich. They are different from you and me." In that spirit, let me tell you about United States Attorneys: they are different from you and me, assuming you are anything like me. United States Attorneys are presidential appointees. The appointment process is entirely political: a candidate for United States Attorney is identified through a largely invisible process overseen by politicians, and is then nominated by a senator (a politician) to the president (a politician) who submits the name for confirmation by the United States Senate (one hundred politicians). It is possible for this process to identify a worthy candidate for the job, and it has, but that doesn't mean the process is particularly sound.

Unfortunately, but unsurprisingly, the inherently political nature of the appointment process typically yields a United States Attorney who is political in nature, his ear to the political ground, his nose to the political wind, tracking progress against a political scorecard. Such a person is fundamentally different from me, and our goals are likely to be mutually exclusive. For example, my measure of the effectiveness of law enforcement is whether it reduces the actual harm caused by criminal activity. If the goal is to reduce violent crime, for example, the measure of success is whether the incidence of violent crime has declined. This might seem obvious, but it is a metric unlikely to appeal to United States Attorneys because it sets a goal that is difficult to reach. In fairness, United States Attorneys do not have an unlimited amount of time in office to achieve their goals, so they tend to be risk-averse, looking for bite-sized objectives.

As a result, United States Attorneys prefer a performance metric over which they have more control: the number of indictments returned by the district. The more indictments returned, the more work the district is doing to combat crime, according to this metric. To my way of thinking, this is completely backward: if the district were succeeding in combating violent crime, for example, you would expect fewer indictments because there would be fewer incidents of violent crime to prosecute.

There is another—and even more troubling—problem with using the number of indictments as the performance metric for a United States Attorney's Office: it creates an incentive to take on numerous, small, and easy cases, rather than fewer, large, and difficult ones. United States Attorneys who evaluate their success in fighting drugs by the number of indictments will encourage AUSAs to charge large numbers of minor offenders among the virtually infinite supply of drug-addicted hustlers arrested on a daily basis by the local police. The result is federal jail cells full of brain-addled users who face federal penalties of up to life in prison while the major offenders continue distributing drugs. Foraging for low-hanging fruit generates high federal indictment statistics, creating the impression of high-tempo law enforcement, but its effect on crime is virtually nil.

More distressing still is the disproportionate effect of this metric on minority-group members. In my experience, the impact of arresting numerous small offenders falls unevenly on African Americans and Latinos. Others have observed this as well, including Attorney General Eric Holder.

A recent study reported that half of African-American men have been arrested at least once by age 23. Overall, black men were 6 times, and Latino men were 2.5 times, more likely to be imprisoned than white men in 2012.

This overrepresentation of young men of color in our criminal justice system is a problem we must confront—not only as an issue of individual responsibility but also as one of fundamental fairness, and as an issue of effective law enforcement. Racial disparities contribute to tension in our nation generally and within communities of color specifically, and tend to breed resentment towards law enforcement that is counterproductive to the goal of reducing crime.

A prosecutor sees this up close: the stream of young men of color coming to court in shackles, mostly charged with low-grade offenses. In individual cases, my view was simple: I prosecute the guilty; if you're guilty, don't expect me to shed a tear because you got caught. Everyone I prosecuted was guilty, and I didn't shed any tears. But when the aggregated results are so extreme—half of all African American men are arrested by the time they're twenty-three—a fair-minded law enforcement officer must at least ask the question, might we be doing something wrong?

Supreme Court Justice George Sutherland's admonition to federal prosecutors rings as true today as it did in 1935:

The United States Attorney is the representative not of an ordinary party to a controversy, but of a sovereignty whose obligation to govern impartially is as compelling as its obligation to govern at all; and whose interest, therefore, in a criminal prosecution is not that it shall win a case, but that justice shall be done. As such, he is in a peculiar and very definite sense the servant of the law, the twofold aim of which is that guilt shall not escape or innocence suffer. He may prosecute with earnestness and vigor—indeed, he should do so. But, while he may strike hard blows, he is not at liberty to strike foul ones. It is as much his duty to refrain from improper methods calculated to produce a wrongful conviction as it is to use every legitimate means to bring about a just one.

The mission of the Department of Justice is to do justice. A federal prosecutor can strike hard blows but must be fair. It is not fair and just, in my opinion, for the federal government to lock up only the minor offenders—the low-hanging fruit—and call it a day. State and local authorities should prosecute the street hustlers, leaving the federal government responsible for taking down interstate and international organizations, locking up the major offenders, and pursuing even more major offenders. That is what citizens expect of their federal government.

You would think this argument would have some appeal. But not so: I made exactly this argument to United States Attorneys throughout my long career and never prevailed. What I could not overcome is the unforgiving fact that United States Attorneys' preferred metric for success—the number of indictments—feeds the political monster. The United States Attorney's Offices compete for resources controlled by the Department of Justice. Individual United States Attorneys justifiably want to demonstrate their office's success to the Department, and the number of indictments is a convenient way of doing so. The Department of Justice embraces this metric, using it both to make resourcing decisions within the Department and to demonstrate the Department's success in reports to Congress. To the political class, this makes sense, and it seems to make everyone involved happy. I am all for happiness, even among the political class. But this is no way to fight crime.

In this context, I had to decide how to initiate the CRACK99 case. Should I walk down the hall to the United States Attorney and tell him I am embarking on a lengthy and potentially costly investigation of a major offender—one located in an inaccessible place, committing acts not yet fully understood but evidently illegal? Maybe show him the CRACK99 website, with the orange pop-up and the Asian girl and the "No maze all is surprised True deal" guarantee?

In my experience, such a pitch is not likely to be supported by United States Attorneys—who would much rather hear about cases that are more of a sure thing, like prosecuting a kid with a rock of crack in his pocket.

So I needed to do a little due diligence to get the CRACK99 case launched. I had to make it look less risky before I could pitch it to the United States Attorney. I would have to offer my own "No maze all is surprised True deal" guarantee. And so, at this early stage, I decided to keep quiet until after we gathered more evidence.

For thirty years I served as an intelligence officer in the Navy Reserve, and during that time I learned many things. One of them is this: it is often wiser to beg for forgiveness than to ask for permission.

To that end, Cullen, Ronayne, and I agreed we would use an undercover approach to CRACK99, posing as U.S. customers. This presented an immediate challenge. The software being offered for sale on the website was not the typical retail software that you might buy from Microsoft. It was sophisticated analytic and design software for high-technology industrial and military applications. An effective undercover approach requires a realistic legend—that is, an appearance that makes sense from the bad guy's point of view. Our undercover legend would require us to appear technologically astute, immersed in the nuances of the most current engineering software. In other words, we would have to appear to be precisely what we were not. Ronayne, Cullen, and I had no professional training in information technology or software design; we needed to get smarter to avoid looking like cops.

AGI, once again, was there to help. We wanted to understand—at least at an elementary level—how CRACK99 provided its customers access to the software being purchased. Generally speaking, such access is gained through licensing files. If you obtain software without the licensing file, you get nothing at all; it's sort of like renting an apartment without getting the door key. My threshold question was whether the high-end software being sold on CRACK99 came with the licensing file, enabling the buyer to actually use the software. The answer to this question would determine whether CRACK99 was a sham, a trap for the unwary Internet wanderer willing to put good money down for software from a Chinese website with an airtight guarantee: "absolutely not deceive!"

AGI officials told us that the way they sold software was to grant potential customers a temporary trial download that would expire after a fixed period. If customers were happy with the product, they would then buy the licensing file, which would thereafter give them continued authorized access to the software, along with upgrades. AGI also taught us about the STK software itself, which enables a user— like AGI's customer, the U.S. government—to track objects in any environment: not only in space but also on land, at sea, in the air. As a result, STK is used for aircraft and unmanned aerial vehicle (UAV) systems; communications and electronic warfare; geospatial intelligence; missile defense; navigation; space exploration; and spacecraft mission design and operations. STK is also utilized for command and control of military and intelligence operations, aiding determinations such as "which sensor to task for an unplanned target, where to direct forces while ensuring communications connectivity, and how to place airborne surveillance assets while avoiding enemy radar."

As the significance of this information washed over us, Cullen, Ronayne, and I thought the same thing: this high-powered multifunctional STK software—so useful in so many military applications—was sitting at that very moment on a website, available for pennies on the dollar to every U.S. adversary, including China. I recalled recent Chinese antisatellite missile tests in which the Chinese had destroyed a weather satellite in polar orbit with a kinetic kill vehicle. The fact that they would conduct such a test in peacetime suggested that China, in the event of war, intended to shoot down U.S. satellites to blind U.S. decision makers and cut off command, control, and communication capabilities. How helpful would it be to the Chinese antisatellite effort to be able to track every satellite in orbit?

Very.

As we were trying to demystify CRACK99 in 2010, the U.S. government was "rebalancing" its national strategy "toward the Asia-Pacific region," the most powerful player in which is China. From the perspective of the Department of Defense (DoD), the challenge derives from China's growing military power and a lack of clarity as to China's "strategic intentions," implying that its improved military capabilities might be directed against the United States. Under the new Pacific-centric U.S. strategy, as stated in the Defense Department's report entitled *Sustaining Global Leadership: Priorities for 21st Century Defense*, one of the primary missions of the military is to:

> *Operate Effectively in Cyberspace and Space. Modern armed forces cannot conduct high-tempo, effective operations without reliable information and communication networks and assured access to cyberspace and space. Today space systems and their supporting infrastructure face a range of threats that may degrade, disrupt, or destroy assets. Accordingly, DoD will continue to work with domestic and international allies and partners and invest in advanced capabilities to defend its networks, operational capability, and resiliency in cyberspace and space.*

In other words, a priority of the U.S. strategy is to achieve and maintain a decisive advantage over adversaries like China in both cyberspace and outer space, so that the United States can maintain command, control, and communications in the event of war. The Chinese do not intend to cede the cyberspace and outer-space theaters to the United States. Instead, they want to deprive the United States of its strategic advantage in these areas. With the embryonic CRACK99 investigation, Cullen, Ronayne, and I had the opportunity to enter this battle space.

Starting an undercover investigation is a little like taking the first swim of the summer. Do you put a toe in the water and carefully descend the ladder, inch by inch—or do you just dive in? Reasonable minds might differ. We decided to dive in.

Our first e-mail was a softball sent on January 7, 2010:

To Whom It May Concern:

I am interested in purchasing the Analytical Graphics STK off of your web site. . . . I noticed this product is free off of the [AGI] website but they charge a very high fee to access their registration keys. The software appears to be useless without these registration keys and I would like some assurance that if I purchased this product with you, I would be getting a registration key that allows me to use this software. . . . Please tell me exactly what I will be getting for my $1,000 (USD). . . . If I am satisfied with this first purchase, I will make many more purchases of this STK and other software from Crack99.

Our main objective in sending this first e-mail was simply to establish initial contact. More than anything, we wanted to know if the CRACK99 operator would answer. We picked the STK software because of its strategic implications; could CRACK99 provide it, and in accessible form? In asking for an "assurance" that we would get a registration key to enable us to use the STK software, we were trying to see how much the CRACK99 operator would say about the crack—that is, the method of bypassing the license file. Nothing ventured, nothing gained.

We sent this first e-mail from an undercover location in Philadelphia maintained by HSI. The place was nondescript and easy to overlook, which was the point. The e-mail would not identify the sender as a U.S. government employee, and it would not correspond to the physical address of any government agency. If he cared to look, the operator of CRACK99 would be able to tell that the sender was in the United States, but that would only confirm our legend as a U.S. business.

The reply from china9981@gmail.com was swift and to the point:

I will give you a registration document. This is the perfect sure!
   Trust from our services.

And there was more: the sender signed his e-mail with a name—Xiang Li. We did not know if this name corresponded to any living human being. But it was a name.

Xiang Li's e-mail was quickly followed by another:

I will provide a detailed installation instructions for you.

how to pay. . . .
Recommended Western Union Money Transfer. This will be one of the most efficient way(Fast!) . . . Call toll-free number . . . tell them you need pay to the a Chinese friend. You can do.

My info:(Please make sure that exactly the same)
   1. Name: First name is ChunYan, Last name is Li
   2. Address: CHINA CHENGDU RENMINNANLU 1 HAO
      Post zip :610041
   3. Phone: +86-13881900147
   4. Chinese citizen ID card: 510681197901071862

This e-mail certainly seemed to confirm our theory that Xiang Li was in China. We now had a physical address in Chengdu, along with a phone number with the Chinese country code of 86, not to mention a Chinese citizen identification number. All we had to do was confirm the information with the Chinese government. But wait, no, we couldn't do that because our interests and theirs were directly at odds—Pacific rebalancing and all that.

There was one point of confusion, however: when Xiang Li provided his identifying information for payment purposes, he provided the name "Chun Yan Li." A little sleuthing led us to conclude that

"Chun Yan" might be a woman's name. Maybe a wife or a sister? Or maybe he was just making it up as he went along.

Many questions were still unanswered, but we had learned something. While we didn't know who Xiang Li was, we did know one thing about him: he was all about the money. This was good news indeed, for in my many years of experience with undercover operations, one lesson has emerged with utmost clarity: greed makes people stupid, and stupid people get arrested. The criminal mastermind's approach might be flawless from his well-protected initial vantage, but once he smells money in the air, he is capable of acting as dopey as a teenage boy with a teenage girl.

We could also see that Xiang Li was persistent. The next day we had another e-mail, very much to the point: "?You no news?" To this e-mail was attached an image file of the STK software we sought to purchase, to further whet our appetite. Cullen showed this image to AGI officials, and they confirmed it was their product, although they could not tell if the required licensing file was included.

Driving home that night, I felt the stirrings of optimism. We were poised to buy stolen software worth $150,000 for a mere $1,000. This really was starting to look like a "perfect sure," as Xiang Li had promised. But I was concerned about how we would get the $1,000 in buy money. On the one hand, when you consider that the U.S. budget is measured in trillions of dollars, $6 billion of which is appropriated to HSI, this might not seem like much of a problem, particularly when the objective is to spend the money on a national security investigation. But money is always a problem. A $6 billion budget is a list of line items, each of which is controlled by a gatekeeper, who might not share my enthusiasm for this particular operation. I was afraid the HSI gatekeeper, whomever it was, would not fund even a measly $1,000 for an undercover investigation when a successful outcome seemed like such a long shot.

Ronayne went to work trying to break the money free and, to my surprise and relief, had it in a matter of days. I didn't ask Ronayne exactly what he had to do to get it; some things are best left alone. Enriched beyond imagination with a cool grand, we sent CRACK99 an e-mail with delivery instructions. Xiang Li wrote back:

Welcome

Step 1 . . . .

However, must be the payment. Do you understand?

Yes, we did understand: nothing would happen until the money was in his hands. So we gambled the $1,000 in national treasure to answer the threshold question: Would Xiang Li deliver pursuant to the CRACK99 "absolutely not deceive!" airtight guarantee?

Xiang Li was explicit about the payment instructions: we were to pay through Western Union to a location in Chengdu. So on January 15, 2010, Cullen drove from the Custom House in Philadelphia to the Western Union at the Food Lion grocery store in Claymont, Delaware, located in a mall near the sprawling chemical plants along Interstate 495.

Why Claymont, Delaware? The answer to this important question derives from a high point of law: the U.S. Constitution. Article III of the Constitution vests judicial power in the Supreme Court and such inferior courts as Congress shall establish and—here's the important part—requires that "Trial of all Crimes . . . shall be held in the State where the said Crimes shall have been committed." This constitutional venue standard left us with a bit of a conundrum: when the offender is most likely in China, in what state are the "said Crimes . . . committed"?

Prior to sending the money, the answer was not clear. But Cullen and Ronayne were sure about one thing: their prosecutor was in Delaware. If they wanted me to handle the case, it would have to be tried in Delaware, and that meant the crime had to be "committed" in Delaware, at least in some sense of the word. The best we could do to connect an offender to the State of Delaware was to send the money—by the means he had requested—from Delaware to China. Hence, we chose the Food Lion in Claymont, a place that is as close to nowhere as you can get, but is in fact in Delaware.

Now came the hardest part of any undercover investigation: the wait. Had we taken the first concrete step in the direction of unveiling CRACK99, or were we just the latest chumps who sent a grand to a stranger on the Internet?

2 | FAST FOOD

SOMETIMES YOU GET LUCKY.

My first trial as a federal prosecutor came just a few months after I was sworn in. I had never tried a case before then. In fact, in my prior employment as an associate in a big law firm, I had spoken only once in a courtroom; in a court of appeals, where I had argued a cross appeal in three minutes and twenty-six seconds, the amount of time the senior partner had left me, out of the thirty minutes allocated to us.

The defendant was a fellow known as Fast Eddie, who was charged with stealing his ex-girlfriend's mail in order to convert her paycheck to his own use. It was a very sad situation, particularly if you consider the betrayed ex-girlfriend's point of view: first you leave me, then you steal my paycheck. Nice. But the case was far from a slam dunk, which is probably why one of the more senior prosecutors was kind enough to provide me with this courtroom experience. I thought I was doing pretty well until the judge called me up to the sidebar and sneered, "Mr. Hall, is this your trial by fire?"

And yet, I emerged victorious. I would like to say that this triumph resulted from a brilliant masterstroke I executed at just the right moment. But the truth is I won because of something Fast Eddie's brother did, or more precisely, didn't do. Fast Eddie's lawyer decided it would be a good idea to humanize his client for the jury, and so he called Eddie's brother to the stand. The brother was a very likable person who made a good impression with the jury. After asking some soft questions and getting helpful answers, Fast Eddie's lawyer confidently asked the brother the money question: "What is Eddie's reputation as a law-abiding citizen?" This is a question commonly asked of a defendant's friends and relations, and I fully expected a resounding endorsement of Fast Eddie's outstanding reputation as a law-abiding citizen. But that's not what happened. Fast Eddie's poor brother couldn't answer the question. He looked at Eddie briefly, and then he looked at his shoes for a long time, obviously engaged in a profound inner struggle. Then he looked at me, and then at the judge. And then he looked at his shoes again. But not a word came out of his mouth. Fast Eddie's brother just couldn't lie, not even for Fast Eddie. The jury convicted on all counts, and I imagine Thanksgiving dinner was a bit awkward after that.

In the matter of Fast Eddie, I got lucky.

And so it was in the matter of CRACK99. When we sent the money to Xiang Li, I was concerned about the possibility of a rip. Theft happens all the time in the underworld, and particularly on the Internet. And an Internet rip is much safer than a rip during a drug deal, where people get shot in the face. But it's still a rip. Had Xiang Li decided to take the money and run, that would have been the end of the case: once you've been burned like that, you can't go back to the U.S. Treasury for more. But that didn't happen: the day after sending the money, we received an e-mail with three .rar files, which are compressed files containing data that must be unpacked prior to use.

The next question was, had we received fully operable STK software for our $1,000? This meant another trip to AGI, so their technology people could examine the files and determine their authenticity and operability. Even the supremely composed Brendan Cullen was

anxious at this point. The stakes for him were high: if the STK software we bought was operable, we would move forward. If not, we
would not, and this false start would be for Cullen an embarrassing
failed opening gambit in a new squad.

The AGI director of technology support opened the software. For
AGI, the news was bad: it was indeed operable STK software, precisely the kind a legitimate user would be able to access in a lawful
transaction with AGI. Except for one thing: the licensing restrictions
had been entirely removed, so a user could, for example, load the
software on multiple computers or redistribute it.

Licensing files provide access to software according to the terms
of the license. If you buy access for one user, the licensing file allows
access to the software only for that one user; if you buy access for
an entire network, then everyone on the network can legally use the
software. You can buy a perpetual license or an annual license, or
something in between. Licensing files also permit access to the specific software program modules the user requires. And of course, you
pay for access; the more you pay, the more you get.

From what we could see, Xiang Li had greatly simplified these
rules: "Step 1 . . . must be the payment"; Step 2, you get unlimited
access. This was, of course, very bad news for AGI; CRACK99 was
selling its flagship STK product from China for a grand. But what was
bad for AGI was good for us: our nascent case was still alive. Cullen
breathed a sigh of relief.

Now that we knew it wasn't a hoax, I had to address this question:
What precisely was Xiang Li's crime? Unfortunately, the answer was
awash in nuance. The world of federal law enforcement abounds with
invisible hazards lurking like mines just beneath the tranquil surface
of an azure sea. One such hazard came from what might seem an
unlikely place: the FBI.

The FBI is the largest and most famous of the federal government's than seventy law enforcement agencies. In addition to

the well-known ones—the FBI, the Drug Enforcement Administration (DEA), and the Bureau of Alcohol, Tobacco, Firearms and Explosives (ATF)—there are dozens of other agencies that have never had their own television show, such as the National Geospatial-Intelligence Agency Police and the Tennessee Valley Authority Office of Inspector General. But the eight-hundred-pound gorilla in the federal law enforcement menagerie is the FBI. The FBI even has a component that assists screenwriters and others in depicting the FBI in mass media. No federal agency is more visible; no federal agency has better brand recognition; and no federal agency spends more time and money protecting its brand.

In startling contrast, when it comes to branding, stands HSI, the agency employing Cullen and Ronayne. HSI is a large law enforcement agency that employs more agents than the better known DEA and ATF, but still only about half the number employed by the FBI. HSI's core problem is not quantitative, however, but qualitative. Its biggest issue is a lack of identity: it just doesn't know what it is. This is ironic because agents like Cullen and Ronayne can proudly trace their pedigree to the U.S. Customs Service, which was created by the fifth act of Congress on July 31, 1789 (the same year in which the office of United States Attorney was created). The FBI wasn't founded until 1908.

Everything went fine for the Customs Service for its first couple-hundred years. But then 9/11 put things sideways. As a result of the Homeland Security Act of 2002, the nation's border agencies were merged into one, including the Customs Service, which had a shotgun wedding with the Immigration and Naturalization Service and became known as "ICE." It has a nice ring to it, and might have been a promising brand except that the "I" in "ICE" stands for "Immigration"—Immigration and Customs Enforcement—and immigration enforcement makes everyone unhappy. So ICE blundered around for a decade or so before addressing the offending "I" and creating Homeland Security Investigations, or HSI.

The persistent problem for HSI is that few people, including members of Congress—which appropriates law enforcement money—know much about it. When a law enforcement crisis confronts the government, the President and Congress think of the FBI, not HSI. So HSI, for all its resources, keeps a humble attitude; head down, it looks over its shoulder to make sure it hasn't attracted the attention of the big dog, the FBI. Because if the big dog thinks HSI has something worth taking, the big dog is going to take it.

At the outset of the CRACK99 investigation, I actively considered whether it was an economic espionage case, and in doing so I was wandering down a dangerous path. From the FBI's point of view, any case relating to espionage, and particularly Chinese espionage, is worth taking. So I had to worry about that big dog.

Cullen and Ronayne, on the other hand, never had any doubt: CRACK99 was a smuggling case, squarely within their purview. From their perspective, the only difference between CRACK99 and old-school smuggling was the digital nature of the contraband. And on this basis, we pressed ahead, brainstorming in Ronayne's office in the Custom House in Philadelphia, talking through the many possible permutations of the CRACK99 enterprise. Was Xiang Li a real person? Was he ten people? Forty people? Was he part of a bigger network we couldn't see? And this led to the question of whether Xiang Li had any connection with the government of the People's Republic of China.

Still, I had to be careful. I didn't know whether CRACK99 was state-sponsored, and I wanted to find out. But if I opened the investigation as an economic espionage case, the FBI would be knocking at my door intending to take it away from HSI. So I kept my own counsel as I assessed whether CRACK99 was selling the fruits of economic espionage—that is, stolen proprietary intellectual property owned by U.S. companies—or the fruits of government espionage—that is, stolen military technology, lifted by cloak-and-dagger tradecraft. Under either scenario, the CRACK99 case might belong more to the FBI than to HSI. And why, you might ask, would I care, other than my steadfast personal loyalty to Cullen and Ronayne? After all, I was an employee of the Department of Justice and the FBI was a sister agency; I was in no way connected institutionally to HSI.

The answer to this question too has its origin in 9/11, when the FBI started morphing gradually away from its traditional law enforcement role into a domestic intelligence agency, like the old MI5 in Britain. In my early days as a prosecutor—in the 1990s—the FBI was unquestionably the premier federal law enforcement agency. Most of my work, and many of my most important cases, were with the FBI. Customs was more a niche law enforcement agency, focused mainly on smuggling offenses. But the FBI handled everything: drugs, violence, corruption, racketeering, frauds in all forms and flavors. It was like one-stop shopping: I could go over to the FBI office and walk from squad to squad, catching up with agents, making progress in my portfolio of cases. This changed gradually after 9/11, when the FBI's priority became counterterrorism. The shift is obviously understandable; it made perfect sense to me in 2002 that FBI resources would be moved away from investigating bank robberies and toward international terrorism. But the FBI is an object of enormous mass, and once it establishes momentum, it is hard to stop. I concluded that the pendulum had swung too far by 2010, when I realized—to my astonishment—that I did not have a single FBI case under indictment.

I'm not the only one who noticed the change. Federal Judge Jed S. Rakoff remarked on the paucity of FBI agents available to investigate financial crime after the crash of 2008 and subsequent Great Recession: "For example, before 2001, the FBI had more than one thousand agents assigned to investigating financial frauds, but after September 11 many of these agents were shifted to antiterrorism work. Who can argue with that? Yet the result was that, by 2007 or so, there were only 120 agents reviewing the more than 50,000 reports of mortgage fraud filed by the banks."

If the FBI took control of the CRACK99 case, I wouldn't be able to work it with Cullen and Ronayne. And the FBI's involvement would also significantly reduce the probability that Xiang Li would feel the cold, unforgiving clasp of steel handcuffs as he was hauled off to face justice. In conjunction with the diversion of agents away from criminal investigations, the FBI's overall emphasis has swung away from traditional law enforcement objectives—like snapping handcuffs on offenders—toward intelligence reporting. I well understood the utility of such reporting, but I also understood that too often it had no end game, like an arrest. My fear was that the FBI's goal would be limited to monitoring Xiang Li's cracked-software operation in order to generate interminable reporting, analysis without objective, and ceaseless discussion among the few cleared for CRACK99 compartmented information.

Despite these misgivings, I continued wondering if the CRACK99 case involved Chinese espionage. While I did not often mention these forbidden thoughts to Cullen and Ronayne, I developed no shortage of scenarios to explain how U.S. technology could end up in the hands of the Chinese government. But I couldn't answer any of the follow-up questions: If CRACK99 was selling the fruits of cloak-and-dagger Chinese espionage, how did Xiang Li get hold of the software products to sell? Did he procure the software officially from the Chinese government for resale on CRACK99? Did he buy it from a corrupt Chinese government employee who was selling it out the back door? Was Xiang Li just a fictional character fronting for the Chinese government, which itself was selling branded U.S. products in a big spy yard sale? If so, why would the Chinese government bother doing that? What—besides a few thousand bucks—would the Chinese government get out of it? And for that matter, wouldn't the Chinese intelligence services want to keep their espionage accomplishments secret, as espionage agencies are wont to do?

Espionage, on the whole, seemed an unlikely theory of prosecution.

Instead, Xiang Li's crime appeared to be one of the most traditional federal violations, originally enacted to give the federal government a jurisdictional basis for pursuing Depression-era interstate gangsters like John Dillinger: the National Stolen Property Act (NSPA). The NSPA, enacted in 1934, outlaws the interstate transportation of stolen property, among other things. It seemed clearly to apply to CRACK99: STK was AGI's property, and it was offered for sale on the CRACK99 website without AGI's permission, having been transported across many state lines, far from its point of origin in Exton, Pennsylvania.

The NSPA approach offered the obvious advantage of keeping Cullen and Ronayne on the case, but there was also a serious flaw, thanks to Elvis Presley. In a case called *Dowling v. United States*, the Supreme Court reversed Paul Dowling's NSPA conviction for the interstate transportation of unauthorized copies of Elvis Presley recordings. Dowling was a devoted Elvis fan, and he noticed that many others were as well, so he started bootlegging Elvis Presley records and selling them by mail. He and another man obtained original recordings to which they were not entitled, made copies of the recordings on vinyl phonograph records—the audio recording medium of the day—and distributed them to Elvis's avid fans, which the *Dowling* Court somewhat gratuitously called a "subculture."

Dowling was convicted of violating the NSPA and appealed. The Supreme Court reversed his conviction, holding that Congress did not intend for the NSPA to be an enforcement mechanism for criminal copyright infringement, because a copyright infringer like Dowling did not take exclusive physical control over the thing actually stolen, the intangible "bundle" of exclusive legal rights protected by copyright law. The Supreme Court held that the NSPA "seems clearly to contemplate a physical identity between the items unlawfully obtained and those eventually transported, and hence [requires] some prior physical taking of the subject goods." The Supreme Court did leave open the question of whether the NSPA would apply where the copyright infringer "obtained the source material through illicit means."

The *Dowling* decision might be worth reading in its entirety if you are interested in better understanding the high level of misery evident in the legal profession. Because, I mean, come on: Dowling stole the copyrighted material in the general sense of the meaning of the word "stole"; there was something that wasn't his, and he took it without permission. But because the goods transported across state lines—the pressed vinyl phonograph records—were not themselves stolen, the NSPA did not apply. This conclusion might be deserving of criticism, but it is, as they say, the law.

Of course, the *Dowling* Court did leave open the possibility that a different result might obtain with more evidence of hanky-panky, like an actual burglary in which copyrighted material was stolen. So maybe the result would have been different had the government introduced evidence of Dowling vaulting the fence at Graceland, crawling across the manicured lawn, picking the lock to the cavernous copyrighted material vault, filling his rucksack with a "bundle" of exclusive legal rights, and effecting silent egress from the premises.

It is a shame that Dowling's prosecutor didn't have such evidence to offer the court. The same might be said of me. Truth be told—and, after all, prosecution is about truth telling if nothing else—I had absolutely no evidence at this stage of how Xiang Li obtained the software he was selling on CRACK99. So I was in much the same position as Dowling's unfortunate prosecutor.

That left the question of whether I should charge criminal copyright infringement, the obvious charge not leveled against Dowling. In that case, the government was constrained by the fact that federal copyright protection did not apply to sound recordings until the Sound Recording Act of 1971. I might face analogous challenges. There are many hazards in criminal copyright-infringement prosecutions, one being that not everyone registers copyrightable material, and another being that the infringement charge lacks jury appeal. A jury wants to see blood and guts—a real crime, not a technical violation of an intangible "bundle" of rights.

So it was clear to me that we needed to understand something about how Xiang Li got hold of the software and how he was able to distribute it globally without permission. We had only two leads in this regard: Xiang Li himself—whoever he might be—and the licensing files, which were the key to accessing the stolen software. Maybe a better understanding of the licensing technology would yield a clue as to the theft itself.

Cullen and a Defense Criminal Investigative Service (DCIS) agent named Tiffany Linn met with AGI to learn how a CRACK99 customer could access STK software without a legitimate licensing file. I was pleased that Cullen was paired with Linn, whom I knew from the Navy, where she had distinguished herself as an intelligence officer.

AGI told the agents that it did not develop the licensing files for STK in-house but procured them from a company I will call "Maxalim," which manufactured executable licensing software I will call "LIMDIS." LIMDIS worked by providing a unique authorized portal into the software: with the proper licensing file in place, legitimate purchasers of STK would get direct access to what they purchased. This is how retail software works in general: if you legally buy Microsoft Office, for example, it comes with a licensing file that installs along with the Office software to give you seamless access.

In addition, LIMDIS electronically tied legitimately purchased STK software to a specified number of workstations, the only locations where it would function. This was intended to prevent a purchaser of STK from buying one copy and then using it in multiple places— or worse, making additional copies for unlawful resale. This physical limitation had been disabled in the STK software we bought from CRACK99, because the LIMDIS code had been overwritten. Therefore we could install our STK software on as many workstations as we desired, and so could anyone else who bought it from CRACK99.

I could see that the secret sauce of CRACK99 was the cracked LIMDIS licensing file. Because the LIMDIS file had been bypassed or overwritten, Xiang Li could sell unlawfully acquired software that actually worked. The question was, how was Xiang Li able to do that?

As a boy, I had the experience of scales falling from my eyes, like Saul in the New Testament, only very different. I grew up in northern California when it was still largely rural, and I spent a lot of time in the woods. This led to many miserable bouts with poison oak, including one particularly disagreeable episode that sealed my eyes shut. The moment when my sight was restored is an early and vivid memory. I was at my brother's birthday party in the long-gone Storyland section of the San Francisco Zoo, enshrouded in pitch darkness, when I felt something fall from my eyes, which suddenly opened, revealing a gigantic multicolored Humpty Dumpty teetering precariously above me on a high wall. It was simultaneously terrifying and exhilarating, as are so many of the best moments in life.

And so it was when the connection between LIMDIS and the CRACK99 mastermind was revealed. Pitch darkness gave way to the bright white of brilliant insight: for that moment, I had the prescience of Tiresias, except that, unlike the mythological blind clairvoyant of Thebes, I was not transformed into a woman.

What was revealed to me was this: the solution to the case was not the CRACK99 website but the LIMDIS licensing file: follow the file to find your offender. I had been distracted by the CRACK99 website and its vivid acid-trip colors and fervent proclamations of future satisfaction, not to mention the orange pop-up with the pretty Asian girl's "100% NO PROBLEM Security" guarantee. I needed to focus on the more mundane LIMDIS file instead. And that originated not in China but in the United States. The key to this case would be found where the LIMDIS file originated: Maxalim.

It was clear to me now: a rogue employee at Maxalim was selling its customers' software out the back door. Maxalim had these products in order to protect them with the LIMDIS licensing file, and the rogue employee was selling them to CRACK99. All we had to do was find the rogue.

Cullen, Ronayne, and I gave some thought to starting an undercover investigation of Maxalim. I am an unabashed proponent of undercover techniques in cases like this, particularly where there might be questions about what an offender knew and when he knew it; there is nothing quite like having an offender answer those very questions on an audio tape recording. But undercover investigations need a starting point, and we did not have one at Maxalim. Even more important was the issue of delay: the rogue employee illegally selling software programs out Maxalim's back door was doing a lot of damage to a lot of companies, and at the same time compromising the national security of the United States. Undercover investigations could take years to complete, and the CRACK99 technology sluice gate would remain open throughout. An undercover approach on the Maxalim rogue was not an option, given the potential negative consequences. We would have to approach Maxalim directly, and try to enlist their help.

AGI introduced Cullen and Linn to one of Maxalim's many fifty-pound-brains. The man from Maxalim looked at the CRACK99 website, noting that many of Maxalim's customers' products were listed for sale there. In other words, it wasn't just AGI's STK software that was compromised by cracked LIMDIS files; a large number of the companies whose software products were for sale on CRACK99 used the same LIMDIS licensing software. This seemed consistent with my theory: the Maxalim rogue had access to the software products of Maxalim's customers, which he then sold to CRACK99, reaping large benefits with little risk of exposure.

It was now up to me to put the hammer down, and I did so by requesting further information from Maxalim. This might not seem much like bringing a hammer down if your idea of bringing a hammer down involves an actual hammer. But you might see the analogy if you've ever received such a request from a federal prosecutor: most people do not find the experience mood enhancing. What typically follows is an anxious phone call to an AUSA from an upscale lawyer who went to all the right schools. So it was in this instance: Maxalim's upscale lawyer was anxious for me to know that the company wished to be completely cooperative, but he was even more anxious to know whether we thought his client had done anything wrong.

This is when I had to deliver some tough news to the anxious upscale lawyer: we had reason to believe there was a rogue employee at Maxalim who was selling customer files out the back door to bad actors like Xiang Li. My revelation did not yield sincere expressions of a citizen's gratitude to a hard-working public servant for a job well done—not that I expected it would.

This was familiar territory: it happens all the time in law enforcement. You investigate the case, figure out the angle, and confront the subject. You have him on videotape selling cocaine to the under-cover agent. You play the tape, and then play it again to make sure he noticed the part where he sold the cocaine to the undercover agent. And what you get in return is "That ain't me."

The upscale Maxalim lawyer didn't say it like this, but he made it clear that he thought I had it all wrong.

That's what they all say.

Nobody likes admitting involvement in something untoward, par-ticularly a successful company full of software engineers with fifty-pound brains represented by an upscale lawyer who went to all the right schools. And, like the rest of us, the mega-brain crowd does not like admitting they've been betrayed by one of their own. So the lawyer's reaction was perfectly understandable, even if it did not have its intended effect. We parted cordially, mutually promising to discuss the matter again soon.

But I had other matters to attend to: the appeal of Kevin Dupree, who straw-purchased a .40 caliber, semiautomatic Glock 22 for his felonious cousin Curtis Boyd, who later used it in a shoot-out with New Jersey state troopers that left Boyd—sadly for no one but Boyd—dead. From Boyd's cold, dead hand the troopers pried the Glock 22.

Felons like Boyd are not allowed to buy firearms, which is why they need non-felonious cousins like Dupree. Straw purchasing is the crime that takes place when someone who is not a felon knowingly buys a firearm for someone who is. Straw purchasers should be prosecuted, as the facts of the Dupree case bear out. There is a reason why felons aren't allowed to have firearms: they often use them with bad results. My task related to none of this, however. Rather, I was assigned to defend in the court of appeals the district court's finding at Dupree's sentencing that the straw purchase of the Glock was part of a drug deal. Specifically, the sentencing court had found that Dupree purchased the gun for his cousin Boyd in order to pay off a debt resulting from the previous transfer from Boyd to Dupree of a small quantity of marijuana. So my job was to zero in on the bag-of-weed aspect of this sordid chapter in human depravity.

You might wonder why an AUSA with twenty years' experience would be selected for this task. The answer is, low-hanging fruit. That's what Dupree was, from the moment of his arrest: risk-free easy pickings. All of the facts of the case were lined up against Dupree; he was literally defenseless. And this is the point where the full weight of the U.S. government descended upon him. Describing it another way, Special Agent Daniel Brazier likes to call it "fast food": easy to prepare, easy to consume, and not good for you. What everyone in federal law enforcement can recite is this mantra: big cases, big problems; small cases, small problems; no cases, no problem. The Dupree case was classic fast food; at no risk and with little effort, Kevin Dupree was going to make the government look good. The United States Attorney could stand thwart the wreckage wrought by Dupree's now lifeless cousin Curtis Boyd and exclaim, This will not stand!

But in the end, I was there to argue about a bag of weed. And my reason for doing so was to increase Dupree's sentence from somewhere between ten and sixteen months to twenty-four months. Not exactly Herculean.

This is, unfortunately, how it works, and it only makes sense if you understand the United States Attorneys' risk-averse approach to law enforcement. Even if you're a twenty-year veteran prosecutor with an enviable record of delivering victory for the home team, you shouldn't be surprised when you pick up an assignment like this— one a rookie could easily handle—especially, if you're not telling the United States Attorney what else you're working on.

I readily admit that, rather than spending my time dealing with Dupree's bag of weed, I might have let the United States Attorney in on my secret. But in February 2010, the time was not right: I was not likely to persuade him to invest resources (including my time) in an investigation against someone whose name might or might not be Xiang Li or Chun Yan Li, who might be a man but might be a woman, who might be a fictional character, who probably is located in inaccessible China, and who seemed to be working with an unidentified rogue employee at Maxalim selling pirated software out the back door. It came down to a matter of faith, and I couldn't take the chance he would try to shut the investigation down.

Under such circumstances, there is only one thing to do: move forward. I took care of Dupree and worked on CRACK99 on my own time. We had to sustain our nascent relationship with Xiang Li even as we tried to figure out the Maxalim angle, and that meant buying more cracked software. Of the thousands of options on the CRACK99 website, we chose QUARTUS software manufactured by the Altera

Corporation, for two main reasons. One was to see whether CRACK99 really could deliver such an advanced, high-tech product. QUARTUS software is not designed for easy use by ordinary mortals. Rather, it is intended for a limited set of users occupying a rarified stratum of humanity: the privileged few who use reprogrammable logic design for the military as well as the automotive, broadcast, computing, industrial design, medical, and communications industries. Given the complex and powerful nature of the software, it was intriguing—to say the least—to know that a cracked version was now in the hands of this Xiang Li person in Chengdu, China. We had considered our- selves lucky to get a fully functioning version of STK, and were still wondering if CRACK99 could deliver on its promises across the board. A successful purchase of a fully functioning version of QUARTUS—a completely unrelated but similarly powerful commercial software product—would suggest the STK purchase was no fluke.

The other reason for acquiring QUARTUS was more mundane. Although QUARTUS software sold for tens of thousands of dollars in the legitimate market, Xiang Li was offering it for around a C note. Lacking a budget for this operation, we were still worried about get- ting buy money. So we aimed low: on February 19, 2010, we e-mailed CRACK99 asking to buy three Altera QUARTUS products that were listed on the website, for a total of $340:

Dear Sir,

Thank you for sending me the STK product (#240001). I am very impressed with this product. However, I noticed that the STK product you sent me was missing the following two parts: STK/Precision Orbit Deter- mination System and STK/Space Environment. Could you possibly send me these products also? Will these products acquire additional costs?

Also, do you still have the following three additional products advertised on your site?

—Altera QUARTUS II Nios Embedded Suite v9.0 (Item # - 440014)
—Altera QUARTUS II v9.0 FPGA Full Working (Item # - 450046)
—Altera QUARTUS II DSP Builder 9.0 (Item # - 450044)

If you have these three products and the other STK products, I will send you the payment. Thank you and I enjoy doing business with you.

In this February 19 e-mail we also took the opportunity to ask about the STK products we had previously purchased, gently complaining that we couldn't get access to two functional layers of the software. We already knew what the problem was, thanks to AGI: the cracked licensing file provided by Xiang Li did not allow access to all layers of the STK software. We were asking Xiang Li to fix this.

Xiang Li wrote back without delay, as he had previously:

happy new year
—Altera QUARTUS II Nios Embedded Suite v9.0 (Item # - 440014)
—Altera QUARTUS II v9.0 FPGA Full Working (Item # - 450046)
—Altera QUARTUS II DSP Builder 9.0 (Item # - 450044)
all is 120+120+100
$USD 340.00

Of course, we noticed that he ignored our query about the two missing layers of STK, so we followed up:

Thank you for your e-mail and Happy New Year to you as well. I will send you the payment for the Altera products next week. Can you also send me the 2 missing products for the STK.

Xiang Li continued to ignore the question about the two missing components of STK. Nevertheless, on February 22, Cullen took the short trip to nondescript Claymont, Delaware, and sent $340 from the Western Union inside the Food Lion grocery store to Chengdu, China, to the attention of Chun Yan Li. On February 24, we sent an e-mail to Xiang Li telling him we had wired the money and were "still waiting for the products to be sent." Xiang Li did not disappoint: the same day, he e-mailed four compressed .rar files, along with instructions on "how to install."

"Check 'crack' help," Xiang Li advised.

Cullen, with the assistance of two DCIS agents, tried to open the four compressed files—without success. Cullen wrote back to Xiang Li: "I attempted to open the links you provided below but they do not work. I receive the HTTP 404 Not Found page when I click on each of the links. Could you please send active links so I am able to download the products I purchased?"

Xiang Li wrote back promptly: "I have already modified." Below these words were four new links. And, after taking several days to download, these worked. We had discovered something new about Xiang Li: he was serious about delivering the goods. CRACK99 was no scam; results really were guaranteed: "No maze all is surprised True deal." And more than that, we learned that Xiang Li was not just a hustler moving product on a website; he seemed to understand a great deal about cracking software files. I concluded that either he was a cracker himself or he had ready access to one.

There was something else we became aware of as well. Prior to buying the QUARTUS products, we applied for and obtained a court order for a pen register. Here's how Title 18 of the United States Code describes a pen register: a "device or process which records or decodes dialing, routing, addressing, or signaling information transmitted by an instrument or facility from which a wire or electronic communication is transmitted, provided, however, that such information shall not include the contents of any communication."

This impenetrable definition illustrates why no one likes

Congress—that and the corruption. Here's my definition: a pen register identifies the outgoing telephone number that a telephone is calling. It all started with Samuel Morse's telegraph in 1840, which included a feature that recorded telegraph signals on a piece of paper. Ink pens came to be used in making these paper records—hence, the name "pen register." In the era of telephones, pen registers were used by telephone companies to keep track of the numbers called, and by law enforcement for the same purpose. As telecommunications moved into the digital age, the concept grew beyond telephones, but the name remained. Pen registers now digitally record the Internet Protocol (IP) addresses of electronic communications. It was a long and involved road from 1840 to 2010, but for us the implication was clear: whoever was sending us e-mails from china9981@gmail.com was using an IP address in Chengdu, China. And he was communicating with people all over the world.

Confirming Xiang Li was in China was helpful in the sense that we could now calibrate the degree of difficulty of our quest. But it did not answer the burning questions: Who is Xiang Li? And where is he getting his software?

3 | DISCORDANT NOTE

IN THE SPRING OF 1976, I FOUND myself in Nepal, at a place called Hinku Cave, en route to the Machhapuchhare Base Camp in the Annapurna Himal. I had planned to sleep in the cave for just one night, but the Himalayan weather gods had other ideas, so I hunkered down in the cold, eating rice and lentils, until the storm blew over. This was a frustrating interlude, being stuck in a dark cave running contrary to the fundamental purpose of mountain climbing, although in retrospect—compared to other places I've been stuck in—Hinku Cave wasn't so bad.

And so it was in March 2010: we were hunkered down, trying to figure out the next step in the CRACK99 investigation. It was obvious to me that the case turned on the rogue employee at Maxalim, but I had no idea who that person might be or how to go about identifying him. Anonymity is a defining aspect of Internet crime. In the old days, if someone was selling stolen product out the back door of a company, you could expect to find him at the back door. As a young prosecutor, I had a case involving an employee of a department store who was stealing (and reselling to his own profit) inventory directly from the sally port of the store's receiving department, and that is exactly where he was arrested. It's not so easy when the product is intangible, the back door is invisible, and the sally port is virtual.

Maxalim had been very helpful in explaining in general terms how LIMDIS licensing software enabled access to software like STK. But the people we talked to didn't have any leads on the rogue employee, and worse, they seemed skeptical—to put it mildly—about the whole rogue-employee theory. And this made me a bit skeptical of their professed desire to be helpful, skepticism being a two-way street and twenty years in federal law enforcement tending to make a person skeptical of just about everything and everyone.

Brendan Cullen and Tiffany Linn had just returned from San Jose, California, where they met with Altera personnel about the Altera QUARTUS II software we had purchased from CRACK99. Altera Corporation is a global semiconductor company with over thirteen thousand customers in the "Telecom and Wireless, Industrial Automation, Military and Automotive, Networking, Computer and Storage, and other vertical markets." Altera manufactures programmable logic devices (PLDs), "which consist of field-programmable gate arrays ('FPGAs') and complex programmable logic devices ('CPLDs')." Programmable logic devices are "standard semiconductor integrated circuits, or chips, that . . . customers program to perform desired logic functions in their electronic systems." In military applications, these devices are used in communication systems, radar systems, and missile guidance systems.

The information provided by Altera put a sharp point on a conclusion we had already deduced: this software was at the top of the software food chain. The QUARTUS II v.9 software we had purchased is used to design and operate programmable chips widely used in producing electronics. QUARTUS II software is thus fundamental to the technology infrastructure in the sense that it is a high-technology product used in still other high-technology products.

The agents brought to San Jose the QUARTUS II software we had purchased from CRACK99. The Altera people examined it and confirmed it was authentic; in other words, it was not bogus or counterfeit, but actual functioning QUARTUS II v.9 software. The next question related to how Xiang Li obtained this software: Was it possible to draw any inferences from the software itself to reveal its path to CRACK99? Like AGI, Altera provided customers with temporary access to free software on a trial basis. Once the trial period expired, the customer needed to purchase a license to continue using the software; otherwise, it would stop working. Altera determined that the software we purchased from Xiang Li was the paid-for version—that is, it wasn't the free temporary trial sample, but the fully licensed software product. This fact struck me as supporting the Maxalim rogue-employee theory: Xiang Li was able to sell the paid-for version because, thanks to the rogue employee, he actually had it. Obviously, I was right about this.

But there was one discordant note in my otherwise pleasing rogue-employee melody. Cullen asked the Altera people if Maxalim was given fully functioning QUARTUS II software in order to develop the licensing file for it. I expected an affirmative answer; it made intuitive sense to me that Maxalim would need the QUARTUS II software in order to write the licensing file to protect it, particularly because I assumed that the process of writing the licensing code involved encryption.

I have never been a cryptographer, but I had some general exposure to cryptology during my years as a naval intelligence officer. What I knew was elementary: an encryption algorithm is used to transform a message (called plaintext) into ciphertext, which cannot be read without the use of an encryption key to transform the ciphertext back into plaintext. There are many different forms of encryption algorithm; among the simplest is the transposition cipher, which shifts the units of plaintext according to a regular pattern, resulting in ciphertext that looks like gibberish without the encryption key—unless you happen to be very good at anagrams. In the digital age, encryption algorithms are many orders of magnitude more complex than a transposition cipher: "It is now routine to encrypt a message . . . so that all the computers on the planet would need longer than the age of the universe to break the cipher." But the goal is unchanged: transforming a coherent message into incomprehensible ciphertext, which is unreadable without the encryption key, and back again.

Regardless of the complexity of the encryption algorithm, encryption starts with the plaintext message. To my way of thinking, the QUARTUS II software was the plaintext message that had to be transformed into something unusable to someone who didn't have the encryption key—in this case, Maxalim's LIMDIS licensing software. To make this transformation occur, Maxalim would need a fully functioning version of the QUARTUS II software as a starting point for the encryption. Obviously.

So I fully expected an affirmative answer to Cullen's question about whether Maxalim would have a copy of Altera's QUARTUS II software in order to write the protective licensing code. But Altera's answer surprised me: there was no reason why Maxalim should have copies of any of Altera's software products.

It was like a belch in the midst of an aria.

Intuition is a powerful human faculty, but it is no substitute for fact. My intuition in this case was based on a combination of ankle-deep knowledge of encryption and the assumption—unadulterated by information—that a licensing file would be based on encryption. The facts were otherwise: Altera told Cullen that Maxalim is simply a supplier of the LIMDIS product; in other words, Altera buys LIMDIS from Maxalim, and then Altera uses LIMDIS to grant its customers access to its software. Maxalim doesn't need access to Altera's QUARTUS II software to perform the limited function of supplying the LIMDIS licensing software.

It took a while for the full import of this information to penetrate my intuition-dulled brain, but eventually it did. If Maxalim doesn't use its customers' software code as the functional equivalent of plaintext, then no Maxalim employee would have the customers' software code to sell out the back door to CRACK99. Maxalim could employ a legion of rogues, but none of them would be in a position to steal the software. And that would mean that my theory was not entirely correct; or to put it another way, it was entirely, fundamentally, and immutably wrong. Fortunately, this was not my first encounter with my own fallibility. One of the benefits of a long career in law enforcement is frequent contact with the hard edge of truth, the ultimate teacher of humility.

Many years before, I had investigated and prosecuted a gang involved in the shooting of a Philadelphia police officer during a car stop. The officer's partner had returned fire as the assailants sped away. The car was recovered later that night, the interior soaked in blood. Bloody fabric swatches were removed and sent to the FBI lab for DNA analysis. This occurred in the early days of law enforcement's utilization of DNA analysis. It was cutting-edge forensic science. I enthusiastically read the lab results, which matched the targets of my investigation to the blood in the car by a method called restriction fragment length polymorphism (RFLP). The FBI report detailed the laborious process required to obtain results by this method and the analyst's findings, and was accompanied by background literature on the RFLP process itself. By the time I made my way through this dense textual thicket—learning how the DNA sample was broken into restriction fragments, which were then organized according to length by gel electrophoresis—I considered myself fluent in RFLP analysis and all that it implied. This is something lawyers do all the time: they learn a few key words and phrases and think they have mastered a new subject. I knew a lawyer who represented construction companies, litigating the unhappy results of unsuccessful commercial building projects, and to hear him talk you would think he could build a skyscraper single-handed; but I happened to know he wasn't good enough with a hammer to hang a picture. I hated to think I had fallen so low, but one meeting with the DNA analyst from the FBI lab showed me I didn't have the dimmest idea what RFLP analysis was or how it worked. I had been schooled.

So, when my cherished rogue-employee theory was dashed and chucked aside like roadkill, I was not entering entirely new territory, and I did not panic. But I did cling to one vestige of the Maxalim rogue-employee theory: the remarkable coincidence that Maxalim supplied the licensing files to so many of the companies whose software was for sale on CRACK99. Was it still possible that a rogue at Maxalim was illegally selling software out the back door: not STK and QUARTUS, but the Maxalim LIMDIS software itself? Or was I grasping for my last shred of pride?

I got back on the phone with Maxalim's upscale lawyer who went to all the right schools. First, we talked about the fact that Maxalim didn't have its customers' underlying software code. He confirmed it, having apparently had a conversation with his client, very similar to Cullen's conversation with Altera. I pressed him on the idea of a rogue Maxalim employee illegally selling licensing software out the back door, and he pushed back: it stands to reason that many CRACK99 products would have licensing files manufactured by Maxalim: LIMDIS is a very popular product in the industry. I agreed that this might be a complete explanation, but I asked if he could pursue the rogue-employee theory just to be sure. He agreed that he would.

What this meant for me, however, was not clear. I was back in Hinku Cave: my forward momentum was stopped; I was stuck in the dark and cold. But I was in good company with Cullen and Ronayne, who were also forward-leaning types. We decided to keep the pressure on Xiang Li, continuing our effort to understand what CRACK99 was about.

On March 18, we sent an e-mail to Xiang Li requesting two products manufactured by Collier Research Corporation: Hyper-

Sizer v.5.3.29 and HyperSizer v.5.3. HyperSizer is used in composite analysis and structural sizing applications, including aircraft and spacecraft design, and is a powerful tool in structural stress analysis. HyperSizer reminded us of QUARTUS II in the sense that it was another building block–type software product available on CRACK99. HyperSizer was part of the engineering infrastructure; it was a tool that enabled engineers to make things, like airplanes and spacecraft.

And we decided to up the ante. We noticed on the Collier Research website that there was a version more current than the HyperSizer v.5.3.29 and HyperSizer v.5.3 advertised on the CRACK99 website. Collier was up to version 5.8. This new software—HyperSizer v.5.8—was not listed on CRACK99. We thought we would test Xiang Li's ability to supply the latest versions of software by requesting HyperSizer v.5.8.

Xiang Li's reply was pithy: "Sorry no 5.8." I did admire his ability to get to the point.

We had learned something: CRACK99's product list was not necessarily current. Wherever Xiang Li was getting the software for CRACK99, there appeared to be a lag, at least for some products. We could surmise that the reason for this is that it takes time to steal software—however it might be done—and then still more time to crack the licensing file. But we didn't really know.

On the other hand, Xiang Li had no problem filling the order for the other HyperSizer products we requested, once we sent him the purchase money from the Claymont, Delaware, Western Union. The cost was only $200, in keeping with our desire to minimize expenses. Xiang Li promptly replied with a link to a HyperSizer.Pro.v.5.3 .rar file, along with instructions on how to install the software:

Check CRACK folder
Bin files
Use iso tools open
"UltraISO"

Following the instructions, Cullen opened the folder labeled "CRACK" and found binary files (known as .bin files), which are image copies of the contents of CD/DVDs. To open the .bin files, Xiang Li provided UltraISO, a converting tool that enables the user to extract files. And it worked. We had purchased for $200 about $50,000 worth of software used for advanced structural engineering on spacecraft and aircraft. The same software was utilized in the design of NASA's Ares V delivery vehicle for the Constellation program, the goal of which was to send an astronaut to Mars (prior to being defunded in 2010). In addition to design, HyperSizer was employed to perform stress analysis on the composite structures of the Ares V vehicle, such as the payload shroud (the covering of the pointy end). A powerful tool, to be sure.

But really, what did we know? None of us was a structural engineer, and I had not forgotten hard-learned lessons—such as those that flowed from my ostensible mastery of RFLP analysis of DNA—about the importance of knowing what you don't know. So Cullen and Linn went to Newport News, Virginia, to interview research and development personnel at Collier. Contrary to my expectations, the company was a small, family-owned business. The size of the firm notwithstanding, its software product is powerful: the Collier people confirmed that because of its advanced nature, effective use of the software, even by highly experienced structural engineers, required significant training. The company had spent considerable effort and money developing its product, and was alarmed to learn that it was available for mere hundreds of dollars on CRACK99. While Collier sold HyperSizer to multibillion dollar aerospace companies, it also sold to a number of small aviation companies. Of particular concern was the possibility of lost sales to the latter class of customers, who might choose to buy their products from CRACK99.

Collier confirmed that the HyperSizer software we purchased was fully functional, and expressed considerable surprise that this was so. Like AGI and Altera, Collier used LIMDIS as the licensing file. However, unlike AGI and Altera, Collier did not provide free trials of the HyperSizer software, and as an added measure of protection from theft, the company physically mailed a dongle (a security key device) to customers to enable access to the software. The dongle had nothing to do with Maxalim, punching another hole in the remnants of my rogue-employee theory. And more than that, getting access to HyperSizer software through illegitimate means required a crack not only of the LIMDIS licensing file but also of the dongle's security key. For the HyperSizer software we purchased from CRACK99, all that had been done: there were no barriers to entry once we opened the downloaded file.

There was a lot going on behind the CRACK99 veil, and it was maddening not to be able to peek behind it. In law enforcement investigations, it is common to pause at certain stages. Suppose you observe a male named Nico selling heroin on Cambria Street, and you want to know where he gets it. At this stage, you pause to formulate a plan. You know that heroin sells best early in the day, when addicts wake up. And you also know that heroin suppliers don't trust their sellers with the inventory, because the street sellers are addicts themselves. So the supplier is going to show up early in the morning to provide product to the street sellers, giving rise to your plan: you show up even earlier, watch the transaction, and arrest Nico's supplier. Piece-a-cake.

It wasn't quite so simple in the case of CRACK99. The corner where Xiang Li was selling cracked software was an abstraction: we couldn't park the surveillance van in front of CRACK99, take some pictures, and make the arrest. We had learned a great deal from the victim companies, but next to nothing about Xiang Li's supply chain; on that score, the victim companies were as mystified as we were. It seemed unlikely that we would be able to deduce his source of supply from what the victims could tell us. And as for Maxalim, the intermediary:

while the rogue-employee theory had not been such a bad theory as theories go, it was now well and truly buried. We had to pause and confront the hard question of how Xiang Li got such sophisticated, expensive software from U.S. companies, to post for sale on CRACK99.

Similar questions were being asked elsewhere in the government: the U.S. Office of the National Counterintelligence Executive (ONCIX) conducted a study on the theft by foreign entities of U.S. economic secrets from 2009 to 2011, the very period when Xiang Li was plying his trade on CRACK99. Here is the central finding of the study:

> Foreign economic collection and industrial espionage against the United States represent significant and growing threats to the nation's prosperity and security. Cyberspace—where most business activity and development of new ideas now takes place—amplifies these threats by making it possible for malicious actors, whether they are corrupted insiders or foreign intelligence services (FIS), to quickly steal and transfer massive quantities of data while remaining anonymous and hard to detect.

The focus of the ONCIX analysis was "trade secrets," defined as "all forms and types of financial, business, scientific, technical, economic, or engineering information," including software programs. ONCIX specifically found that "sensitive US economic information and technology" had been targeted both by foreign intelligence services and by private entities, the latter in the form of both private-sector companies and individual foreign nationals—like Xiang Li. It didn't take ONCIX long to drill down on China:

> Chinese actors are the world's most active and persistent perpetrators of economic espionage. US private sector firms and cybersecurity specialists have reported an onslaught of computer network intrusions that have originated in China, but the IC [intelligence community] cannot confirm who was responsible.

Thus were our efforts framed by a strategic context considerably broader than the purchase of stolen software in $200 increments via the Western Union in the Claymont, Delaware, Food Lion. Foreign adversaries in China were systemically stealing U.S. trade secrets, including technology like the software for sale on CRACK99. Whether the Chinese government was directing Xiang Li or not—something we did not know—the CRACK99 enterprise fit within the pattern ONCIX identified.

The ONCIX report was not released to Congress until 2011, and so we did not know its contents in 2010, but we were generally aware of the "onslaught" of Chinese computer network intrusions. This was no secret, and we thought these intrusions could have some relation to CRACK99. What we didn't have, however, was evidence. Assumptions and intuition had already sent me down the wrong path in this case. The time was ripe for some actual, verifiable, empirically observed facts. But the problem with facts is that they're not always there when you need them.

One theory was that Xiang Li was a hacker who sold the fruits of his endeavors on CRACK99. By "hacker," I mean someone who effects an unauthorized intrusion into a computer or computer network. This definition is not universally accepted, and there is lively debate on the question of how to distinguish malicious behavior from brilliant innovation in this field. Steve Jobs and Steve Wozniak, before they invented Apple, developed their famous Blue Box, which enabled them to control telephone switches using in-band signaling, to make free long-distance phone calls. Jobs said that this accomplishment gave the two Steves the confidence to go on to found Apple. It took two fifty-pound brains to make the Blue Box, but it was at base a device to commit fraud on the telephone company. I'm willing to guess Jobs would have taken a dim view of contemporary young geniuses inventing similarly dazzling methods of defrauding Apple.

The range of hacking techniques is wide and ever growing. Some are thuggishly crude, others mind-bendingly ingenious. On the thuggish end of the scale are social engineering techniques such as the extortionate phone call: "Give me your password or I'll set your husband on fire." Or the somewhat less intimidating call from the IT department: "Hello, Jake, it's Marcel from IT. Time to install some updates and I'll need your password." More advanced and subtle techniques include installing a rootkit, without the user's knowledge, along with apparently legitimate software. However access is gained, the hacker's objective is to load malicious software—known as "malware"—that provides the hacker ongoing access to the victim computer. Malware includes worms and viruses that self-replicate throughout a computer network, and Trojan Horses that appear to be doing something legitimate while setting up a back door for subsequent unfettered access by the hacker. The surreptitiously installed malware can in some cases turn the victim computer into a bot (short for "robot")—also known as a "zombie"—performing automated tasks over the Internet to the hacker's advantage. Malware development is an area where having a fifty-pound brain is propitious.

Regardless of the level of ingenuity evident in the technique employed, hacking is about stealing. My question was whether Xiang Li was the one doing the stealing. An affirmative answer would have seemed obvious if CRACK99 offered a small number of software titles for sale. If it listed only STK and QUARTUS II, for example, I could easily imagine that resulted from Xiang Li or a confederate hacking into the AGI and Altera networks, lifting the STK and QUARTUS II software, and posting them for sale on CRACK99. The problem was the scope and scale of CRACK99, where thousands of software titles were available. We hadn't purchased and authenticated them all, but every one we did buy was fully functional, leading me to believe that the entire inventory of CRACK99 likely was as well. It was the scale of the operation that steered me to the Maxalim rogue-employee theory to begin with; the rogue was an economy of scale; a way to explain the presence of thousands of software titles in the CRACK99 inventory. Without the rogue, I still had to explain how all this had come to be.

Chinese government sponsorship was another theory that might account for the scale of the operation: perhaps Xiang Li had obtained the thousands of software titles from his government. I had serious doubts about this theory though, because I did not see how this benefitted the Chinese government. And ONCIX had made a special point of saying that the U.S. intelligence community could not verify involvement of the Chinese government in intrusions originating from China:

> *US corporations and cyber security specialists also have reported an onslaught of computer network intrusions originating from Internet Protocol (IP) addresses in China, which private sector specialists call "advanced persistent threats." Some of these reports have alleged a Chinese corporate or government sponsor of the activity, but the IC has not been able to attribute many of these private sector data breaches to a state sponsor.*

The source for the software sold on CRACK99—whether government sponsored or not—certainly could be characterized as an "advanced persistent threat" (APT). What, other than an advanced and persistent effort, could produce the kind of software inventory—thousands of high-technology programs—available on CRACK99?

The computer security company Mandiant released a report in 2010—foreshadowing its even more explosive report in 2013—on APT activity, the "vast majority . . . [of which was] linked to China." Here is Mandiant's key finding in 2010:

> *Over the past five years, MANDIANT has seen a dramatic change in information security incidents. Superbly capable teams of attackers*

> *successfully expanded their intrusions at government and defense-re-*
> *lated targets . . . to researchers, manufacturers, law firms, and even*
> *non-profits. These intrusions appear to be conducted by well-funded,*
> *organized groups of attackers. We call them the "Advanced Persistent*
> *Threat"—the APT—and they are not "hackers". Their motivation, tech-*
> *niques and tenacity are different. They are professionals, and their*
> *success rate is impressive.*

I understood Mandiant's dismissive use of the term "hackers" to mean disorganized amateur thieves and vandals. This demonstrates the lack of consensus on the definition of "hacker," my preferred definition being much broader. However the term "hacker" should be employed, it was clear that what Mandiant discovered was similar to what our investigation revealed: a systematic, organized, and professional operation. Not everyone, of course, finds a correspondence between such positive characteristics and governmental activity, but Mandiant could not help but ask the question in 2010 of whether the Chinese government was involved:

> *The scale, operation and logistics of conducting these attacks—against*
> *the government, commercial and private sectors—indicates that they're*
> *state-sponsored. The Chinese government may authorize this activity,*
> *but there's no way to determine the extent of its involvement. None-*
> *theless, we've been able to correlate almost every APT intrusion we've*
> *investigated to current events within China.*

I could see Mandiant's point: it was hard to resist the conclusion that the Chinese government directed such APT intrusions, just as it was hard to resist the conclusion that a cache like CRACK99 was somehow the result of government-sponsored activity. But there was no direct proof of Chinese government involvement, in the sense of an ample body of evidence pointing unwaveringly to that one and only conclusion, the balm to soothe a prosecutor's troubled mind. Instead, there were lots of indications, suggesting lots of theories, leading to lots of questions—and we needed answers. In 2010, we didn't have those answers. The advanced persistent threat was very much like CRACK99 itself: it was known to exist but was operating from behind a veil we could not penetrate.

Whether Xiang Li was acting at the direction of his government or not, it is hard to miss the parallel between CRACK99 and the technological modernization that has marked the twenty-first century in China. The ONCIX report identified the Chinese government's stated policy goals, revealing an uncanny similarity between the Chinese government's priorities and Xiang Li's. ONCIX found that "Beijing's Project 863, for example, lists the development of 'key technologies for the construction of China's information infrastructure' as the first of four priorities." This goal brings to mind Altera's QUARTUS II and FPGA chips, the semiconductors that can be programmed by the purchaser to customize the chip to its ultimate intended function; QUARTUS II would appear to be an archetypal example of software useful in the construction of "China's information infrastructure."

Moreover, according to ONCIX, a priority of the Chinese government was the development of "advanced materials and manufacturing techniques," specifically:

One focus of China's 863 Program is achieving mastery of key new materials and advanced manufacturing technologies to boost industrial competitiveness, particularly in the aviation and high-speed rail sectors.

The Collier Research Corporation could not have said it better: this is the purpose of advanced software like HyperSizer, which is used to perform structural analysis on vehicles subjected to enormous stress, including airplanes, spacecraft, and high-speed rail vehicles.

Similarly, ONCIX noted China's "particular interest" in military technologies, including:

> *Aerospace/aeronautics. The air supremacy demonstrated by US military operations in recent decades will remain a driver of foreign efforts to collect US aerospace and aeronautics technologies. The greatest interest may be in UAVs because of their recent successful use for both intelligence gathering and kinetic operations in Afghanistan, Iraq, and elsewhere.*

Another rather obvious fit: AGI's STK was an advanced technology for aerospace and aeronautics, whose applications included the tracking of UAVs. It seemed Xiang Li's plays were called right out of ONCIX's version of the People's Liberation Army (PLA) playbook.

Of course, this is the problem with small samples: they give rise to faulty conclusions. We had made at this stage only three controlled purchases from CRACK99. If three points define a plane, then, ipso facto, CRACK99 is government sponsored, and I was right back where I had started, wondering if this was really an espionage case. But three points don't necessarily define a single plane; the three points could represent three parallel planes or a cube or a polyhedron or some *n*-dimensional shape I am not trained to understand. Experience had taught me to hesitate before jumping to conclusions. I thought back to lessons learned from past mistakes. Many years before, I had opened an investigation of a minority-owned company alleged to be defrauding the government by taking on federal construction contracts, and then flipping the contracts to someone else, retaining the margin for doing nothing. Under different circumstances, this would be smart business. But in the case of government procurement, it was fraud because the minority-owned contractor was required to perform work equal to a minimum percentage of the value of the contract itself, and was required to so certify. The company in question did none of this work, according to a reliable confidential informant. The fact that the woman who owned the company was young, diminutive, and pretty seemed to corroborate the allegations in the minds of the all-male investigative team of manly men, including me; she just didn't look like a construction contractor. As it turned out, the allegation was entirely false, motivated by a failure of the informant's romantic aspirations. We should have seen it coming, given the propinquity between vengeance and the keen sting of love's loss.

Things are not always what they seem. Despite my suspicions to the contrary, we could not, based on the evidence we had amassed to date, connect CRACK99 directly to the advanced and persistent effort of the Chinese government to steal U.S. military and corporate trade secrets. We needed more information of an overarching nature: not just another undercover purchase, but something that would give us a broader perspective, a ten-thousand-foot view.

That something was an e-mail search warrant, which we could now obtain on the basis of our investigation to date. A search warrant is a court order authorizing the government to search a particular place for evidence or fruits of a crime, based on probable cause, the standard set forth in the Fourth Amendment of the U.S. Constitution. Probable cause is one of the most fundamental concepts in law enforcement, and yet it is not precisely defined, not for lack of opportunity to do so, but because the Supreme Court has explicitly refused to.

Notwithstanding the invocation in the term "probable cause" of the mathematical concept of probability, the Supreme Court has said, "The probable-cause standard is incapable of precise definition or quantification into percentages because it deals with probabilities and depends on the totality of the circumstances." This statement, of course, capsizes the entire concept of probability in a sea of words: the probable-cause standard is quantifiable into percentages precisely because it "deals with probabilities."

That said, it is true that the concept of probable cause is not subject to true mathematical precision because the underlying facts are often not quantitative in nature. So, even if the Supreme Court had said that "probable cause" means a probability equal to or exceeding 50.00001 percent, how would that help answer the question of whether the probable-cause threshold is met when a prostitute named Kiki reports that Frankie "Fats" Fontana is currently holding a pound of methamphetamine in the shed behind Red's Tavern on Route 1? The answer is that it would not, leaving judges in much the same position as Justice Potter Stewart when he famously admitted not being able to provide a rigorous definition for hard-core pornography, but concluded, "I know it when I see it." So it is with federal magistrates: when it comes to probable cause, they know it when they see it, or believe that they do.

In the case of our e-mail search warrant, we had to convince a judge that we had shown probable cause that evidence or fruits of a crime would be found in the e-mail messages stored on Xiang Li's e-mail account. But, given the evidence we had accumulated, our task here was not difficult: the crime itself was occurring over the subject e-mail account. The CRACK99 website invited customer inquiries, which we had made, to order stolen and cracked software, which had been delivered—all through the same e-mail account. Thus the e-mail account was itself an instrument of crime; it was hardly a logical stretch that the e-mail account would contain evidence of that very crime. We did not spend a lot of time worrying about what degree of probability was inherent in probable cause because we were at about 100 percent.

What we did wonder is what the search warrant would yield. I hoped that answer would not be a mass of e-mail communications in Mandarin that would have to be translated at great investment of time and money. The expense of an interpreter was something that might raise the profile of the CRACK99 case to our disadvantage. Mike

Ronayne had been artful in obtaining funding for our frugal under-cover purchases, but a mass of Mandarin e-mails might require a more serious funding stream, elevating the approval level beyond wher-ever it was Ronayne had been liberating funds. On the other hand, I was reasonably optimistic that we could avoid that result because the website and Xiang Li's e-mails were written in English—even if it was a bit broken. We knew from the pen register that CRACK99 had many U.S. customers—like ourselves—who would be communicating in English, and we wanted to know who they were.

We also wanted to know who the foreign customers were. Where was this U.S. technology traveling after it left CRACK99? Was it in the hands of adversaries other than China, like Iran or North Korea? And, of course, we wanted to know if Xiang Li's e-mail communications would identify his suppliers. This was the outsized question looming over us: How did this high-tech software get to CRACK99?

To answer these questions, Brendan Cullen got to work on an e-mail search warrant affidavit in April 2010, summarizing our inves-tigative activities to date, particularly the three undercover purchases of STK, QUARTUS II, and HyperSizer. The affidavit was a typical Brendan Cullen product: thorough, detailed, and accurate, a prosecu-tor's dream. Working twelve-hour days, he produced a tour de force.

I had a few questions about the scope of the search warrant and directed them to Ed McAndrew, who occupied the office next to mine. Ed is that rare lawyer who is actually likable, even funny. People with extensive experience with lawyers will find this difficult to believe, but it's true. And Ed is that one in a hundred thousand lawyers who is just as effective in the chaos of the courtroom as in the measured and deliberate realm of legal writing. The fact that Ed also has an actual, verifiable personality makes him more like one in a million.

More than that, as a veteran cyber prosecutor, Ed knew a great deal about computers. Most of his work on cybercrime to this point had taken the form of child pornography prosecutions. I had handled some child porn cases in the days before the Internet, back when the postal service delivered the plain brown packages from Amsterdam without return addresses. We would get an anticipatory search warrant, dress an agent as a letter carrier, deliver the package, wait fifteen minutes, and execute the warrant. I really hated those cases; a glance at the evidence was enough to make you give up on humanity altogether. To avoid that result, I consoled myself with the refrain that child porn defendants represented a tiny fringe at the farthest end of the continuum of humanity. Unfortunately, I was wrong. As the Internet exploded in its ubiquity, so did child porn; the offenders were seemingly everywhere. Ed—God bless him—handled these cases so the rest of us didn't have to.

It occurred to me that Ed would be a valuable addition to our team, and he was only too happy to join. After Brendan and I summarized the case for him, I was interested in his reaction; it's always good to get the perspective of someone who is not committed to a case, to see if he shares your enthusiasm. And Ed certainly did; if anything, he thought CRACK99 was an even more important case than I did. I put this down to his superior knowledge of computers.

So, with Ed's help, we put together the search warrant application. On a nondescript day in the nondescript city of Wilmington, Delaware, Ed, Brendan, and I walked from my office to the federal courthouse to present the search warrant and supporting affidavit to a magistrate judge. We sat quietly in chambers as the judge reviewed the affidavit, which was unlike most other affidavits she read, involving gun possession and drug seizures. When she was finished, she looked up at us, shook her head, and signed the warrant. As to probable cause, evidently the judge knew it when she saw it.

Then she said something troubling: "This is an economic espionage case." This was the question that had worried me from the beginning, and I continued to be concerned that the FBI would show interest once we had laid the groundwork. Cullen was the first to respond. "The way

I look at it," he said, "this is a smuggling case. We're used to thinking of smuggling in terms of shipping containers being moved across borders. In this case, you don't need the shipping containers, because the technology can be smuggled electronically." I was supposed to be Cullen's mouthpiece, but he could do just fine on his own.

As we walked back from the federal courthouse with our search warrant approved, I wondered, Would we get a peek behind the CRACK99 veil? Would we finally be able to determine the source of Xiang Li's software?

4 | HACKER, CRACKER, SATELLITE TRACKER

I'M NOT SAYING I WON the Cold War. But I did serve in the U.S. Navy during the Cold War, which we won. You can draw your own conclusions.

I deployed to the Arctic several times in the late eighties and early nineties as part of the Navy's effort to conduct airborne antisubmarine operations in that region. The general idea was to locate and track Soviet submarines under the ice, something the Soviets would rather we not do. I was flying in a P-3C, a four-engine turboprop antisubmarine patrol aircraft, somewhere in the vicinity of the North Pole when the flight engineer advised the pilot of a fuel leak. This is not good, but things like this sometimes happen, particularly in harsh Arctic conditions. Moments later, the flight engineer announced a bleed air leak. This too is not good, but it also can be expected where the extreme cold makes everything fragile. The mission commander decided we would return to base in northern Greenland. A junior officer, I was disappointed in the early termination of the mission and said so to a more senior officer, Commander John F. Roscoe.

"You think you fully understand this situation?" asked Commander Roscoe.

"No sir," I said, having learned that a junior officer never fully understands the situation.

"If the fuel vapor and the hot air come into contact, do you know what we are?"

"No, sir."

"A bomb," said Commander Roscoe. Then he started laughing. "They won't even find our femurs," he concluded. And then he laughed some more.

That we made it back with our femurs intact did nothing to undermine the lesson that sometimes things don't go according to plan. After securing the e-mail search warrant for Xiang Li's account, my budding optimism gave way to resignation as I was assigned to investigate a postal worker I will call "Russo." A part-time rural letter carrier, Russo had been given a Voyager credit card to purchase gasoline for his postal delivery vehicle. Someone noticed he was buying an unusual amount of gasoline and took a closer look, determining that he had purchased $2,047.21 worth of fuel for his personal use. This, unfortunately, is a fairly routine scam: The government worker gets a government credit card to purchase gasoline for government business only. He knows if he uses the credit card at a liquor store or a strip club, he will set off alarms, so he uses it at a gas station, figuring it will not attract attention. He fills up the family wagon a few times, and nobody says anything, so he fills up his buddy's minivan for cash. This works out well, so he does it again. And then again. Before he knows it, he has purchased more gasoline than he could possibly use on a rural postal delivery route. I had another case like this involving a Veterans Administration drug counselor who used his government-issued Voyager credit card to buy cocaine: he would meet his supplier at the gas station and pump enough gas to buy a gram or so. Then he would counsel combat veterans suffering the scourge of drug addiction.

Eventually, Russo confessed, got a lawyer, and signed a plea agreement. Everyone was happy: the United States Attorney got an easy conviction, and Russo didn't go to prison. I try to be a team player, and prosecuting Russo fell into the category of taking one for the team. Although the time spent on Russo's theft might have been better spent on Xiang Li, Russo deserved to be charged. You can't have postal workers stealing the gas money. Someone had to prosecute him, and I tried to be philosophical about why that someone had to be me; I don't like paying taxes, but I do pay them because it is part of the deal: if you want the benefits of living in America, plan on paying some taxes. Likewise, serving as an AUSA: if you want the benefits—such as investigating an epic case like CRACK99—you're going to have to handle a petty crime from time to time to keep the authorities happy. Cases like *United States v. Russo* are like taxes: you pay what you owe, and move on.

You might be thinking that the Russo case presented an opportunity for me to let the United States Attorney in on the CRACK99 secret, and you might be right. But I still did not consider the time ripe: there were too many unanswered questions to make the sale. In contrast, Russo was right in the United States Attorney's sweet spot: fast food. And as an added bonus to the United States Attorney, the Russo conviction would be recorded in the Justice Department's books not as a petty theft but as government corruption, Russo being a government employee who stole government funds. This meant that the United States Attorney would get credit for a conviction of ostensible consequence, as if he had convicted a corrupt state senator. In contrast, CRACK99 was an unsolved mystery that had the potential to go off the tracks in any direction; CRACK99 could not compete with a sure thing like Russo.

I tried to minimize distractions like Russo by focusing on the possible implications of CRACK99—and specifically STK and the Chinese antisatellite program. I was keenly aware in 2010 that only a few years earlier, the People's Republic of China (PRC) had shot down a weather satellite with a medium-range ballistic missile. The Congressional Research Service summarized the event as follows:

On January 11, 2007, at 5:28 pm EST, the PRC conducted its first suc-cessful direct-ascent anti-satellite (ASAT) weapons test, launching a ballistic missile armed with a kinetic kill vehicle (not an exploding conventional or nuclear warhead) to destroy the PRC's Fengyun-1C weather satellite at about 530 miles up in low earth orbit (LEO) in space. . . . A National Security Council spokesman issued the White House's public response on January 18, stating that "China's develop-ment and testing of such weapons is inconsistent with the spirit of cooperation that both countries aspire to in the civil space area." He stated that the PRC used a land-based, medium-range ballistic missile.

This was no routine event. "It was the first such destruction of a satellite since the ASAT tests conducted during the Cold War by the United States and the Soviet Union in the 1980s." Why would China do this? It was a highly provocative step geopolitically, as indicated by the White House response, calling the test "inconsistent with the spirit of cooperation." This is pretty close to trash talking in the world of diplomats. And more than that, shooting down the satellite was a costly endeavor: not only the obvious expense of a medium-range bal-listic missile launch, but also the second-order effect of the destroyed satellite creating a debris field estimated to remain in the earth's orbit for twenty years, putting at risk other satellites, not to mention manned spacecraft, including those from China.

The reason for China's provocative step, in the end, was simple: China needed to test the ability of its antisatellite weapon to kill a satellite with a direct ground launch. A successful test would confirm China's antisatellite warfare capability. And the test was a success. The question of whether China intended to pursue an antisatellite capability had been debated within the U.S. government right up until the time of the test, but the answer was now clear. The remain-ing question was, why did China desire an antisatellite capability? According to the Congressional Research Service:

The longer-term implications concern some questions about China's capability and intention to attack U.S. satellites. Whereas the Secretary of Defense has reported publicly to Congress since 1998 that China's military has been developing an ASAT capability, some observers doubted the Pentagon's assertions. China's January 2007 test confirmed China's long-suspected program to develop ASAT weapons, a program that could potentially put at risk U.S. military and intelligence satellites that are needed to provide tracking and targeting for rapid reaction or other operations.

Intelligence officers try to divine an adversary's intentions from his capabilities. The strategic intentions implied by China's revealed antisatellite capabilities were grave, even dispositive under the right conditions: the Chinese strategic goal might be to "decapitate" U.S. leadership, cutting off senior decision-makers from command and control by destroying the satellites connecting them to a remote battle space, such as the western Pacific. If that was in fact China's goal, it was an ambitious proposition: if you want to decapitate the U.S. command and control architecture, it will take more than a single kinetic kill.

I could not ignore the obvious conclusion that it would be helpful indeed, from the strategic perspective of the People's Republic of China, to have AGI's Satellite Tool Kit (STK) available to track and target U.S. satellites. I did not know whether the Chinese government was using STK at all, much less for this purpose. But I did know STK was sitting on a server in China. It was hardly a stretch to imagine the Chinese government obtaining STK for use in its antisatellite program. Was it so difficult to imagine Xiang Li as an acquisition agent for the PLA?

Maybe so. My background as a naval intelligence officer complemented my career as a federal prosecutor in many ways, starting with the fact that both vocations involved the collection and analysis of information in order to determine an appropriate course of action. But intelligence officers are trained to think in geopolitical terms, and sometimes criminal activity isn't so strategic. Maybe Xiang Li—far from being a Bond villain—was just a Chengdu punk living in his mom's basement, or a fence hustling hot software to feed a bad junk habit. The truth is, I didn't know.

What I did know is that CRACK99 offered for sale thousands of high-tech software programs, mostly originating in the United States. Even if Xiang Li had nothing to do with the PLA, he got those programs somewhere. How? There were a number of possibilities, one of which was that Xiang Li or his confederates were self-sourcing through a hacking enterprise: taking what they could on an as-needed basis. It did not take much imagination to come up with this theory: 2010 was the year when the Department of Defense confirmed a significant data loss from two years before:

In 2008, the U.S. Department of Defense suffered a significant compromise of its classified military computer networks. It began when an infected flash drive was inserted into a U.S. military laptop at a base in the Middle East. The flash drive's malicious computer code, placed there by a foreign intelligence agency, uploaded itself onto a network run by the U.S. Central Command. That code spread undetected on both classified and unclassified systems, establishing what amounted to a digital beachhead, from which data could be transferred to servers under foreign control. It was a network administrator's worst fear: a rogue program operating silently, poised to deliver operational plans into the hands of an unknown adversary.

The previously classified 2008 breach was described as the "most significant breach of U.S. military computers ever," and was accompanied by an even more alarming revelation:

Over the past ten years, the frequency and sophistication of intrusions into U.S. military networks have increased exponentially. Every day,

U.S. military and civilian networks are probed thousands of times and scanned millions of times. And the 2008 intrusion . . . was not the only successful penetration. Adversaries have acquired thousands of files from U.S. networks and from the networks of U.S. allies and industry partners, including weapons blueprints, operational plans, and surveillance data.

The Department of Defense did not disclose what the "adversaries" had acquired, which "weapons blueprints." But it seemed reasonable to believe that China—the source of the intrusions highlighted by ONCIX and Mandiant—might be one of those adversaries.

What was the U.S. government doing about this threat? On the military side, there were some organizational changes. Reporting to the Secretary of Defense are four-star combatant commanders with responsibility over the joint forces assigned to their areas of responsibility. For example, EUCOM is the European Command, and its commander has responsibility for U.S. forces in Europe. CENTCOM is Central Command, and its commander has responsibility for U.S. forces in the Middle East region. PACOM is the Pacific Command; AFRICOM covers Africa; and so on. One of these combatant commands is the U.S. Strategic Command (USSTRATCOM), which does not have regional responsibility like EUCOM or CENTCOM, but a more conceptual mission:

USSTRATCOM conducts global operations in coordination with other Combatant Commands, Services, and appropriate U.S. Government agencies to deter and detect strategic attacks against the U.S. and its allies, and is prepared to defend the nation as directed.

In 2010, USSTRATCOM gained a subcommand called U.S. Cyber Command, known as "CYBERCOM," whose stated purpose is as follows:

Cyber Command has three missions. First, it leads the day-to-day protection of all defense networks and supports military and counterterror-

ism missions with operations in cyberspace. Second, it provides a clear and accountable way to marshal cyberwarfare resources from across the military. A single chain of command runs from the U.S. president to the secretary of defense to the commander of Strategic Command to the commander of Cyber Command and on to individual military units around the world. To ensure that considerations of cybersecurity are a regular part of training and equipping soldiers, Cyber Command oversees commands within each branch of the military, including the Army Forces Cyber Command, the U.S. Navy's Tenth Fleet, the 24th Air Force, and the Marine Corps Forces Cyberspace Command.

CYBERCOM was also tasked with working with "a variety of partners inside and outside the U.S. government. Representatives from the FBI, the Department of Homeland Security, the Justice Department, and the Defense Information Systems Agency work on-site at Cyber Command's Fort Meade headquarters."

Despite this apparent effort to coordinate governmental cybersecurity efforts at CYBERCOM, Cullen, Ronayne, and I hadn't received any calls from Fort Meade. This was no surprise; I cannot think of a single instance in my long career as a prosecutor when I had a call from the intelligence community offering to help with a law enforcement objective. There were many disincentives to such a call, the most legitimate being the risk of ending up in the witness box in federal court, exposing classified information to public view.

Although rhetoric was abounding in 2010, there was no concerted federal law enforcement effort to address the threat of foreign cyber intrusions and the corresponding illegal proliferation of technology from the United States. No one in the Department of Justice suggested that I shift my effort from the thrilling hunt for Russo and his gasoline credit card to support national cybersecurity. Likewise for Cullen and Ronayne, which is why they had to keep a low profile within their own agency, money-wise. In fact, their group—the counter-proliferation group—had not been tasked with addressing the proliferation of technology that results from cyber intrusions. They were assigned to investigate more traditional smuggling of tangible items, such as missile components. There was an intellectual-property group, but it was focused on the importation of counterfeit retail products like knock-off Gucci handbags. Software piracy was not really anyone's mission.

Just the year before, on April 21, 2009, the *Wall Street Journal* reported a hack, apparently from China, resulting in the theft of terabytes of design and electronics data relating to the $300 billion F-35 Lightning II stealth joint strike fighter. The F-35 is a fifth-generation tactical fighter developed to ensure future American air superiority with features such as low probability of intercept radar (LPIR), which makes it possible for the F-35 to acquire a target without giving away its position to an adversary, like, say, the PLA Air Force. The F-35 also features advanced avionics and integrated computer networking to give the pilot the ability to maintain situational awareness while engaging an adversary. The *Wall Street Journal* wasn't specific about what precise data were stolen among the terabytes apparently now in the hands of the Chinese government. But Joel Brenner, the National Counterintelligence Executive, was quoted as expressing concern about U.S. pilots not being able to trust their radar, implying that the hack would enable an adversary such as China to develop counter-measures to defeat advanced systems like LPIR.

Although the information available in 2010 was far from complete, it was alarming. China targeted U.S. technology and now possessed it. Given the immensely high stakes, and the abundant and growing evidence of a concerted and aggressive Chinese cyber effort to diminish U.S. national security, one might have expected an equally concerted and aggressive defensive cyber effort. But no one from the Department of Justice laid down a strategy, much less a tactical plan, for addressing the threat. There were documents called "strategic plans," and some even had the word "cyber" in them. But they were not, in fact, strategies. They were more like shopping lists of desired end states and conclusory statements about how to achieve them. They did not direct a prosecutor's actions, much less establish cybersecurity as a priority compared to, say, the Russo case. They were pablum.

We were alone: a handful of agents and two prosecutors scraping together cash for undercover buys, trying to figure out the mystery of CRACK99, Xiang Li's astonishing Chinese software piracy operation. We wouldn't be getting any help from headquarters; we had to solve the CRACK99 mystery on our own. If the cyber intrusions being reported in 2009 and 2010 originated in China, could Xiang Li be involved—on his own behalf or on behalf of the People's Republic of China? Was he sitting on top of a hacking pyramid, sending out orders to add to his inventory?

One way to address this question was to determine the currency of Xiang Li's inventory; if he had the most recent versions of software, we could infer he was making a concerted effort to steal software as it was being developed and improved. In March 2010, he failed this test when we asked him to provide the most recent version of HyperSizer—version 5.8. "Sorry," he wrote, "no 5.8." Was this anomalous or was he always slightly behind in his inventory? On April 13, we sent an e-mail seeking to answer this question.

Sir,

    Greetings. Do you have the latest versions of the following software products?
1. STK 9.0?
2. BizIntel08?
Thank you for your time.
Regards,

The STK product we requested was the most recent version of AGI's Satellite Tool Kit, a product we were particularly focused on due to our concerns about its application to China's antisatellite program. The other program we requested, which I will call "BizIntel 2008," was a business intelligence product that interested us because it was cheap—just $200, so we could buy it without upsetting the bean counters. But more than that, it was a powerful piece of software used to integrate large amounts of data—including technical data—into understandable reports. An effective tool for IT professionals and application designers, this software product fell into the category of "information infrastructure," one of China's strategic priorities according to ONCIX. BizIntel 2008 was analogous in that sense to Altera's QUARTUS II v.9 software, used to design and operate field-programmable gate array (FPGA) chips.

As usual, the reply from Xiang Li was prompt.

BizIntel --------------------- $USD 200.00

STK 9.0 ------------ Time in the future, not now. Any news, I will inform you

So, it was a split decision. I wasn't sure exactly what conclusion to draw from this. If China was using STK in its antisatellite program and Xiang Li had some role in that, wouldn't it stand to reason that Xiang Li would have the most current version of STK?

On the other hand, he did have the most recent version of BizIntel, for which we paid him via the Western Union in the Claymont, Delaware, Food Lion supermarket. There was an error in the information provided to Western Union, however, but as soon as that was straightened out—and not until then—Xiang Li sent us the BizIntel 2008 .rar file, along with installation instructions and a comforting note: "100% cracked."

Xiang Li also sent us a training file for use with BizIntel 2008, without charge. "More . . . . . gifts," he wrote.

A few weeks later, on May 21, Xiang Li wrote:

good news
STK 9.0 ----------------$USD 3000.00
LATEST VERSION
ANALYTICAL GRAPHICS STK 9.1.0

We confirmed with AGI that this was the most current version. So with points off for lack of timeliness, Xiang Li had passed the test. But where did he get it? From a hacker in a virtual network? From someone in the PLA? What explained the three-week delay?

We had by this time obtained the results of the search warrant on Xiang Li's e-mail account, china9981@gmail.com. I harbored hopes that the e-mails might show evidence of the PLA asking for specific software, for example, a request for proposal for STK sent by the PLA's General Armaments Department at ASAT.Program.Manager@ GDA.PLA.cn.mil, followed by Xiang Li's reply:

Welcome
Step 1 . . . .
However, must be the payment. Do you understand?

The volume of e-mails seized was enormous—there were ten thousand to slog through—and it took many weeks to analyze them. The brunt of the effort was borne by Cullen. His approach was typically methodical, first identifying e-mails sent by Xiang Li, as opposed to those sent to Xiang Li, on the operating assumption that e-mails sent by Xiang Li would reflect deals he was working on actively. Cullen set up an Excel spreadsheet listing customer names, countries of origin, products sold, and any other identifying information. He worked into the night and on weekends to complete the process, with the goal of reviewing 250 e-mails a day. It is a commonplace that government workers are lazy and unfocused, and for good reason; Cullen, however, is a striking exception.

Beyond the sheer mass, the most difficult aspect of analyzing Xiang Li's e-mails originated in the fact that there were hundreds of unrelated threads of conversation because Xiang Li was dealing with hundreds of transactions during the period under review. Each transaction had to be unwound to determine the customer inquiry that ultimately resulted in a sale. Once Cullen untangled this mess, we counted—between April 2008 and April 2010—over 450 illegal software sales to customers located throughout the world.

We could see that when it came to money, Xiang Li was egalitarian: no matter who you were or where you were, you paid before he delivered. Payments were usually sent via Western Union and Money Gram, although some customers made bank transfers or used Pay Pal and Ali Pay, an overseas online payment medium popular in China and Russia. Xiang Li usually supplied his other customers with software in the same manner he supplied us: after receiving payment, he would send an e-mail containing a uniform resource locator (URL) web address through which the customer could download large compressed electronic files. And all of his customers—like us—paid pennies on the dollar.

In one typical exchange, on January 9, 2009, a customer in the United States named Kris M. (last name withheld) purchased a software product called Rockwell RSlogix5000, manufactured by Rockwell Automation, a U.S. company. This software is used in industrial automation to provide a single process control platform to enhance the speed of information transfer. The price on the legitimate market—that is, when purchased legally—was between $2,500 and $8,000, depending on what features were included. Xiang Li's price was $200. Records from Western Union revealed that on January 9,

Kris M. sent Xiang Li $200 via a Western Union branch located in the United States, which Xiang Li picked up at a Western Union branch located in Chengdu, China, on January 10.

On other occasions, Xiang Li provided the pirated software by sending discs through the mail. For example, on January 13, 2009, a U.S. customer named Dan G. (last name withheld) e-mailed Xiang Li to confirm that he made a $60 Western Union payment for a software product called Vericut 6.2. This software, manufactured by CG Tech, a company based in the United States, is used to simulate computer numerical control (CNC) machining to control precision tools. Its purpose is to detect errors, prevent tool collisions, and improve efficiency by increasing machine-cutting speeds. Dan G. also sent Xiang Li an additional $35 to ship a disc containing this software by mail to his residence in Illinois.

But mail was not Xiang Li's preferred method of transferring software. As he explained to one customer on July 21, 2008, "Now CD-ROM by mail is illegal. Customs may be destroyed." On January 14, 2009, another customer asked Xiang Li to mail him a copy of the cracked software. When Xiang Li demurred, the customer asked what the problem was. Xiang Li replied, "Because the end of the strict customs checks. This is contraband."

Aha. This was important. Whatever his station in life—Chengdu punk in mom's basement, underworld fence, or Bond villain working for the PLA—Xiang Li knew that what he was doing was illegal: he was knowingly trafficking in contraband. If I could ever get my hands on him, I could prove to a jury that Xiang Li's actions were willful, that he was not acting out of ignorance of the law.

To this end, it would also be helpful to have Xiang Li himself—through his e-mails—answer for the jury a question asked by a customer on April 19, 2010: "Can you please explain how your service can provide this software for just 80 dollars? I am aware that the cost of Compusoft is much much more than this." Xiang Li responded the same day with utter clarity: "this is cracked version software." When another customer asked on February 11, 2010, if the software he was buying from CRACK99 was "a complete version" and whether a "dongle [was] needed or included," and "what about updates," Xiang Li replied, "This is cracked version . . . no need dongle . . . only the version no updates." There certainly was no question in Xiang Li's mind about the fact that the software was cracked. This was no honest mistake.

The e-mails also demonstrated Xiang Li's shamelessness in conducting his cracked software enterprise. For example, a customer asked on January 8, 2010, about the installation process, reporting that he had received a message that access to the license would expire on "22 JAN 2010." Xiang Li explained helpfully—both to the customer and now to us—that the software would remain operational beyond the trial period because he had altered the trial period's time limit in the license file source code: "this is cracked versin! There is no limit you know?? you see? I edit the time . . . ." Xiang Li's answer to this e-mail was also helpful in gaining an understanding of how the crack worked, at least in this case: Xiang Li was altering the expiration date of the software license so that it would never expire.

There was more evidence of Xiang Li's willfulness as well. We found numerous cease-and-desist e-mails from businesses demanding that their software not be sold on CRACK99. These e-mails stated that CRACK99 was violating the laws of the United States and other nations by illegally advertising and selling software products without authorization. Xiang Li had a standard reply to these demands: he would promise to remove the products in question from the CRACK99 website. And sometimes he did. But he also told his customers that he had products for sale he was not allowed to advertise on CRACK99, and he sold those software products despite the cease-and-desist letters.

The CRACK99 e-mails appeared to confirm that Xiang Li was an actual person—at least in the sense that he had a date of birth, which is a good first step in becoming an actual person. The e-mails also seemed to make clear that Xiang Li and Chun Yan Li were two different people, not two aliases for the same individual. Their division of labor was clear: Xiang Li directly communicated with customers, quoting prices and assisting with technical difficulties, while Chun Yan Li collected the money. Chun Yan Li had a separate Chinese identification number and birth date, but the same address, leading us to conclude she was probably a wife or sister. The e-mails—along with an analysis of financial records such as Western Union receipts, Money Gram receipts, and PayPal data—led us to conclude that her primary responsibility in the operations of CRACK99 was to collect proceeds from the website's customers.

We also learned that Xiang Li and Chun Yan Li were not the only people involved in the operations of CRACK99. On November 29, 2008, a potential customer contacted CRACK99 inquiring about a software product called Plant Simulation, version 8.2.4, manufactured by Siemens PLM Software. Xiang Li responded that he did have the software but an earlier version. The customer then wrote back asking if Xiang Li knew anybody who could crack the more current version of the software. Xiang Li responded by stating that he could arrange for that—for $1,000. The customer agreed, asking who will do the job: "Yes ok tell me who do this." Xiang Li replied, "Experts crack, Chinese people Sorry can not reveal more."

If true, this meant Xiang Li was not himself the cracker but instead employed—or at least had access to—expert Chinese crackers. This theory was corroborated by a February 2, 2009, exchange with a potential customer in which Xiang Li described his role as follows: "I am not a crack production engineers (my job is to collect)[.] This is an international organization created to crack. . . ." And in May 2009, during an e-mail dialogue with a customer who was hesitant to pay for a software product, Xiang Li explained, "Engineers do not have the money will not begin work Do you understand? . . . I need to use your money to seek the help of experts to cracker master I earn 10% of the profits." If Xiang Li was telling the customer the truth, it meant that he employed other individuals to do the actual cracking of the software. Thus was Xiang Li at the head of a conspiracy, directing the actions of "cracker masters" for a 10 percent piece of the action.

Although Xiang Li appeared to direct others—the "cracker masters"— to crack the software, he demonstrated a strong working knowledge of cracking methodology. There were many customer e-mails—not unlike our own—requesting assistance opening a cracked software file. Time and again, Xiang Li walked his customers through the process. Often, this involved bypassing the time restrictions of the licensing files—in some cases, simply by eliminating those restrictions from the licensing code; in other cases, by instructing customers to set the internal clocks in their computers to a particular date to conform to the date in the cracked licensing file. This enabled CRACK99 customers to bypass the dissemination restrictions and time limitations originally imposed by the license file, thereby allowing unlimited sharing and duplication. Xiang Li was more than a mere fence; he really was making the market work.

The scope of Xiang Li's enterprise was enormous, extending to sixty countries. In February 2009, Xiang Li sold software to a customer in Indonesia I will call "Kadek." According to their e-mail dialogue, Kadek purchased a software product called Agilent Advance Design System, manufactured by Agilent Technologies. This is electronic design automation software for radio frequency, microwave, and high-speed digital applications in the wireless communication, aerospace, and defense industries, offered to the legitimate market at a retail price beginning at $10,000. CRACK99 sold this product for $60. Western Union records revealed that on February 5, 2009, Kadek transferred the Indonesian equivalent of $60 from Indonesia to Xiang Li in Chengdu, China. One wonders to what use Kadek put this advanced software in Indonesia. Any scenario is possible once it landed in his hands.

Then there was the exchange with a man I will call "Nasir" who wanted to buy Ansoft Simplorer software, manufactured by ANSYS in the United States. Here is how ANSYS describes its product:

> *ANSYS Simplorer is an intuitive, multi-domain, multi-technology simulation program that enables engineers to simulate complex power electronic and electrically controlled systems. Simplorer's powerful technology allows you to analyze all aspects of large-scale systems, from detailed component analysis to system performance, in a single virtual design environment.*

Simplorer is high-end, engineering design simulation software to predict system performance, particularly in "building complex power electronic and electrically controlled systems." Why would anyone want it?

> *With Simplorer, engineers working in the early stages of the design cycle can identify problems that other simulation or build-and-test methods cannot detect, allowing them to maximize product performance and reduce time-to-market. . . . For industries where products depend on precise interaction between electromechanical components, power electronic circuits and system-based electrical and mechanical control, Simplorer cuts through the technological chaos and delivers an unequalled level of usability and numerical power. Whether the challenge is developing an electric propulsion system, integrating an electric drive with a motor or developing a new alternative energy system, Simplorer provides the technology you need to virtually explore every aspect of the design and deliver it fast and under budget.*

In other words, Ansoft Simplorer can be used in a wide range of electronic and electrical engineering system simulation environments, including electric propulsion systems, which are used in spacecraft and satellites.

On February 7, 2010, Nasir attempted to buy Simplorer software directly from ANSYS, indicating he was located in Syria. As indeed he was: we determined that although Nasir used an e-mail account created using a Ukrainian IP address, he had recently accessed the account from multiple IP addresses located in the Syrian Arab Republic. More than this, Nasir said he was working for the government of Syria, providing "IT solutions to governments and educational institutions in Syria."

On February 9, ANSYS wrote back saying it is "prohibited by the U.S. government from doing business with Syria. Therefore, we are unable to satisfy your request to buy our software." Nasir, undeterred, wrote back asking for the "student version," as if this would satisfy ANSYS's concerns about the Syrian embargo. ANSYS wrote back: "Just to re-iterate . . ." Rebuffed, Nasir turned the next day to CRACK99, and was immediately rewarded with a price quote and wiring instructions. Nasir sought clarification, asking if he would be buying the "complete version . . . I mean software and crack?" Xiang Li's response was clear: "this is cracked version." This answer was more to Nasir's liking.

On February 15, Xiang Li received e-mail confirmation that $185 had been sent by Western Union from Syria to China. Making matters more intriguing: that e-mail was not sent by Nasir; it was from someone whom I will call "Yusuf" who said he was acting on behalf of his brother. Xiang Li did not appear to be as intrigued as we were; to Xiang Li, a sale was a sale, so on February 19, he sent five download links to Nasir's e-mail account. Yusuf responded by asking Xiang Li to mail the software to Syria because "the download is impossible here because of very slow internet." Xiang Li—always focused on customer satisfaction—did as requested. The software, purchased for $185, was worth $26,000.

Xiang Li thus circumvented the U.S. embargo of Syria for only $185. What use Nasir, Yusuf, and their friends and relations in Syria had for the ANSYS simulation software, we did not know. It might be that Nasir was going to design an electric car with it, for the benefit of all. But the possibility of nefarious uses cannot be ignored, particularly when you consider that Nasir was located in Syria, home of the House of Assad, which is why Syria is embargoed. The Assad regime might find Simplorer useful in developing or improving electric systems in military hardware, for example. And from the House of Assad, it is a short step to Hezbollah, and from there, where? The most ominous implication from this single transaction with Syria is the broadest: once control of technology is lost, there is no getting it back. The potential uses of Simplorer—for good or ill—will be determined by whoever holds the software.

Based on our review of the e-mails, we found that the majority of CRACK99's sales were to Australia, Canada, China, Germany, Italy, Singapore, the United Kingdom, and the United States. In fact, one-third of Xiang Li's customers—including Kris M. and Dan G.—were from the United States. Xiang Li sold hundreds of different software programs to his customers, the majority of which were originally produced in the United States. This meant that Xiang Li was sitting at the epicenter of a strangely circular distribution system in which stolen software originated in the United States, traveled by unknown means to China, and then was redistributed back to the United States. This made sense in a perverse way: as a technologically innovating country, the United States both creates new technology and consumes it; so it is both the victim of software piracy and the consumer generating demand. But this pattern did not negate the fact that CRACK99 also sold to customers in China—and elsewhere—nor did it negate the possibility that Xiang Li was disseminating software by means other than the e-mail account we had searched—china9981@gmail.com—in which case we would not know of the transaction.

It all fit a pattern—and a familiar one. CRACK99 was a thriving enterprise; we were just one of hundreds of customers of a web-based retail business that was efficient and customer oriented. But in all the data from the e-mail search warrant, we did not find a single instance in which the PLA ordered software from Xiang Li: not a single request for proposal for STK sent by the PLA's General Armaments Department at ASAT.Program.Manager@GDA.PLA.cn.mil. Maybe he was supplying the PLA, but not by means of china9981@gmail.com.

And more than that: we did not uncover any evidence demonstrating the method by which Xiang Li acquired his massive inventory of software. However he was getting it, it wasn't through the china9981@gmail.com e-mail account. So how was he getting it?

5 | THAT GIANT SUCKING SOUND

I HUSTLED TOWARD THE TOWER OF the USS *America*, CV 66, my flight suit sticking to my back. The late spring air was warm and humid, but the exhilaration of landing on a rolling flight deck might have contributed to the perspiration situation. That day, we experienced the added thrill of a bolter, which occurs when the tailhook fails to engage any of the arresting wires and the aircraft has to circle back for another try. For what it's worth, the pilot's back was even more soaked. He wore a patch on his shoulder that said, "U.S. NAVY: ONE GOOD DEAL AFTER ANOTHER."

There are a lot of people on the flight deck of an aircraft carrier during air operations: plane handlers in blue shirts, aviation fuelers (called "grapes") in purple, ordnancemen in red, and others. If you're not one of these people, the flight deck is no place to linger. I remember thinking that that particular place at that particular time was a particularly dangerous place to be. And yet, nothing went wrong and no one got hurt; for all those people on the flight deck, it was just another day at the office. My brother was a carrier aviator who trapped over a hundred times aboard the USS *Theodore Roosevelt*,

93

CVN 71, without a single mishap. No one conducts carrier air operations better than the U.S. Navy, and no one ever has.

In my experience, there are two U.S. Navies. There is the administrative Navy, which is a monument to incompetence. These are the people who lose your vaccination record, causing your orders to be disapproved until you get a second, unnecessary flu inoculation. These are the people who can't manage to pay your travel claim within a month of your return, and act like they're doing you a personal favor when they do. These are the people who lose a sailor's service record and then refuse to consider his promotion because his records are incomplete. This administrative Navy stands in marked contrast to the other side of the U.S. Navy: the real Navy, the operational Navy. This is the Navy whose fleets are powered by nuclear reactors operated by youngsters just out of school; the Navy that sends ballistic-missile submarines on uninterrupted underwater operations for months at a time; the Navy that deploys SEALs into impossible circumstances to accomplish the implausible. Not to mention the United States Marine Corps. There are many reasons for this astonishing level of operational competence, including the courage and skill of naval aviators and "grapes" and marines and SEALs and submariners. Another reason is American technology, which is highly evolved, not only because of the military's direct investment but also because of the private innovation on which military technology depends. There is no separating the two: the U.S. military has always benefited from the ingenuity and inventiveness of American enterprise.

The U.S. military is an integral part of the U.S. economy, the success of which is dependent on intellectual property. As innovation goes, so goes the economy, including the military sector. The Commerce Department has identified 75 out of 313 industries as being intellectual property (IP)–intensive, and found that these particular industries accounted for 27.1 million American jobs, or 18.8 percent of all employment in the economy, in 2010. The IP–intensive sector also supported one supply-chain job for every job within the IP-intensive-sector. So, directly or indirectly, this sector of the economy accounted for approximately 40 million jobs, or 27.7 percent of all employment, in 2010. Thus is the theft of American technology a threat to national security in two senses: one is the direct loss of combat effectiveness caused by the proliferation of closely held technology; the other is the loss of the technological infrastructure that drives the American economy, which in turn supports the military. When employment in IP-intensive industry declines, innovation declines, thereby degrading military readiness.

And then there is the direct economic harm: the dollars taken out of American pockets. "Intellectual property accounts for approximately 33 percent of the value of U.S. corporations," or $5 trillion. In 2010, CYBERCOM commander General Keith B. Alexander said, "Of that [$5 trillion], approximately $300 billion [6 percent] is stolen over the networks per year." In 2012, General Alexander continued the theme: "The ongoing cyber-thefts from the networks of public and private organizations, including Fortune 500 companies, represent the greatest transfer of wealth in human history."

When these intellectual-property assets are stolen, American companies lose value, which diminishes the incentive to innovate because the innovators are deprived of the full benefit of their innovations. Moreover, declining revenue is reflected in declining payroll; in this way, theft of intellectual property accounts for the loss of "millions" of jobs in the United States, according to the 2013 report from the Commission on the Theft of American Intellectual Property, also called the IP Commission. In February 2014, 10.5 million people in the United States were unemployed, an unemployment rate of 6.7 percent. The IP Commission did not say how many "millions" of unemployed people were indirectly the victims of the theft of intellectual property, but if by "millions" the IP Commission meant 2 million, then intellectual-property theft accounted for about 20 percent of the total unemployment figure of 10.5 million. So, if intellectual-property theft suddenly stopped before February 2014, the 6.7 percent unemployment rate would have only been around 5.3 percent. Many economists consider a 5 percent unemployment rate to be "full employment."

Intellectual-property theft imposes other costs as well, such as corruption of supply chains, including those of the Department of Defense, by components that are counterfeit—that is, unauthorized copies of legitimate components. A 2013 study by the U.S. Senate Committee on Armed Services "uncovered 1,800 cases of suspect electronic parts [in the Defense Department supply chain]. The total number of individual suspect parts involved in those cases exceeded one million." Seventy percent of the counterfeit parts originated in China.

Counterfeit parts are by definition not manufactured to specification, which makes them fundamentally unreliable. No one wants to fly in an airplane—civilian or military—with unreliable electronic components. In addition to the threat of unreliability, counterfeit software introduces malevolent second-order effects, such as malware. According to a 2013 study from IDC, "the direct costs to enterprises from dealing with malware from counterfeit software will hit $114 billion." The same study estimated that the probability of encountering malware in the course of using "pirated" software is one in three.

The IDC study distinguished between "counterfeit" and "pirated" software as follows:

> *"Pirated software" refers to software that is improperly licensed or not licensed at all, and "counterfeit software" refers to a subset of pirated software that is deliberately presented as genuine when it is not.*

We had determined that the software being sold by Xiang Li was not counterfeit in the sense of being fake; rather, it was authentic software that had been pirated. We based this determination on the manufacturers' confirmation that the software we bought on CRACK99 was the actual software they had produced. Admittedly, the distinction between counterfeit and pirated software can become a bit blurry; since software code can be copied and pasted, a counterfeit version might just be an unauthorized copy, which is pretty close to the definition of pirated software. But we need not get bogged down in definitions. Both counterfeit software and pirated software present the serious threat of introducing malware, and represent two faces of the same global problem: stolen intellectual property.

And where does the lion's share of this intellectual-property theft originate? China—approximately 70 percent. According to Richard Clarke, former special adviser on cybersecurity to President George W. Bush, speaking in 2011:

> *What has been happening over the course of the last five years is that China—let's call it for what it is—has been hacking its way into every corporation it can find listed in Dun & Bradstreet. Every corporation in the U.S., every corporation in Asia, every corporation in Germany. And using a vacuum cleaner to suck data out in terabytes and petabytes. I don't think you can overstate the damage to this country that has already been done.*

Stories abound. There is the sad tale of Massachusetts-based American Superconductor (AMSC), which lost its wind-energy software code to its Chinese customer Sinovel Wind Group, and then lost 84 percent of its stock value. The software, which controlled AMSC's wind turbines in the Gobi Desert, was illegally downloaded from an AMSC computer in the United States to a computer in Austria. This caused AMSC a loss of more than $800 million when the Chinese decided that since they had the software, they didn't need AMSC anymore. Then there is the Chinese hack of iBAHN, a U.S.-based company that provides broadband Internet access for many hotel chains, including Marriott. The iBAHN hack not only enabled the Chinese to monitor e-mails—a potential treasure trove of business intelligence—but also established a potential backdoor for entry into corporate computer networks.

In another reported case, Microsoft sold a single license of an advanced business software product to a Chinese buyer. When Microsoft issued an upgrade to that product, the upgrade was downloaded 30 million times, meaning the one legitimate license had been cracked and replicated an astonishing 30 million times.

Reported cases of employee theft from U.S. employers for the benefit of Chinese competitors have become commonplace. David Yen Lee was the technical director of Valspar Corporation's architectural coatings group. He downloaded 160 secret formulas from Valspar's network in order to turn them over to Valspar's Chinese competitor, Nippon Paints, where Lee had recently accepted employment. The formulas were valued at between $7 million and $20 million. Chinese national Kexue Huang stole trade secrets from his employer Dow AgroSciences relating to the production of organic insecticides, in order to turn them over to Chinese universities controlled by the Chinese government. Tze Chao stole trade secrets from his employer DuPont relating to titanium dioxide (TiO_2) manufacturing and turned them over to Pangang Group, a company that manufactures TiO_2 and is controlled by the People's Republic of China. Chao acknowledged that "the PRC government had placed a priority on developing chloride-process TiO_2 technology in a short period of time and wished to acquire this technology from western companies."

In some of these cases, the U.S. company employee was actually an agent of the Chinese government. Dongfan "Greg" Chung worked at Rockwell International and Boeing from 1973 until the time of his arrest. During this period, Chung stole trade secrets relating to the Space Shuttle and the Delta IV rocket for the benefit of the Chinese government. The Chinese aviation industry began sending Chung "tasking" letters as early as 1979, directing him to collect specific technological information, including data related to the Space Shuttle and various military and civilian aircraft. On one occasion, Chung responded, "I would like to make an effort to contribute to the Four Modernizations of China." Among the engineering manuals Chung sent to his handlers was the one relating to the U.S. B-1 supersonic strategic bomber.

If this Chinese theft of American technology and know-how seems targeted and systematic, it's because it is. In 2013, the IP Commission reported, "National industrial policy goals in China encourage IP theft, and an extraordinary number of Chinese in business and government entities are engaged in this practice." This means that whether directly government sponsored or not, Chinese intellectual-property theft—even by privateers such as Xiang Li—is state sponsored in the sense that it is encouraged by the Chinese government.

Between 1820 and 1950, the world economy grew nearly eightfold, and since 1950 more than sixteen-fold. Technological innovation was one of the predominant drivers of this dramatic increase in wealth. The innovators and inventors were rewarded, creating an incentive to develop newer technologies and products despite the fearsome risks and burdensome upfront investment. The astonishing rate of discovery in the past hundred years—particularly in areas like aerospace, aviation, information technology, and biochemistry—has driven further innovation, motivated by the tremendous benefits awaiting the innovators. The giants of today—Microsoft, Apple, Google, Boeing, Lockheed, and many others—are monuments to this cycle of risk and reward.

That is the American story. China wants a different story, one where the Chinese skip the risk and toil of research and development but enjoy the benefits. The United States has been innovating for the past century and China has not, but China wants to compete with the United States as its equal in the world economy. To do this, the Chinese need U.S. technology. So they've decided to steal it. The Office of the U.S. Trade Representative reports that China has stolen "all forms of trade secrets," characterizing Chinese theft of intellectual property as "escalating." The U.S. Trade Representative found that, as one means of acquiring trade secrets, "Chinese agencies inappropriately require or pressure rights holders to transfer [intellectual-property rights] from foreign to domestic entities." Between 50 and 80 percent of the theft of intellectual property from the United States and elsewhere is committed by Chinese actors.

The Chinese government's strategy of global intellectual-property theft has succeeded. According to the IP Commission,

> *By legal as well as illegal means, China has done a Herculean job of absorbing American and other countries' technology. China now manufactures more cars than any other country, in 2012 producing almost as many as the United States and Japan combined; launches astronauts into orbit; assembles and makes many components for sophisticated consumer products like the iPad; leads the world in many green industries; builds most of the world's new nuclear power plants; is rapidly advancing its military technology, often at a quicker pace than most experts predict; and makes some of the world's fastest supercomputers. China is projected to pass the United States in total economic output between 2016 and 2030, depending on the source and methodology used.*

One measure of China's success in this "Herculean" technology transfer effort is the accelerating rate of development of military aircraft. Multiple news sources reported in 2014 that technology stolen from the U.S. F-35—the most advanced fifth-generation stealth tactical fighter in the U.S. arsenal—has appeared in China's fifth-generation stealth fighter. Specifically:

> *The F-35 data theft was confirmed after recent photographs were published on Chinese websites showing a newer version of the J-20.*

The new version of the radar-evading aircraft had incorporated several design upgrades since the first demonstrator aircraft was revealed in 2011. According to the officials, the J-20 has progressed from prototype to demonstrator. One of its most significant weapons enhancements is a new electro-optical targeting system under its nose. Additionally, protruding engine nozzles seen in the earlier version have been hidden, an attempt to further reduce the jet's radar signature. The newest J-20 also appeared with a different radar-absorbing coating.

According to these press reports, the technology transfer took place as a result of "Chinese cyber spying against the Lockheed Martin F-35 Lightning II . . . under what U.S. intelligence agencies codenamed Operation Byzantine Hades, a large-scale, multi-year cyber program that targeted governments and industry." The means by which the PLA Air Force has moved from the fourth to the fifth generation of military aviation is theft of U.S. technology.

Ironically, U.S. technology enables the Chinese to steal U.S. technology with relative ease, and nowhere is this more evident than on the Internet. It is precisely because of American success in developing web-based applications, microcircuitry, and computer hardware that China is able to use the Internet as an efficient method of theft. CRACK99 is a gleaming monument to this aspect of China's success: thousands of other people's inventions and innovations, posted on the Internet for sale at pennies on the dollar.

Figuring out how this had come to be was one of the goals of our April 2010 e-mail search warrant, and the results helped discipline my imagination. For one thing, we did not see any evidence of tasking of Xiang Li by the Chinese government, nor did we find any proof of Xiang Li selling to the government directly. But what we did discover was shocking: the scope of Xiang Li's enterprise was enormous—so much so, that we could not be sure we were seeing it all. It reminded me of looking at the ocean from the rail of a ship: you know it's the ocean, and you now it's big, but you can't see where it ends.

This is what pushed me over the United States Attorney's transom. The results from the e-mail search warrant settled the question of whether we were on to something significant. The level of Xiang Li's activity and the scope of his global operation demonstrated that— whoever he was—he wasn't some pimply geek in his mom's basement having fun with his laptop. He was a righteous target, someone who was doing real damage to the United States, whether measured in terms of harm to national security or in terms of more broad economic costs. The United States Attorney needed to be advised that, like it or not, his office had a significant case. And he needed to be informed that this case would be taking up a large portion of my time going forward.

So I told him all about the CRACK99 enterprise, emphasizing the scope of its Internet sales activity, as revealed by the e-mail search warrant, and the nature of the high-tech software being sold. The United States Attorney knew nothing about the Chinese government's sponsorship and encouragement of cyber intrusion and espionage, so I briefed him on that as well. I explained in some detail the consequences, both in national security and in economic terms: lost jobs, stolen innovation, military technology proliferation, and U.S. strategic disadvantage. I thought I delivered a stem-winder, if you will forgive a bit of self-congratulatory preening. Alas, to no avail: his reaction was about as half-hearted and noncommittal as you might expect, assuming your expectations were as low as mine. He didn't say anything particularly memorable, just something along the lines of, "Well, okay, thanks."

Life is about balance. On the one hand, after my humdinger of a speech, the United States Attorney did not tell me to cease and desist, which was good. On the other hand, soon after giving the United States Attorney my CRACK99 stem-winder, I was assigned the matter of a young fellow named "Juco" (not his real name) who was arrested after delivering heroin. The lure of fast food is difficult to resist.

Juco had been caught in the act of delivering the heroin from Philadelphia to a parking lot outside Wilmington. Having been caught red-handed, Juco wanted to talk, as do so many who are caught red-handed. I don't know why exactly, considering that we come from very different places, but I happen to be particularly good at talking to the Jucos of this world. A similarly situated offender told me that I reminded him of his father.

"Was your father bald like me?" I asked.

"I don't know," he replied.

Juco was full of actionable information, which he was only too happy to provide when asked. The asking part, that's the art of law enforcement, and I learned at the feet of the master: Philadelphia Police Detective Jim Moffit. Above all, he taught me to go slow. Smoking filterless cigarettes, which he always offered to the subject, Moffit would follow up on everything. "Let's explore this," he would say, letting the subject know that everything—and I mean everything—would be explored. Moffit was rarely confrontational; in fact, he was downright amiable, even in the company of the most utterly vile people you can imagine, people who rape and hurt and kill without regret. There is a time for confrontation and a place for outrage, but in the ordinary course, I learned that subjects react better to sweet than to sour. "I'm not here to judge," he would say, having learned that people in trouble often seek an opportunity to explain. Moffit was only too happy to oblige.

Juco's information led to more arrests, which in turn led to opportunities to excel in the courtroom, including the cross-examination of a woman claiming to be the long-time girlfriend of one of the new round of defendants. She testified under oath that during their five-year relationship, the defendant lived on Roosevelt Boulevard in Philadelphia, but she couldn't say where—except to helpfully add that he lived on the second floor with someone named Juan, whose last name she did not know. She said her boyfriend had worked at a bodega in north Philadelphia for five years, "eight to eight," twelve hours a day. However, the defendant had previously stated he worked in construction, although he could not provide the name of his employer.

In the context, her testimony made perfect sense because nothing makes sense once you enter the world of narcotics trafficking, a place where down is up and up is down. Likewise, there is little that makes sense in the government's never-ending and never-winning war on drugs. That is because there is no strategic plan; I wouldn't even say there is a tactical plan. There is only low-hanging fruit like Juco and his codefendants: they get locked up more or less at random, others replace them, the replacements get locked up and then replaced, and nothing changes. This is why I had a hard time viewing this heroin caper as important enough to justify taking time away from the CRACK99 investigation. Tragically for me, the assignment meant that my breathtakingly eloquent speech to the United States Attorney about national security, our intellectual property–intensive economy, and the fate of nations had exactly zero effect.

In the face of life's disappointments, we must soldier on. And so, our appetites whetted by the results of the April e-mail search warrant, Ed, Brendan, and I got to work on another warrant. Part of our motivation was sheer avarice: we liked what we saw, so we wanted more. But we also needed to stay current on Xiang Li's activities and gain more insight into the CRACK99 enterprise. In August, a federal magistrate judge approved a new warrant, giving us access to Xiang Li's activity on the account between April 20 and August 23, 2010. The results were consistent with those of the April warrant. During the four-month period, Xiang Li conducted eighty-five separate illegal software transactions with approximately sixty-six different customers, about half of whom were in the United States. The remaining customers were from the United Kingdom, the United

Arab Emirates (UAE), Germany, Kuwait, Uganda, and Saudi Arabia, among other nations.

I was particularly concerned about Xiang Li's traffic with the UAE and Kuwait given their proximity to Iran, to which I was afraid American technology was being transferred. This was an old habit from years of investigating Iranian arms trafficking, which was often conducted using transshipment points in the Persian Gulf, such as Dubai. But my concern was not well grounded in the context of Internet sales. After all, Xiang Li's customers could have resold software to Iran just as easily from Uganda as from the UAE. But the general concern was valid: we had no idea what happened to the software after Xiang Li sold it; it could have been transferred to any number of American adversaries, whether Iran, China, or someone else.

As we had in April, we observed a wide range of software products sold during this four-month period, for use in engineering, manufacturing, space exploration, aerospace simulation and design, and mathematics—even storm-water management. Likewise, the majority had been produced by U.S.-based companies. In most of the transactions, Xiang Li sent his customers the software via URL links embedded in e-mails, the same method employed in his dealings with us. We determined that the most commonly used URL was registered to "li xiang" of Chengdu, China, with the same telephone number as that provided on CRACK99's website.

We found more evidence in Xiang Li's e-mails of his willfulness, demonstrating that he knew he was committing a crime. For example, he instructed his customers not to disclose to their banks the purpose of the money transfers because the transactions were prohibited by law. Likewise, in a June 29, 2010, e-mail, a customer asked Xiang Li, "Is this a full legal version? . . . I will require a legal copy. . . . Will they be inclined to pursue legal persecution of me . . . ?" Xiang Li responded, "Sorry I am www.crack99.com all software is cracked version[.] Is not the official version."

Other e-mail exchanges revealed something about the scale of CRACK99's operations. On May 7, 2010, a Turkish customer requested one thousand products and asked Xiang Li if he could handle such a large request. Xiang Li wrote back, "My office the biggest computer market in Chengdu. CHINA I understand the market dynamics." Indeed he did, at least the market dynamics in China.

His understanding of the market dynamics in the United States, however, was another matter altogether. Fences always sell hot merchandise at steep discounts; this is true whether they sell hot ice, hot art, or hot cars. It is self-evident that the same dynamic would apply in the context of hot software. Xiang Li's production costs were zero, given that his inventory was stolen, and his overhead was otherwise low, since he sold over the Internet; ipso facto, he could sell at a discount. In that sense, it was not shocking that Xiang Li sold STK software at less than the $150,000 market price. But $1,000? Where did he come up with that number? His price was less than 1 percent of the market price. Did he know this?

I assumed the answer to be negative. Prices for high-technology software are often hard to determine; they are usually not listed on company websites and are often considered proprietary information, only given out at the point of sale—although it must be said that someone who is able to steal the proprietary software ought to be able to obtain the proprietary pricing information as well. But if Xiang Li's knowledge of the American market was limited, we might have an opportunity to take the undercover case to the next level. He might need us to take better advantage of that market.

As the summer of 2010 gave way to fall, I had to recognize that, for all we had learned, we still did not really understand how the cracking method worked. Most of what we knew we had learned from Xiang Li himself, in the form of his software installation instructions. Here is an example:

How to install Altair Hyperworks v10 in windows XP standalone version

1. *Do not install the altair license manager after the installation of the software.*
2. *Open the ALTAIR_LIC.DAT file in Magnitude folder*
3. *After installation Right Click on My computer → Advanced → Environment Variables → Click on New.*
4. *Enter the Variable name as ALTAIR_[LIMDIS]_LICENSE_FILE. make sure no spelling mistake is there and variable value as 7788@this_host*
5. *Copy the license file from magnitude folder to installation location. For example : D:\Altair\hw10.0\security*
6. *Copy the two ... .exe files from magnitude to For Example (D:\Altair\hw10.0\security\win32).*
7. *D:\Altair\hw10.0\security\win32 open the [LIMDIS].exe utility.*
8. *Caution : Don't install installer . . .*
9. *Follow the screenshots in this document*

Click on the start server . . . . . Job done !!!!!

The installation was not intuitive, to say the least. And I knew that we—or at least I—probably would never fully understand exactly how the cracks were applied. But I thought it made sense to acquire as much understanding as possible before finding myself in a position— such as at the bar of a federal court—where I might be expected to provide a coherent explanation of the cracking process. This is why I called Maxalim's upscale lawyer who went to all the right schools.

On September 23, 2010, Brendan Cullen, Tiffany Linn, and I met with Maxalim executives at their lawyer's tony offices in Chicago. Sitting on a well-polished mahogany table was a large, tantalizing tray of pastries. I really like pastries. I sincerely wanted to eat those pastries. I abstained, as did the agents, worried about the appearance of impropriety, but I did spend an undue amount of time staring at that tray.

Prior to this meeting, we had provided Maxalim with several examples of the license files obtained from CRACK99. We asked them for a tutorial on how the LIMDIS licensing file could be cracked. This meeting must have been unusual for the Maxalim executives, not only because we were from law enforcement, but also because we were not software types. Art connoisseurs talk to art connoisseurs, and baseball fans talk to baseball fans. But a Yankees fan talking to a Neo-Impressionist connoisseur might learn that the connoisseur is not current on the latest standings. And, conversely, the connoisseur might find the Yankees fan's knowledge of pointillism somewhat disappointing.

So it was at the Maxalim meeting. We were pretty good at what we did for a living, and had a reasonable idea of what hacking and cracking were about. But putting us in the same room with these guys was a lot like sitting a Neo-Impressionist connoisseur down with Joe Torre to talk baseball. The conversation was one-sided.

I started things off by letting the Maxalim people know we weren't there to accuse them of doing anything wrong. I had already told their lawyer this; otherwise, we probably wouldn't have been sitting in the same room. He seemed relieved that I had finally let go of my rogue-employee theory once and for all. The company executives said they were happy to help, and started out by giving us an overview of Maxalim's business objective, which is to facilitate application usage management for software companies. They were at pains to emphasize that Maxalim is not a security software manufacturer that provides encryption for software. Rather, Maxalim provides the "plumbing" to enable the customers of software companies to access software according to the terms of the license. The way they put it was that Maxalim products help "keep an honest customer honest." For example, Maxalim provided licensing software for an accounting program used by a major automobile manufacturer. If, say, ten licenses for the accounting software were sold to the car manufacturer, Maxalim provided the "plumbing" to ensure that only the ten licensed users used the software. If it turned out the car manufacturer needed more than ten licenses, it could buy more. In this way, Maxalim products help "monetize" the accounting software.

The executives told us that when customers requested additional security beyond this licensing protection, Maxalim would recommend that they procure tamper-resistant licensing, which provides extra security through a process called binary hardening. Maxalim, however, does not offer that type of product—it does not view its products as having a security role.

"So why doesn't everyone get tamper-resistant licensing?" I asked.

The answer was that the extra security is cumbersome and irritating to use. "Think," I was told, "how much you enjoy enhanced computer security processes in your workplace, and you'll get the idea."

I got the idea.

Then we got around to a tutorial on how the Maxalim license files had been cracked. One method was what they called a "binary hack," in which the cracker approaches Maxalim's software code like a puzzle. The general idea is to remove an original piece of the puzzle and replace it with the cracker's piece, thereby enabling the cracker to bypass a licensing restriction. Another, more difficult method is to hack the entire license file, meaning to take it apart and put it back together in a manner that enables unlimited access.

The Maxalim personnel emphasized that it is unlikely that there is one generic method that can be applied to cracking a wide spectrum of software products. Each software product would likely require its own unique approach. So a crack written for an AGI software product would probably differ from one created for an Altera software product. In the case of the cracked license files we provided prior to the meeting, the Maxalim people told us the cracks were executed by a binary hack because the CRACK99 instructions told customers to "drop" their information into the cracked files. Having cut out Maxalim's code—which causes the licensing software to act as Maxalim intended—CRACK99 pasted substitute code into the license file to make it work as CRACK99 intended.

This sort of cutting-and-pasting process, we were told, is indicative of a binary hack. Similarly indicative of a binary hack was another feature of CRACK99's cracks: the substitution of the illegitimate user's identification for that of the licensed user. Maxalim's licensing software operates by sending out a series of "calls" to the software under license. These calls determine which user is permitted to use the software, and what functions are available to that user. The CRACK99 crack removed the code causing the call to go to the vendor and replaced it with new code directing the call to the unlicensed user.

Another method employed by CRACK99 was to reset the time limits of the license, in order to bypass restrictions such as those placed on temporary licenses. Many of the cracked licensing files we had obtained from CRACK99 were accompanied by instructions to reset the date on our computer to September 8, 2008. I asked if that was a metaphysically significant licensing date. Maxalim said no, it was not a magical date; it had no significance at all. We surmised that this date was simply prior to the date the crack was performed, giving the user access after September 8, 2008. Maxalim also told us that this method of cracking might enable the cracker to gain access to updated software products.

This summary from Maxalim helped me to better understand the mechanics of cracking, but it certainly did not qualify me as an expert on the subject, any more than my limited exposure to DNA forensics made me a DNA expert. I didn't know how to crack licensing files when I left Chicago, but I did have a greater appreciation for the complexity of Xiang Li's operation, and his sophistication in being able to assist customers—including us—in applying the cracks to the software he sold.

We also left Chicago with a clear idea of our way forward. In addition to our meeting with the people at Maxalim, Brendan, Tiffany, and I spent our time in Chicago brainstorming on where to take the investigation. We started doing this in a taxicab on Michigan Avenue and decided a better place would be Ditka's. Iron Mike was not there, but, judging from the cigar smoke on the second floor, we had just missed him. Over calamari and nachos—and maybe an onion ring tower—we considered what additional information we needed in order to bring charges. By the time the steaks arrived, we were planning how to arrest Xiang Li. These are the standard questions agents and prosecutors discuss in the course of the investigation—although not always over steaks and jalapeno hash browns at Ditka's—but in this case the main challenge arose from the thousands of miles separating us from our target. We had accumulated evidence against Xiang Li by conducting undercover Internet purchases, utilizing Xiang Li's website against him, and could continue to do so. But the question was, to what end? We could keep buying his products, but what would we gain at the margin from each additional purchase?

I proposed two answers to these questions, with the consequence that it took quite a while to eat my filet. The first was that additional purchases would help us determine if Xiang Li was able—as he appeared to be—to deliver on the promises of the CRACK99 website. In other words, I wanted to test the proposition that Xiang Li could actually deliver on a big order of the software in his extensive published inventory. My second proposal was that we become particularly good customers of CRACK99 to increase our influence with Xiang Li. We knew from the e-mail search warrants that CRACK99 had some repeat business, but not an extensive amount. I thought we could become, at reasonable expense, a significant part of the CRACK99 business model. The reason I wanted to do this was to give Xiang Li an incentive to meet with us. His e-mails—and his pricing in general—had made me wonder how much he knew about the U.S.

market. Maybe if we became significant enough customers, he would be interested in discussing a partnership with us to expand his revenue opportunities in the United States—in particular, maybe he would want to meet with us to discuss these possibilities face to face.

In order for us to put the bracelets on him, that is. This is the turning point in every undercover case: Will the target show up to be arrested? The intoxicating smell of money has dulled even the sharpest criminal minds, and we were counting on that dynamic to work here. But would it?

6 | THE LAST WAR

IT IS AXIOMATIC THAT GENERALS PLAN for the next war by preparing for the last one. Even though there is an axiom involved, this approach is not necessarily good. One of the reasons the United States was not ready for World War II is that U.S. military leaders in 1941 were preparing for World War I, the last war of the dreadnaughts, failing to fully appreciate the defining role of the aircraft carrier. This was a strategic failure, but it was understandable in the sense that we humans are not prescient; preparing for the next war by reference to the last is inevitable. And some lessons from the last war are applicable to the next.

For Ronayne and me, the last war had been about Iran. The case against Iranian arms dealer Amir Ardebili started in 2004 and ended only weeks before Brendan Cullen's fateful visit to AGI. I will spare you all the details because someone else already wrote a book about that caper. However, I will tell you a little about the case because it proved a concept—obvious but controversial—advocated by Ronayne, his boss John Malandra, and me: in national security cases like these, you are not likely to find adversaries conveniently waiting for you in the United States; they are overseas, and if you want to arrest them, you will have to leave the comfort of your home turf. The vast majority of people charged by U.S. authorities with arms proliferation offenses are arrested in the United States, not abroad. Often, they are arrested at the border; low-hanging fruit, waiting to be picked. So the fast-food concept applied in the context of arms proliferation as well as other types of prosecutions: the easier, the better.

But randomly arresting the easiest people to arrest is a poor strategy; indeed, it is no strategy at all. A better approach is to identify the offenders causing the most harm and to target them. In the context of arms dealing, you will find them overseas. And in the case of Iranian arms dealers, you will find most of them in Iran. In the past, this daunting fact caused agents and prosecutors to give up on investigations because they were too hard. What we were advocating was a different approach: We should make a special point of going after the overseas targets, the degree of difficulty notwithstanding, precisely because they are causing the most harm. And to accomplish that goal, we should take the show on the road. It is astonishing in retrospect how much the government resisted—and continues to resist—this idea, particularly given that arresting the guilty and bringing them to justice is a fundamental goal of law enforcement. But to return to an old theme: big cases, big problems.

We had an undercover storefront, a bricks-and-mortar place originally leased with the idea that arms dealers would flock there to be arrested. Unsurprisingly, this did not come to pass. But working from this storefront, we did identify an abundance of potential targets, including Ardebili. There was little about Ardebili's first e-mail inquiries in 2004 to clue us in to his significance; he was one among many who troll the Internet looking for illicit sources in the arms trade. And he was maddening in his inconsistencies: He would request that we quote a price for an aircraft part, telling us it was urgent. We would move heaven and earth to research the part number promptly, respond to Ardebili with a quote, and then . . . we'd hear nothing. Ardebili would be unresponsive, remaining in the wind until his next urgent request for a price quote. We repeated this pattern of self-debasement for an indefensibly long period of time before we finally fired him, telling him to take his business elsewhere. That seemed only to encourage him. I considered whether this was a cultural phenomenon or a demonstration of the commonplace that nothing is truly valued until it is lost.

By 2005, we were focused on another arms dealer I will call "Sameer," who wanted to buy an airborne high-definition forward-looking infrared radar (FLIR) system used for air-to-surface missile targeting. We negotiated the deal with Sameer by e-mail, but Sameer made it clear that he would not take delivery in the United States. He was located in the Middle East, a less-than-friendly region in terms of law enforcement cooperation. Where then could we meet?

Enter "Darius" (not his real name). An HSI agent posted overseas, Darius had been making friends in unlikely places, including the national police in a former Soviet republic I will call "Notrussia." The Notrussians might, Darius told me, entertain the idea of an undercover meeting in their country. And there was more: Darius had been working with the Notrussian national police to create a Notrussian undercover storefront for just such a purpose. If we could get official approval from the Notrussian government to use this storefront, it would provide a plausible basis for inviting Sameer to meet in Notrussia to take delivery of the FLIR system. At which point we would arrest him.

There was one problem: an AUSA is not allowed unilaterally to fly off to former Soviet republics and negotiate deals. I would have to go through Main Justice, specifically, the Office of International Affairs (OIA). The OIA would have to approve my written Mutual Legal Assistance Treaty (MLAT) request. I knew that if I just wrote up an MLAT request and sent it down there, I would be guaranteed months of anguish—and more importantly for the case, months of delay in arranging a meeting in Notrussia. This is something Sameer was unlikely to tolerate.

Darius and I came up with a plan to expedite matters. Darius knew that the national police already concurred in our plan and were willing to assist in any way they could. He also knew that the Notrussian prosecutor general wanted to meet with me to discuss the parameters of the agreement so there were no misunderstandings about what we would be authorized to do in Notrussia. So Darius and I decided to get ahead of the OIA. Darius would ask the national police to submit our plan to the Notrussian prosecutor general, who would then request a meeting with me to negotiate a final agreement. The meeting would be scheduled for a date only weeks away, creating a deadline OIA could not ignore.

The plan worked. I prepared an MLAT request asking the Notrussian government for permission to create an undercover storefront in Notrussia as a prelude to an undercover meeting there with Sameer, during which we would show him an actual FLIR system and accept his purchase money. We also asked the Notrussians to arrest Sameer at the end of the undercover meeting and extradite him to the United States. The OIA actually approved it on time, mainly to avoid the embarrassment of telling the Notrussian prosecutor general that we could not meet with him on his desired schedule to discuss our proposal because we couldn't manage to write our proposal in time. Of course, the OIA didn't leave much room for error, approving the request mere days before the scheduled meeting.

There was one more obstacle: the United States Attorney. AUSAs can't travel overseas without the approval of the United States Attorney. So I had to ask. I summarized the case for him and the importance of the undercover meeting, and the necessity of getting Notrussian approval. Evidently, I was not very convincing; although he did give his concurrence, he viewed the trip as a lark. I might have seen his point if I had proposed a February meeting in Antigua.

But this particular lark involved travel to a former Soviet republic in February, which might qualify if your idea of a lark involves feet that are always cold, pickled herring and beet soup, and a cramped seat in coach class. As it turned out, however, the beer in Notrussia was quite good, something I chose not to disclose to the United States Attorney, given the whole lark situation.

I flew to Frankfurt to make a connecting flight to Notrussia. Unfortunately for me, President George W. Bush was traveling to Frankfurt the same day, so the airport was shut down for hours, canceling my flight. This was a good-news, bad-news situation. The good news was I took a nice nap. The bad news was I knew Darius was waiting for me in Notrussia, and 2005 predating the era of the ubiquitous cell phone, it was not easy to contact him. I managed to reach HSI headquarters, which patched me through to him. He arranged an alternative flight on a Notrussian airline war-surplus turboprop. I landed a little before midnight.

It was cold as I stood alone in the dark. Notrussia is a place whose version of darkness is much darker than mine. I thought I saw something move on my flank. Probably nothing. But it stayed with me as I walked toward the terminal. When I approached immigration, it came into form: a tall silhouette. When I arrived at the counter, the silhouette swooped down on me.

"I'm guessing Dave Hall?" asked Darius.

This is how we met. In the cab, he let me know our meeting with the prosecutor general was scheduled for the next day. We had breakfast early the next morning at the hotel, which featured a spectacular buffet. I loaded my plate with eggs and a diverse variety of sausages before sitting across from Darius, who had a small bowl of fruit and yogurt.

"Don't judge me," I said.

"I don't judge," he replied. "I observe."

The prosecutor general's office was located in a Soviet-era building that from the outside looked as brutal as the Soviet regime itself: harsh, gray, and ugly. Inside was the same, except for one important thing: the people, who were very friendly. They all liked Darius, who appeared to be a regular. He said things in Russian, and the Not-russians all laughed. Then they took us to a conference room with a large wooden table in the center to await the prosecutor general. With us was an interpreter from the U.S. embassy.

The prosecutor general entered with a flourish. He was a large man accompanied by a posse of other large men, all appearing to wear the same boxy dark-gray suit. I too was wearing a boxy dark-gray suit, the style being ubiquitous in law enforcement, except in France. So we had something in common from the beginning. That and baldness. The prosecutor general grabbed my hand firmly and shook it vigorously. His face was like stone.

He sat down, placed his palms on the highly polished table, and started talking rapidly in Russian. The U.S. embassy interpreter said nothing. This was irritating, but not entirely unexpected, given my many years of government service. When the prosecutor general finished talking, I looked at Darius, whose fluency in Russian, fortunately for me, rendered the U.S. embassy interpreter superfluous.

"Tell him what you want," said Darius.

So I did, with Darius doing the translating and the U.S. embassy interpreter remaining silent, evidently lost in his own world. There was a certain amount of back and forth between Darius and the prosecutor general, most of which was not interpreted, reminding me of a previous interaction with the Russian language. I was interviewing a Russian-speaking witness in an insurance fraud case who provided a long-winded answer to a question, reduced by the interpreter to: "Yes." I said, "Well, I can tell he said a great deal more than that." The interpreter replied: "It was lyrical digression."

Finally, Darius looked at me with a pleased expression. The prosecutor general reached across the table with his large hand and grabbed mine again. He smiled—an action he did not seem accustomed to taking.

"We have a deal," said Darius.

I returned to Ronayne and Malandra with the Notrussian green light to proceed with the undercover plan, which we executed without delay. We told Sameer we would be working the deal through a Notrussian sister company to protect us from prying American eyes. We invited him to meet us in Notrussia as soon as possible to close the deal and inspect the FLIR. Our sister company would ship the FLIR wherever Sameer liked. Sameer agreed to our terms and said he would get back with a date. We were elated.

And then he disappeared.

We had been through this before with Ardebili, this coming to terms and disappearing. We did not like it. But Ardebili always reappeared, and we hoped Sameer would do the same. But no, Sameer was gone for good. Ardebili, in contrast, was relentless in his efforts to reestablish contact. We weren't playing hard to get; we were sincerely fed up with him. But we finally gave in, engaging in price quotes and the endless back and forth of negotiation. It seemed that every time I went to the undercover storefront for an update on Ardebili, Special Agent P. J. Lechleitner would start out with, "Freakin' squirrel." Then I would hear the latest tale of woe, always following the same pattern: request for a price quote, quote provided, negotiation over price, followed by silence, followed by a new request for a quote. Repeat cycle.

Our efforts to arrest Sameer in Notrussia were not entirely wasted. By 2006, Darius, posing as the president of the Notrussian sister company, handled the better part of our undercover communications with Ardebili. So we were able to present a credible Notrussian front to Ardebili. Although the interactions were tedious, Darius established a rapport with Ardebili and even seemed to win his trust. On May 30, 2006, Ardebili wrote:

Working Via [your Notrussian] company is very perfect way which long time we are looking for such chance. [You] . . . could have new packing with new description to send our needed goods. We have do same method with companies in UAE, Kuwait but this Areas are restricted you know.

Darius replied:

What you can say can perhaps be good business, but I stress to you what we are do is ILLEGAL in US. . . . With more discussion it is possible we do good business—but patience and good planning will keep us out of jail!

Darius, in an astonishing exhibition of patience steeled by sheer will, continued his communications with Ardebili through 2006 and into 2007 before actually coming to terms on a concrete transaction. Both Darius and I like to fish, and it can be said that fishermen must like to cast because they do a lot more casting than catching. So it is with undercover investigations: Darius spent sixteen months casting, before hooking Ardebili on April 9, 2007:

This is urgent inquiry. You are kindly requewsted to quote us for following P/N urgently: "P/N MAPCGM0003 903218B Description: Phase Shifter, S-Band, 6 Bit 2.3-4.1 GHz Required quantity: 1500 Mfg: M/A-COM Inc."

This e-mail marked the beginning of the end for Ardebili. Phase shifters are microchips used in phased array radar, which is employed in a number of military applications, including missile defense and missile guidance. For example, the U.S. Navy uses phased array radar in the Aegis system, which enables combatant ships to acquire and attack multiple targets simultaneously. By April 30, we had a deal on the phase shifters: we would sell 1,400 microchips for a total of $88,837 with a 12 percent cash deposit.

Things couldn't have been better. Except that Ardebili didn't send the required deposit, sending instead one excuse after another. On June 1, Ardebili sent Darius an e-mail suggesting we use a letter of credit. This was surprising. A letter of credit would be a standard method of conducting an international transaction of this kind—if the transaction were lawful. In such a case, a letter of credit from a bank would guarantee payment by the buyer. Ardebili's proposal to use a letter of credit was baffling because he knew very well we couldn't go to a bank to guarantee an illegal deal. I concluded that Ardebili was stalling. But why?

The next day, Ardebili answered that question. He contacted Darius using Yahoo Messenger, asking Darius to lower the down payment to $3,000. Darius objected. Ardebili replied that we have the purchase order in hand, so "what is your problem?" Darius replied, "I have no problem. You have a problem. You have told your customer that you could deliver product after I tell you over and over that deal will require pre-payment of 12%."

Darius and I spent a lot of time talking about this one. Ardebili's request for a lower down payment—after already agreeing to terms— was maddening. But we were so close.

Darius asked me, "Is there any legal minimum payment required to make this case?"

If we readily agreed to a reduction in the down payment, we would look like saps or, worse, cops. And at trial, we might be accused of entrapment. On the other hand, if we said no, he might walk away, as so many—including Ardebili—had done in the past. We were so close.

"There is no minimum," I said. "At some point we're going to look stupid, but we might already be there. Let's take the money and move forward."

On June 7, Ardebili and Darius communicated using Yahoo Messenger: "I have decided your terms are good enough." Darius went on to say that he must see money in the Delaware bank account before this deal becomes real. Ardebili replied that he has "the formal agreement with my customers in Iran."

As we closed in on the deal with Ardebili, we had a new problem. The British government had lodged an objection to our continued use of the informant who had introduced Ardebili to our undercover storefront in the first place. The informant was a British subject and a former arms dealer. We had met with British authorities before on this subject, and they were aware that the informant was working for us, but now there was a new problem: the Crown Prosecution Service wanted to charge him with export offenses. The Brits proposed a meeting in London at Secret Intelligence Service (SIS, formerly MI6) headquarters to discuss their objection. The United States Attorney viewed this trip as another lark—and, in fairness, this time it was to London.

The stakes were high. As we planned the end game with Ardebili, we were considering giving the informant an active role in pushing Ardebili forward, given his proclivity to disappear at critical moments. And whether or not we used the informant with Ardebili, we were planning to use him with other Iranian arms dealers we had targeted. The British had the ability to bring this to a sudden stop, and they were threatening to do just that.

The meeting at SIS headquarters was like most diplomatic meetings: many things were said, but little was accomplished. I asked if the British authorities could be precise about their plans to charge the informant: specifically, when and with what offenses? This, they did not wish to share. In that case, would they be willing to share their evidence that the informant was still dealing arms? Our agreement with the informant prohibited such activity and we had no evidence that he was violating it, but we would end our relationship if we had concrete proof. They declined. I offered to share the burden of the investigation and help them arrest the informant if he was in fact still dealing arms. Again, they declined. After a day of dickering, we reached a temporary solution: we would agree not to use our informant for six months while they finalized the charges against him. If the informant was charged, we would drop him. As it turned out, he was never charged.

A frustrating interaction, all in all. But there was one consolation: a good meal. The British side wanted to show that there were no hard feelings and that our special alliance was still special. So we went out to dinner. But first, as is the custom in the British Isles, we had drinks. I'm not a mind reader, but I drew the firm conclusion that the Brits were trying to get us drunk; they were pushing the cocktails pretty hard, even for Brits. I cannot prove it, but I think they were hoping to compromise us, maybe catch somebody saying something he shouldn't. To this end, one of the Brits cornered Malandra, and asked, gesturing toward me across the room, "Wot's 'is story?"

Malandra didn't miss a beat. Referring to my recent hip-replacement surgery, he replied, "Hall? Amazing. Only one hip, that guy. One hip. And he walks, talks, rides a bike, the whole deal. Amazing."

The Brit wore a look of profound bafflement throughout the remainder of the evening. No one can crack Malandra.

Darius was having a similarly frustrating experience with Ardebili, who continued to object to the down payment, raising again the idea of using a letter of credit. Darius responded to this idea on June 13, via Yahoo Messenger:

> *A letter of credit from an Iran bank is garbage anyway. If your bank refuses to pay, what do we do? Ask the UN to help us? We are violating the law by selling you these devices. What court is going to help us?*

I laughed pretty hard at the UN jab. Darius was right: in a deal like this, no neutral third party would arbitrate disputes—hence, the need for a cash deposit.

We were seriously questioning whether Ardebili would ever send the deposit. This was a moment when we could have used the informant's assistance: cheerleading the deal, or at least vouching for us again. But we stuck to our agreement with the Brits.

On June 23, Ardebili contacted Darius using Yahoo Messenger to ask if Darius had received the payment, claiming he had sent the deposit "last week." Darius said no, and on June 28, Ardebili e-mailed to say there was a problem with the transfer of euros to a U.S. bank. This was obviously balderdash, given that euros are routinely transferred to U.S. banks all day, every day. It looked like, after getting so close, this deal would evaporate like all the others.

The sea change came on July 25. Malandra, Ronayne, Harry Ubele, and I were eating in a Mexican restaurant called La Tolteca outside Wilmington when we got the call from P. J. Lechleitner: a wire transfer had just been received in our undercover account in the amount of $2,980.00. The little weasel had stiffed us for the $20 transfer fee. But we were in business. We celebrated with enchiladas and extra hot sauce.

Darius got right to work arranging a face-to-face meeting with Ardebili to deliver the phase shifters. This might sound easy, and it would be in the commercial world, but in the world of law enforcement, it is one of the hardest of all problems. Like Sameer, Ardebili was unwilling to meet us in the United States. So the question was, what other nation would permit us to lure an Iranian, conduct an undercover transaction, arrest him, and extradite him? If you are thinking that one of our NATO allies in Western Europe would be only too willing to volunteer to improve the security of NATO nations from the Iranian threat, you would be wrong. Western Europe, for reasons political and legal, is not hospitable to this kind of joint law enforcement operation. One of the main legal obstacles to an undercover meeting in Western Europe arises from a significant difference in the law governing undercover activity. In Europe, generally speaking, undercover law enforcement agents are considered agents provocateur, and the results of their efforts are often suppressed on the ground of entrapment.

Darius proposed the Republic of Georgia as a meeting place. Ardebili's first question in response was, "Where is Georgia?" We expected that from Ardebili's point of view, Georgia would be an attractive venue for a meeting because it was close to Iran. From our point of view, it was an attractive venue because Darius had good relations with the Georgian police. But how would this look from the Georgian government's point of view? To find out, P. J. Lechleitner, Darius, and I went to Tbilisi, Georgia, to meet with the prosecutor general. She was very young, smart, and incorruptible, according to our police sources. We faced a challenge in that there was no MLAT between the United States and Georgia, nor was there an extradition treaty. But we looked on this as an opportunity to forge a relationship that could lead to an MLAT. So we made our proposal, and after a number of probing questions, she agreed. We were delighted until we heard that she would need the approval of Georgia's president, which sounded like it would take some time. I said I understood as I frequently confirmed my decisions with the President of the United States. She didn't laugh.

When we got to our hotel, we decided to see if we could contact Ardebili on Yahoo Messenger. Sure enough, there he was. Darius told Ardebili he was in Georgia at that moment and was making preparations for their meeting. Darius asked if Ardebili could send proof of identity so Darius could make arrangements for his entry into Georgia.

> ARDEBILI: i will send you copy of my pasport
> DARIUS: OK and please to make your flight reservation now—my cousin will make reservation to match when you come.
> ARDEBILI: when will he receive to tibilis
> DARIUS: 28SEP would be good.

. . .

ARDEBILI: did you asked him to come to Dubai ?

DARIUS: Yes and he say no

ARDEBILI: because i should be Dubai on this time

ARDEBILI: please ask him again

DARIUS: When can you come Tbilisi?

ARDEBILI: i prefer to meet each other in Dubai

ARDEBILI: is it impossible?

DARIUS: Stop this

ARDEBILI: i will cancle my meeting in Dubai

ARDEBILI: do not be worry

With Ardebili, the negotiation never ended. He initially agrees to a 12 percent deposit, then wants to drop it to nearly 3 percent. No sooner does he agree on Tbilisi, then he wants to meet in Dubai. So I laughed hard over Darius's shoulder when Ardebili capitulated to Darius's command: "Stop this."

There was one moment of astonishing good luck that day when Ardebili asked Darius—who was supposed to be a Russian speaker from Notrussia—to write something in Russian. Because we were in Georgia, we had a keyboard with Cyrillic script so Darius could comply with ease, enhancing his credibility with Ardebili.

This was also the first time we confirmed who Ardebili was. He had used a number of different aliases in the past, and we were not sure of his real name. And then after agreeing to send a copy of his passport, he wrote the following:

ARDEBILI: do you know my real name?

DARIUS: Amir AMIR A.?

ARDEBILI.: no

ARDEBILI.: Amir Hossein Ardebili

ARDEBILI.: this is my real name

DARIUS: Very nice to meet you.

The next day, the prosecutor general called: the president of Georgia had approved our plan; we were good to go. I asked her what she needed from us to go forward. She told us we would need a diplomatic note, making the request for assistance, and documentation of the criminal charges against Ardebili. This was, on the whole, good news. But I also knew that the next several months would be anguished: to send a diplomatic note meant I would have to return to the OIA at Main Justice. I would also have to push the diplomatic note through the entire bureaucratic morass of the State Department in order for it to travel in cable form from the State Department in Washington to the U.S. ambassador in Georgia to the Georgian Ministry of Foreign Affairs to the Georgian prosecutor general. And even though the diplomatic note would do nothing more than make a request that had already been granted, many U.S. officials would insist on being involved, rather like a hundred dogs trying to pee on the same fire hydrant.

I decided that the fastest way to bring charges against Ardebili was to obtain a criminal complaint from a magistrate judge. This would also have the benefit of an accompanying affidavit substantiating the charges, so that the Georgians would have a summary of the evidence to use in the extradition proceeding. So far, so good. But there was a wrinkle. We had learned that Ardebili had been dealing with others in the United States and, in fact, had engaged in a transaction with undercover HSI agents in Boston. This gave us the opportunity to conclude both our deal and the Boston deal at the same time. But how would we do that? In Ardebili's mind, there was no reason to combine the two deals because he had no reason to believe his supplier in Boston was related to Darius.

The Boston deal involved BEI GyroChip Model QRS11 Quartz Rate Sensors. These are military gyros used for fire control, range finding, optical, and guidance control equipment in advanced aircraft, missile, and space applications. Boston's involvement with Ardebili began in

July 2005, sometime after ours. On October 26 of that year, Ardebili sent via e-mail a request for a price quote for ten QRS11-00300-100 gyro chips, and the Boston undercover agents quoted a price of $30,000. On November 28, Ardebili wired a $7,000 down payment to an undercover bank account. In June 2006, the Boston agents sent the gyros per Ardebili's instructions but arranged for them to be seized at the U.S. border. Boston kept the $7,000.

Now it all made sense. This explained Ardebili's squeamishness when it came to sending Darius the down payment for our deal: he had been ripped off once and didn't want that to happen again. He didn't seem quite so unreasonable after all.

We were wringing our hands trying to figure out how we could merge the two sales. It would seem ridiculous for us to tell Ardebili that we just happened to know this other company in Boston with whom he just happened to have a pending transaction. We decided not to mention the Boston deal in advance, complete our own sale in Tbilisi, and then at the last minute offer to help with the Boston situation. If he smelled a rat, it wouldn't matter because it would be too late; our business would be otherwise concluded.

But our hand wringing was for naught, as it so often is. Sometimes you get lucky, and as my friend Bob Wittman—the storied FBI art-crime undercover agent—likes to say, "Better lucky than good." To our amazement, once Ardebili agreed to meet in Georgia, he asked Darius to arrange for the Boston gyro supplier to join the meeting in Tbilisi to deliver the gyro chips. Darius agreed. Better lucky than good.

I contacted the United States Attorney's Office in Boston to coordinate the two cases. I talked with an AUSA whose voice betrayed dissipation and defeat. He said he had had problems with the case—which is why he had not charged it—and mentioned a few that I thought were easily overcome. I pointed out that the undercover meeting in Georgia would be a perfect time and place to address those problems.

"But if they're not addressed," he moaned, "I'll be stuck prosecuting a problematic case."

I promised to prosecute the case, telling him that if he got a criminal complaint in Boston, I would include his charges in my indictment. So all the problems would be mine. There was more whining, but he finally agreed. It was rather like dealing with Ardebili.

The reason it was important to charge the Boston case at this stage is that under the Rule of Specialty, a defendant extradited from a foreign country cannot be tried on charges other than those in place at the time of the extradition. So, if our adventure in Georgia succeeded, we would need to present all charges against Ardebili prior to his extradition. Anything we left out would be lost forever.

The stage was set for the final act in Tbilisi.

On October 1, 2007, John Malandra and I stood in the Tbilisi airport, awaiting Ardebili's arrival. Darius was nearby, looking good in a black suit, black shirt, and wrap-around black shades, flanked by beefy Georgian bodyguards. Another bodyguard waited outside the terminal, at the wheel of an idling armored black Mercedes. And when I say Darius was looking good, I mean he was looking bad, the way you would expect an Eastern European arms broker to look while awaiting an Iranian arms dealer at the Tbilisi airport.

Malandra and I were trying to blend in: two guys waiting for a friend. Malandra was licking an ice cream cone. "What looks less than a cop," he asked, "than a guy licking an ice cream cone?"

"This," I said, putting on a large, fuzzy Georgian shepherd's hat I had just purchased. I looked ridiculous.

"That's nothing," Malandra said, "compared to how ridiculous we're going to look if this bird doesn't show."

To our relief, Ardebili did show. When he did, we quickly left the airport and headed for the Hotel Tbilisi, where the undercover meeting would take place. As I crossed the front courtyard of the hotel, I was intercepted by a Georgian officer who spoke excellent English.

He told me there was a problem with the diplomatic note: it had not arrived in time to be submitted to the Georgian court for approval. So our undercover operation that day would not be usable in U.S. court.

You might be wondering, as I was then, how this could have happened. I had, immediately upon returning from my August trip to Georgia, submitted a diplomatic note for the OIA to transfer to the State Department to transmit to Tbilisi. I knew there would be an unconscionable amount of dithering, which is a varsity sport in Washington, D.C. Compounding this, because there was no precedent for what I was doing, the bureaucrats at the Departments of Justice and State would be nervous about putting their names on the routing slip. Something could go wrong. So I was on the phone with people at the OIA pretty much every day, pushing them to move the note forward to the next level. Once it left the Department of Justice, I was on the phone with staff at the State Department to move it out of their building to the U.S. ambassador in Tbilisi. The U.S. ambassador was the one guy I was not worried about. I had briefed him on the operation when I was in Tbilisi, and he enthusiastically approved. The week before the scheduled October 1, 2007, meeting, I was assured by the State Department that the diplomatic note had already left Washington for Tbilisi.

Not so. The diplomatic note did not leave the State Department until the very end of the week, making it impossible for the Georgians to get court approval in time for our Monday meeting. Darius and P. J. were brilliant in their undercover roles that first day. We had discussed this meeting for weeks, preparing the questions, going over a checklist of facts we wanted Ardebili to acknowledge on tape: he was buying U.S. military goods for the government of Iran, he knew the deal was illegal under U.S. law, and he knew what the military goods would be used for. After an exhausting day, Darius and P. J. had done their duty. And then I had to give them the bad news: someone else had not done his duty, so they would have to do their duty twice. We would have to reconstruct Day One on Day Two. They were not pleased, but they manned up and did it.

In the end, putting aside bureaucratic blundering, the results of the undercover meetings could not have been better. There were extensive discussions about the phase shifters between Darius, Ardebili, and P. J., who was playing the role of Darius's cousin from the United States. Ardebili was completely sold on the two of them, as he demonstrated by calling Iran with instructions to transfer by wire approximately $60,000 to our undercover bank account in further payment for the phase shifters. Ardebili also negotiated the acquisition of an additional four thousand phase shifters, telling us that he believed that five thousand phase shifters were required for each radar system that employed them. This was significant because thousands of phase shifters are required to build phased array radar. We concluded that Ardebili was buying them for someone who was building phased array radar—someone like the government of Iran.

The undercover meetings answered the question of who was behind Ardebili: he said his "only customer" was Iran. That is about as clear as it gets. But more than that, he said he procured directly for Iran Electronics Industries, the organization that acquired electronic components for the government of Iran. He even gave us the shipping account number needed to ship the phase shifters on Iran Air airline to Iran. As for money, Ardebili confirmed that there is no direct way to transfer money to the United States from Iran. Instead, he used an exchange in Iran to transfer funds to cooperating European banks, from which the funds were sent to the United States. The intermediate bank used by Ardebili to pay for the phase shifters was in Germany.

Ardebili and the agents also discussed the acquisition of a DADC-107, a digital air data computer to replace the central air data computer in Iran's U.S.-made F-4 fighter aircraft. Ardebili had previously indicated his interest in acquiring this piece of equipment in an August 7, 2007, e-mail, shortly after he had sent the down payment on the phase shifters:

> *Also we need your update about the , P/N: DADC-107 .*
> *As I aware this unit is manufacturing in Israel and install in F-4 .*
> *Could you supply?*
> *This is too urgent.*
> *Best Regards*
> *Amir*

Ardebili and undercover agents completed the DADC-107 deal in Tbilisi, after Ardebili explained that the reason for the Iranian government's urgency is that Iran is the only country that has the F-4 aircraft in its inventory—and none of them work. This put a sharp focus on the Iranian perspective. The United States supplied Iran with fighter aircraft—F-14s, F-5s, and F-4s—during the regime of Shah Pahlavi, when the United States and Iran were allies. After the 1979 revolution, the United States cut off the supply of spare parts and upgrades, leaving Iran in the position it finds itself today, thus requiring acquisition agents like Ardebili to find parts to keep the aircraft flying.

To what end?

"They think," Ardebili explained, "the war is coming."

Ardebili covered a lot of other ground as well. When asked about "nuclear issues" and whether he was interested in something "radioactive," Ardebili said, "Yes." He was just as unequivocal when asked if he wanted "proliferation equipment" for "nuclear weapons" or "nuclear power." He said, "Everything. . . . I can do anything."

The final act at the Hotel Tbilisi was a visit by Special Agent Harry Ubele—posing as the Boston gyro supplier—who delivered the gyros to Ardebili. Ubele asked Ardebili to sign a receipt—a nice piece of evidence to show the jury—which he was only too happy to do. It was Harry's first undercover role, which is like playing your first football game in the NFL. As that final transaction was being conducted, Malandra and I were in the monitoring room next door talking to the Georgian police arrest team. They didn't speak English, and we wanted them to know who the good guys were. So Malandra sketched a map of the room and put a big "X" where Ardebili was sitting. We watched the arrest go down over the video monitor, and heard P. J. saying, "What's going on, Amir?" staying in role until the very end. As the cuffs were being placed on Ardebili, a Georgian officer's cell phone went off, playing *The Godfather* theme. We laughed at that and shook hands all around. A Georgian prosecutor showed up at the end and spoke agitatedly with the police. He obviously had not been told about this in advance and was looking utterly bewildered by all the Americans standing around.

After Ardebili was taken away, we went across the street to the hotel. I thought I might have a beer but that didn't happen. The FBI LEGATT from the embassy handed me his cell phone. It was the United States Attorney calling with congratulations. This was a surprise because I hadn't yet informed him of the arrest. After saying, "Way to go, buddy," he came to the point: Main Justice had scheduled a press conference for the next day to announce the arrest.

"They can't do that," I said.

Malandra, who has a sixth sense for these things, knew at once what was happening: "Don't let them do that," he said in the menacing way only Malandra can pull off.

"It's already been scheduled," said the United States Attorney.

"Unschedule it," I said. "They can't do it."

"Well, they're doing it," said the United States Attorney.

"It's a sealed case," I said. "They can't say anything about it."

"We can unseal it."

"I won't unseal it. Do you have any idea what's at stake here?" I asked. Deciding that the question should not be rhetorical, I answered it. First of all, publicizing the arrest will make it less likely the Georgians will extradite Ardebili; it will put them in an untenable position with the Iranians, who will press for his release. Second, we just seized his laptop, which is full of leads for future cases. If you publicize it, we won't be able to pursue those leads.

This went on for quite a while, and ended when I told the United States Attorney to tell the people at Main Justice that they could expect me to testify against them in Congress, as well as making formal complaints to the Inspector General and the Office of Professional Responsibility. It was no bluff.

"You don't want to be making threats," I was warned.

"I am making threats," I said. "You should feel free to quote me on that."

I don't know exactly what happened after that call, but I do know that Main Justice postponed the press conference and scheduled a phone call to discuss it on my return in two days.

Before leaving Tbilisi, we had a ceremonial meal called a supra with our Georgian partners. We drank wine out of ornate bullhorns and gave impassioned, long-winded toasts. Mine was about freedom, something Americans take for granted, I said, but cherished by Georgians who had lived for so long under the heavy jackboot of the Soviet Union. I meandered over a lot of ground, but in the end I thanked them sincerely. Then I turned to the still-bewildered Georgian prosecutor and said, "I feel your pain."

When I got home, the United States Attorney—under pressure from Main Justice—and I got on the phone with the National Security Division at Main Justice. They had rescheduled the press conference for the following week. I repeated what I had told the United States Attorney: going public would put the extradition at risk and would eliminate the possibility of taking action on the leads we knew awaited us in Ardebili's laptop. We would be squandering the full benefit of the arrest, which had been the culmination of three years' effort. The Main Justice people were not impressed. They persisted in their demand for a press conference, and I just kept saying no. The conversation was utterly dysfunctional. Finally, I wore them down— this is what you have to do to save the government from its own bad impulses—and they said they would delay the press conference until Ardebili had been extradited to the United States.

The conference call was followed by many phone calls to me from the National Security Division deputy, who continued to advocate a press conference. I understood the appeal of a press conference from the division's point of view: it created the impression that the National Security Division was actually doing something about national security. But the level of effort surprised me—that is, until the following week, when the National Security Division chief announced the formation of a counter-proliferation task force designed to stem the loss of weapons technology to China and Iran.

> *Foreign states and terrorist organizations are actively seeking to acquire U.S. data, technological knowledge and equipment that will advance their military capacity, their weapons systems and even their weapons of mass destruction programs. . . . This initiative is a coordinated campaign to keep sensitive U.S. technology from falling into the wrong hands and from being used against our allies, against our troops overseas or against Americans at home.*

All was now clear. Our case would have been a perfect example of the National Security Division's exceptional efforts to stem the flow of weapons components to our adversaries, if you disregarded the fact that the National Security Division had nothing to do with the case.

We got the laptop back from the Georgians shortly after the arrest. We went to court for a search warrant and then started a careful review of its contents. This took time, but eventually the laptop revealed the full scope of Ardebili's activities. It contained forty gigabytes of data, including twenty-six thousand e-mail messages and over a hundred thousand files. A search for the word "missile" resulted in 1,498 hits. Ardebili had been involved in arms deals worth millions of dollars, involving aviation components, stealth technology for ships, and microprocessors used in improvised explosive devices employed against Americans in Iraq and Afghanistan. Ardebili's laptop demonstrated the scope not only of his own arms dealing but also of the Iranian government's acquisition activities. And worse, it showed how much the U.S. government had missed over the years. The very make of microprocessor acquired by Ardebili had been used against U.S. forces in a theater of war, thus illustrating the ultimate point about technology transfer: once it's gone, it is uncontrolled. It can end up anywhere to be used by anyone, against anyone. It's like getting shot by your own gun.

Once the press conference crisis had passed, the time came to worry about extradition, an unpredictable process in the best of circumstances but particularly so in our case because this extradition was a first for Georgia. Understandably, the Georgian authorities wanted to do it right, not only for the sake of their new legal system but also for their prestige in the international community. Having suffered under the suffocating burden of Soviet oppression, they looked to the West, and wanted to satisfy Western expectations. This was quite a change from past, Soviet-era practice. Our self-centered question was, how long will all that take?

As it turned out, the answer was, not long at all. After Ardebili's October 2, 2007, arrest, I called the OIA regularly for updates, which they never had. The agents on the ground were much better sources of information than my own organization. This was no surprise to me, given my many years of relying on agents for the ground truth. We learned in November that extradition was proceeding quickly and might be completed as early as December. The Georgians made it clear that once the extradition process was over, they wanted Ardebili out of the country as quickly as possible, an understandable request under the circumstances, given the rage exhibited by the Iranians who, among other things, threatened to cut off Georgia's natural gas supply on the eve of winter.

Malandra and I started making phone calls to figure out the most expeditious way of extracting Ardebili once the Georgians gave us the word. We asked around to see if any government VIP jets were available; not surprisingly, all the government VIPs had plans for their jets for the foreseeable future. We tried to arrange military transport, but military transport aircraft were fully employed in Iraq and it was hard to justify the diversion of military resources from a theater of war to transport one prisoner. In the end, Malandra lobbied his own organization, HSI. Malandra is a formidable force, and most people find it difficult to resist his will, including senior people in HSI. But he was asking a lot: chartering a Gulfstream IV jet to get us to Georgia was expensive, as much as $250,000. But Malandra forged ahead and got funding.

Our original plan was to fly to Germany, refuel, fly to Georgia, return to Germany with Ardebili, refuel, and return to the United States. However, there was a problem: if we refueled in Germany, Ardebili would have the right to deplane and seek sanctuary there, defeating the entire purpose of our enterprise. So I started looking for other refueling venues. The problem was, given the distance to Georgia and the range of a Gulfstream IV, those venues tended to be in Western Europe, where similar rules applied. In the end, we worked out an arrangement to stop in the Netherlands on our return trip. As December blended into January, I was receiving a stream of updates from Georgia on the likely date of the final extradition order. Finally, I heard it directly from the Georgian prosecutor general.

We prepositioned at Dulles airport and were ready for departure well before dawn on January 21, 2008. But as soon as we were on the plane, there was a problem: the pilots told us HSI headquarters hadn't filed the appropriate paperwork with Germany, and we therefore were not authorized to land there. (The Germans can be sticklers about paperwork, as you might have heard.) Compounding the problem, we were departing on President's Day, and the people who might be expected to sort this problem out were not in the office. Malandra called the unit chief responsible for the blunder, who said that he wouldn't be able to straighten it out on a holiday and that we were not authorized to launch. Malandra explained why that was an unacceptable answer. The unit chief explained to Malandra that it was Malandra in fact who held the unacceptable position. Malandra held the phone away from his head and said, "Bad connection; can't hear you; you're breaking up." I could hear the unit chief screaming in frustration. Having previously discussed alternative destinations with the flight crew, who advised that we could fly to Amsterdam, we walked up to the cockpit and Malandra said, "Amsterdam it is."

We landed at night and dined on Dutch chicken wings at an airport hotel. Here's the thing about Dutch chicken wings: they are truly awful. I mean, just awful. But there was one good thing about them: they were food. The next morning, we met for coffee and an update on the extradition. We all had the same question: When would we make the last leg to Tbilisi? "Not today fellas," said Malandra, hanging up the cell phone. We had a day to kill, so we took the train to Amsterdam, where we saw all the usual curiosities, mainly hashish shops and prostitutes behind glass windows, an object lesson in the thin line that separates the libertarian from the libertine; the sequence of events that ends with a young woman dancing listlessly in a glass box is never a happy one.

Malandra's phone was ringing again. I hoped it was the call telling us to launch for Tbilisi, but it was not; instead, someone was telling us to get out of Amsterdam because our security had been compromised. We didn't get a lot of details, but we headed back to the hotel to pack. The question was where to go, and the answer soon came: Vienna. On the one hand, this made some sense because Vienna is closer to Tbilisi than Amsterdam is. On the other hand, Vienna has long been famous as a hotbed of espionage, so I wondered if it was the best place security-wise.

When we landed in Vienna, the attaché met us at the airport and whisked us to the Grand Hotel Wien, a beautiful five-star venue on the Ringstrasse. It was the height of the ball season, and the lobby was filled with ladies in gowns and gents in tails, sipping champagne before spending the evening waltzing. The hotel manager, flanked by his welcoming staff, greeted me at the door.

He asked breathlessly, "Mr. Hall? Is it Mr. Hall?"

"Yes, it is."

"Welcome to our hotel, Mr. Hall. We do hope you enjoy your stay."

Whereupon, surreally, I was given flowers and chocolates and escorted to my room; rather, it was a two-story suite with a fruit basket on each floor.

I collared the attaché: "Who did you tell these people I am?"

"Someone important," he explained.

The illusion was pleasant, I admit, but in truth, I had little use for a two-story suite. I did eat an apple though.

The next morning, we met for coffee, Vienna being a particularly good place for coffee. Malandra's phone rang again, and we all leaned toward it expectantly. "Not today fellas," he said. So we wandered around Vienna, a place much more wholesome than Amsterdam, and full of history. At the Schwarzenbergplatz, we stood before the equestrian statue of Field Marshall Karl Philipp Schwarzenberg, who was instrumental in the defeat of Napoleon Bonaparte at the Battle of Leipzig in 1813 and ultimately the Battle of Paris in 1814. I said something to this effect to the agents, one of whom (who will not be named) said, referring to the movie *Napoleon Dynamite*, "Oh, I thought it was Napoleon riding to Kip's wedding."

"Different Napoleon," I advised. "Although it's an understandable mistake."

Soon thereafter, we noticed something was amiss: we were being followed.

I've been tailed before, and the threshold question is whether the tail is worth shaking. This depends on many factors, including who is doing the tailing. In many countries, you should expect to be followed, and should probably just put up with it. I couldn't think of any reason why the Austrians would be interested in keeping tabs on us, but you never know. They might just be training a new guy. Or maybe they wanted to know who was staying in the two-floor suite at the Grand Hotel Wien. But the tail didn't look Austrian. He looked distinctly Middle Eastern. We wondered if he might be Iranian; if so, this would indicate an extremely high level of coordination within the Iranian intelligence service, a level I would expect within Iran but not necessarily in Austria. Since we weren't doing anything in Vienna other than waiting, we settled for meaningless gestures like staring at the tail and arbitrarily moving in random directions, more for fun than anything else.

When the call came, we were standing in front of St. Stephen's Cathedral. "They want to talk to you," said Malandra. I got on the line and was told the Supreme Court of Georgia would be ruling the next day.

"How can you be so sure?" I asked, thinking that in the United States I could rarely tell someone when a court would rule.

"Is confident prediction," said the Georgian caller.

We mustered at dawn the next day and boarded our Gulfstream IV. After landing at Tbilisi, we immediately taxied to the far end of the airport and parked by an abandoned shed where feral dogs roamed. We kept getting calls telling us Ardebili was on his way, and finally we saw tiny red lights at the far end of the runway. The tiny red lights were not moving toward us, so we turned on the Gulfstream IV landing lights to broadcast our position. Then the tiny red lights got bigger. When the convoy finally reached us, Malandra and I alighted, and Ardebili was led out of a police van in handcuffs. They handed Malandra something written in Georgian and asked him to sign it. He looked at me, we both shrugged, and Malandra signed it. "What're ya gonna do?" he said resignedly.

The agents and I had discussed the issue of questioning Ardebili on the flight home. I thought it was important not to start right in on an interrogation for several reasons, one of which was that we didn't know anything about his physical or mental condition. "Let's take our time," I reasoned. "Feed him, let him take a nap, then see if he wants to talk to us." I also didn't want him to invoke his right to remain silent as we were taking off; an invocation is forever, and it would be a long, quiet ride home. Everyone seemed to agree with my counsel.

I was surprised therefore to hear what came from the after section of the fuselage during takeoff. The Gulfstream IV rolled out fast and climbed steeply out of Tbilisi as I called from memory the ranges of Soviet surface-to-air missiles, to the enormous delight of those seated near me. Then I heard the following words tumble down the tube: "You have the right to remain silent; anything you say can and will be used against you in a court of law. . . . "

"It's like raising teenagers," I thought. "They never listen."

This was an entirely unfair conclusion, as it turned out. Ronayne let me know what happened: as soon as he was strapped in, Ardebili started making a statement, so Ronayne interrupted him to read him his rights—prudent and appropriate under the circumstances. Ardebili talked for quite a while and ate a large number of sandwiches. Then he fell sound asleep.

We landed around one a.m. on Sunday, January 26, at New Castle airport in Delaware. Judge Leonard Stark had agreed to come in for an initial appearance in the courthouse at three a.m. Then—with Ardebili's consent—we housed him in the Philadelphia detention center under a false name, due to the death threats he had received from Iran. I got home and went to sleep a little before dawn. But it didn't take long for the phone to ring: Washington again. The National Security Division wanted to do a press conference. Again.

"No," I said. "We just got him back and we are going to start an undercover operation where we pose as Ardebili. Announcing he is in custody will make that plan impossible."

"How do you know that plan will work?" the caller wanted to know.

"I don't," I said. "You never know. But I do know we won't arrest anyone in the U.S. if we don't try."

I wish I had quoted the Great One: "You miss 100 percent of the shots you don't take."

This argument went on for weeks, but I persisted, and in the end the National Security Division found something else to do a press conference about. And—although I had apparently hurt the feelings of the sensitive souls in the National Security Division—someone in Washington decided the commander in chief needed to know what was going on. Malandra called my cell phone to let me know. I was in a CVS parking lot on my way home from work, having been previously instructed by Mrs. Hall to buy milk, orange juice, toilet paper, and other odds and ends. I had just received at the CVS checkout counter the ultimate retail badge of shame: the declined credit card. I handed over my debit card: same result. I looked in my wallet: nothing. The fruits of a long government career.

I excused myself and returned to my car, where I searched under the seats for loose change. Malandra's call came just as I was on my hands and knees fumbling under the driver's seat. I had forty-nine cents so far.

"Just had a call," said Malandra. "President's getting briefed."

"On what?"

"Our case."

"Have you seen the brief?"

"No."

"How do you know they have it right?"

"Don't. Out."

I hung up and went back to coin fishing. I returned to CVS with a fistful of change, made the walk of shame back to the cash register, and bought a single roll of toilet paper. I returned to my happy home in failure, tendering my loyal and faithful wife of thirty years a single roll of toilet paper as the President was briefed on my recent activities. It all made sense.

The President evidently did not need any further briefing, and so we pressed on: We found 150 or so companies in the United States that had done business with Ardebili. We couldn't prove from the e-mail traffic that they knew they were dealing with an Iranian because he presented himself as "Alex Dave" from Dubai. This is why the undercover approach was so important. When the undercover agents made it clear they were soliciting an export to Iran, most of the 150 companies ceased communication. Notably, and sadly, not one contacted law enforcement authorities. Malandra sent leads to other HSI offices on more than fifty companies, not one of which resulted in charges. This too was sad. For our part, we charged eleven companies and individuals.

There were other positive effects from the Ardebili case: we had proved a concept, and the agents—having seen it work—were encouraged to press ahead. In one instance, shortly after the Ardebili arrest in Georgia, we received informant information from Europe that an American in Los Angeles named Paul Taylor was exporting controlled U.S. military communications equipment. In February 2008, we initiated undercover e-mail communication with Taylor about an antigravity flight suit he was trying to sell on eBay. This led to phone calls in which Taylor agreed to sell military aviation helmets with embedded communications devices, admitting that they were controlled by the military and illegal to export. When the undercover agent pressed him on this, Taylor said—to his enormous subsequent regret—"I don't give a fuck."

After Taylor exported a sample helmet to an overseas undercover location, the undercover agent and Taylor met in Los Angeles in February 2009 to talk about a bulk purchase of ten to twenty helmets. During this meeting, Taylor volunteered that Iran needs F-14 parts and that he would be happy to provide them. A month later, Taylor agreed to supply an F-14 ejection seat for export to Iran, delivering it in April in a crate marked as movie props. On December 10, 2009, the undercover agent and Taylor met in Delaware, and Taylor was arrested. He identified the source of the F-14 ejection seat as a man in California named Marc Knapp.

Taylor introduced the undercover agent to Knapp by phone, and on December 24—the day after Brendan Cullen's consequential brief at AGI—Knapp called the undercover agent to discuss future sales of F-14 and F-5 ejection seats. On January 4, 2010—days before our first undercover contact with Xiang Li—the undercover agent and Knapp met in Philadelphia, where they discussed the sale of ten F-14 ejection seats at $25,000 each. Knapp also offered to sell search-and-rescue radios so the enemy can "just listen in" when a U.S. airman is downed. He also advised that he knew of two F-5B fighters for sale, suggesting the Iranians might be interested.

The undercover agent met again with Knapp in Los Angeles in January 2010. Knapp took the undercover to Van Nuys Airport to inspect the F-5B offered for sale. We agreed to purchase the F-14 ejection seat and continued discussing the F-5B deal throughout February and March. Knapp and the undercover agent decided that the F-5B would be transshipped through Hungary, and to that end they met in Budapest on April 29 and 30. To make this happen, I negotiated with the Hungarians, obtaining an agreement to support an undercover meeting in Budapest. In a cafe, Knapp and the undercover agent met with a second undercover officer who was posing as an Iranian acquisition agent. They finalized their transshipment plans, emboldening Knapp to the point where he felt compelled to share his innermost feelings: "I'm starting to hate the U.S. more and more."

Knapp and the undercover agent continued arranging for the F-5B export until their final meeting on July 20 in Wilmington, Delaware, where Knapp presented his final plans. He was arrested and pled guilty to all counts.

For his part, Ardebili pled guilty to all counts—ours and Boston's—in 2008 and was sentenced in December 2009, just weeks before AGI told Brendan Cullen about CRACK99. By this time, the HSI office in Philadelphia had two counter-proliferation groups, one headed by Malandra and the other by Ronayne. They worked an active portfolio of investigations of foreign arms dealers, mostly Iranian. Software piracy was another matter, however. It was a bastard stepchild; no one knew where it belonged. Intellectual-property crime was not handled by Ronayne's counter-proliferation group but by a property-crime group that focused on brand infringement, seizing knockoff perfumes and Rolex watches. No one was focused on software piracy. Even the HSI annual reports of seizures for fiscal years 2010 and 2011 did not list software, although they did list just about everything else imaginable, including handbags, watches, consumer electronics, footwear, pharmaceuticals, optical media, digital media, apparel, perfume, and toys.

The Ardebili case and its spin-offs had proved a concept and provided us with a template for future investigations. And it had given us "street cred." But even with that recent success, the question was, would we get the support we needed to go forward with the CRACK99 investigation?

7 | THE NEXT WAR

"DO YOU THINK WE SHOULD BE doing only Iranian cases? I mean, what about China?"

This question came at me from Special Agent Harry Ubele, leaning his solid frame across the table to make his point. It was very late on an unusually warm summer night in an eastern European capital in 2010. I had a wet towel behind my neck. We had just concluded a meeting with an Iranian procurement agent based in Europe who was trying to acquire civil aviation components, among other things. Harry had cut his eyeteeth on Iranian procurement with the Ardebili case, but he did not have tunnel vision. A Navy vet, he well understood the strategic importance of China, an adversary the Navy has kept in its sights throughout the post-9/11 war on Middle Eastern–based terrorism. The Navy had to keep its sights trained on China because the Navy was responsible for the Pacific theater, and when you're in the Pacific theater, you would have to make an effort to miss the significance of China. Harry was aware of the Xiang Li case, but in the summer of 2010, it was hard to say where the investigation was headed. And Harry knew that it was our team's only one involving

China, in contrast to dozens of Iranian cases. Harry's question was prescient and timely.

As it happened, Harry Ubele and President Barack Obama were thinking along similar lines. "At the very outset of his Administration, the President made a strategic decision to increase the United States' focus on the Asia-Pacific region by rebalancing U.S. engagements, activities, and resources toward this vital region." In 2011, the President made this clear in a speech to the Australian parliament:

> Our new focus on this region reflects a fundamental truth—the United States has been, and always will be, a Pacific nation. . . . Here, we see the future. As the world's fastest-growing region—and home to more than half the global economy—the Asia Pacific is critical to achieving my highest priority, and that's creating jobs and opportunity for the American people. . . . As President, I have, therefore, made a deliberate and strategic decision—as a Pacific nation, the United States will play a larger and long-term role in shaping this region and its future, by upholding core principles and in close partnership with our allies and friends.

And to put a fine point on it, in case someone in the back row was not paying attention, the President continued:

> My guidance is clear. As we plan and budget for the future, we will allocate the resources necessary to maintain our strong military presence in this region. We will preserve our unique ability to project power and deter threats to peace. . . . Our enduring interests in the region demand our enduring presence in the region. The United States is a Pacific power, and we are here to stay.

I do think that qualifies as clear guidance. The President said the Pacific region was his "highest priority," meaning Iran and the Middle

East were no longer number one on the presidential punch list. Maybe a close second, but definitely not number one. This represented a significant change in strategic focus, partly for economic reasons—the Pacific is the "fastest-growing region" and represents "half the global economy"—and partly for military purposes—"We will . . . . maintain our strong military presence . . . [in order to] project power and deter threats to peace."

His clarity notwithstanding, the President didn't have much to show for this rebalancing, and by February 2013, an acute strategic imbalance was made public in a report from the cybersecurity firm Mandiant. After years of diligent and proactive investigation, Mandiant had managed to establish that a hacking group known as the "Comment Crew" was in reality the "2nd Bureau of the People's Liberation Army (PLA) General Staff Department's (GSD) 3rd Department," also known as "Unit 61398." This PLA unit, Mandiant found, had "systematically stolen hundreds of terabytes of data from at least 141 organizations," including major U.S. defense contractors.

These revelations were followed by more. In April 2013, FireEye Labs, another cybersecurity firm (which has since acquired Mandiant), reported observing "a series of related attacks against a dozen organizations in the aerospace, defense, and telecommunications industries as well as government agencies located in the United States and India which have been occurring at least as early as December of 2011. . . . We have linked these attacks back to Operation Beebus [the PLA's campaign to steal U.S. technology]."

Operation Beebus was a resounding success, to the detriment of the United States.

As if that wasn't bad enough, shortly before the release of the Mandiant and FireEye investigations, in January 2013 the Defense Science Board (DSB)—a group that advises the Secretary of Defense—released the *Task Force Report: Resilient Military Systems and the Advanced Cyber Threat*. The Defense Science Board had been charged with evaluating the resiliency of Department of Defense (DoD) systems to cyber attack. Based on data collected over an eighteen-month period ending in August 2012, the findings were not good:

> *The DoD, and its contractor base are high priority targets that have sustained staggering losses of system design information incorporating years of combat knowledge and experience. Employing reverse engineering techniques, adversaries can exploit weapon system technical plans for their benefit. Perhaps even more significant, they gained insight to operational concepts and system use (e.g., which processes are automated and which are person controlled) developed from decades of U.S. operational and developmental experience—the type of information that cannot simply be recreated in a laboratory or factory environment. Such information provides tremendous benefit to an adversary, shortening time for development of countermeasures by years.*

In short, as a result of the loss of U.S. technology and know-how to cyber theft, the United States has lost strategic advantage. Particularly ominous was this finding:

> *Should the United States find itself in a full-scale conflict with a peer adversary, [cyber] attacks would be expected to include denial of service, data corruption, supply chain corruption, traitorous insiders, kinetic and related non-kinetic attacks at all altitudes from underwater to space.*

And who is this "peer adversary"? The report did not say, although it identified only two countries as occupying the top tiers of the adversary pyramid: China and Russia.

The report went on to say that as a result of the cyber threat, U.S. forces in combat might experience the following adverse consequences:

- *Degradation or severing of communication links critical to the operation of U.S. forces, thereby denying the receipt of command directions and sensor data*
- *Data manipulation or corruption may cause misdirected U.S. operations and lead to lack of trust of all information*
- *Weapons and weapon systems may fail to operate as intended, to include operating in ways harmful to U.S. forces*
- *Potential destruction of U.S. systems (e.g. crashing a plane, satellite, unmanned aerial vehicles, etc.).*

The Defense Science Board drew the following conclusions:

- *The cyber threat is serious, with potential consequences similar in some ways to the nuclear threat of the Cold War*
- *The cyber threat is also insidious allowing adversaries to access vast new channels of intelligence about critical U.S. enablers (operational and technical; military and industrial) that can threaten our national and economic security*
- *Current DoD actions, though numerous, are fragmented. Thus, DoD is not prepared to defend against this threat*
- *DoD red teams, using cyber attack tools, which can be downloaded from the Internet, are very successful at defeating our systems*
- *U.S. networks are built on inherently insecure architectures with increasing use of foreign-built components*
- *U.S. intelligence against peer threats targeting DoD systems is inadequate*
- *With present capabilities and technology, it is not possible to defend with confidence against the most sophisticated cyber attacks*
- *It will take years for the Department to build an effective response to the cyber threat to include elements of deterrence, mission assurance and offensive cyber capabilities.*

Imagine that you are Secretary of Defense Robert Gates, and you are reading this report early on a Tuesday morning in January 2013. You are a busy man and don't have time to read the whole thing. So you just skim the conclusions. Wouldn't that pretty much ruin your Tuesday? Maybe even the whole month? This is not just some blog. This is from the Defense Science Board, which has just told you that the cyber threat to the Defense Department has "potential consequences similar . . . to the nuclear threat of the Cold War." That is about as "serious" as it gets, particularly given that you remember the Cold War for what it was: a stalemate that could have ended at any moment with the sudden destruction of the world.

I don't think the Defense Science Board's report ruined Secretary Gates's Tuesday or even his January. I don't think it surprised him at all. Secretary Gates himself had given a similar warning in November 2010: "There is a huge future threat and there is a considerable current threat [from cyber attacks]." The Defense Department had also established CYBERCOM that year, evincing awareness that the cyber threat was looming. And 2010 was when the Defense Department confirmed the 2008 breach of Central Command's network, the "most significant breach of U.S. military computers ever": "The 2008 intrusion . . . was not the only successful penetration. Adversaries have acquired thousands of files from U.S. networks and from the networks of U.S. allies and industry partners, including weapons blueprints, operational plans, and surveillance data."

In 2010, the Department of Defense was at least starting to look at the cyber threat. Likewise, CIA Director Leon Panetta, in April 2010, outlined the CIA's blueprint for the future, highlighting among his priorities "the proliferation of dangerous technology [and] cyber threats." Thus can it be said fairly that by 2010 the U.S. government had recognized the danger posed by cyber attacks. Nevertheless, government disclosures to the public were far from fulsome. This is nothing new. I well understand the reasons for withholding certain kinds of information from the public. For one, anything that gets released to the public for its own good also gets released to U.S. adversaries for their own good. And there is the "mosaic" principle, under the tenets of which tidbits of information—harmless in isolation—can be reassembled in ways damaging to U.S. national security. In fact, the government does have to be careful about what it discloses.

In the end, it was Mandiant and FireEye and the press—not the government—that turned a bright light on China, publicly demonstrating the magnitude of the Chinese cyber threat. On May 2, 2013, journalists from Bloomberg news reported a massive hack by the PLA of the defense contractor QinetiQ, which produces robotics, satellite systems, and military control software, among other things. The hack reportedly started in 2007 and lasted three years:

> "We found traces of the intruders in many of their divisions and across most of their product lines," said Christopher Day, until February a senior vice president for Verizon Communications Inc. Terremark security division, which was hired twice by QinetiQ to investigate the break-ins. "There was virtually no place we looked where we didn't find them."

The consequences were significant: the PLA stole twenty gigabytes of data, including software for robotic systems, apparently for the purpose of reverse engineering them for Chinese production:

> Among the victims was a specialist in the embedded software on microchips that control the company's military robots, which would help in China's own robot-building program, said Noel Sharkey, a drones and robotics expert at Britain's Sheffield University. The PLA unveiled a bomb disposal robot in April 2012 similar to QinetiQ's Dragon Runner.

The PLA hackers are also believed to have utilized their access to QinetiQ to break into the computers of the U.S. Army Redstone

Arsenal—home of the U.S. Army Aviation and Missile Command—through a shared network. "God forbid we get into a conflict with China but if we did we could face a major embarrassment, where we try out all these sophisticated weapons systems and they don't work," said Richard Clarke, special cybersecurity adviser to President George W. Bush. Amazingly, QinetiQ was awarded a $4.7 million cybersecurity contract by the U.S. Department of Transportation in 2012.

In May 2013, its hand no doubt forced by the public disclosures of Mandiant and others, the Department of Defense publicly accused the People's Republic of China of cyber espionage directed against U.S. networks:

> In 2012, numerous computer systems around the world, including those owned by the U.S. government, continued to be targeted for intrusions, some of which appear to be attributable directly to the Chinese government and military. These intrusions were focused on exfiltrating information. China is using its computer network exploitation (CNE) capability to support intelligence collection against the U.S. diplomatic, economic, and defense industrial base sectors that support U.S. national defense programs.

Since then, the government has made other disclosures as well, including the acknowledgment that the Chinese had breached TRANSCOM—one of the nine combatant commands. TRANSCOM is the U.S. Transportation Command, headed by a four-star general. Its mission is to provide "full-spectrum global mobility solutions" to other combatant commands, the services, and Defense Department agencies. TRANSCOM handles logistics, making it a ripe target for cyber intrusion. The Senate Armed Services Committee conducted an investigation into the cyber penetration of TRANSCOM in 2013. Its declassified findings were released in a report in 2014. Central among them are the following:

The committee's inquiry identified approximately 50 successful intrusions or other cyber events targeting TRANSCOM contractors between June 1, 2012 and May 30, 2013. Of those 50, at least 20 were successful intrusions into contractor networks attributed to an "advanced persistent threat" (APT), a term used to distinguish sophisticated cyber threats that are frequently associated with foreign governments.

You might be wondering which foreign governments. "Of the at least 20 successful cyber intrusions attributed to an APT, all were attributed to China."

The committee's report also noted that:

Chinese military analysts . . . have identified logistics and mobilization as potential U.S. vulnerabilities "given the requirements for precision in coordinating transportation, communications, and logistics networks." In fact, Chinese military doctrine "advocate[s] targeting adversary command and control and logistics networks to impact their ability to operate during the early stages of conflict."

On January 30, 2014, the U.S.-China Economic and Security Review Commission, which was created by Congress to investigate and report to Congress on the national security implications of economic relations with China, heard the following testimony:

Cyber espionage has been and continues to be a godsend to China's economic and technological modernization. For military equipment, a 2012 Defense Science Board report identified a range of systems as compromised by Chinese espionage. These included the PAC-3 Patriot missile system, Terminal High Altitude Area Defense (THAAD); the Aegis ballistic-missile defense system, the F/A-18 fighter jet, the V-22 Osprey, the Black Hawk helicopter, the F-35 Joint Strike fighter and the Littoral Combat Ship (LCS). These targets not only improved China's own manufacturing capabilities, but provided it insight into air and air defense system most likely to be used in combat a maritime and air combat and allowed China to try to develop countermeasures to evade or defeat US missile and air defense.

It is difficult to exaggerate the gravity of this threat. The question is, what will the U.S. government do about it? As a nation, we have found ourselves at such strategic crossroads before. In 1947, the Soviet Union—our former ally—posed a significant strategic threat that the U.S. government did not fully recognize until George Keenan, using the pseudonym "X," wrote his famous strategy of containment:

In these circumstances it is clear that the main element of any United States policy toward the Soviet Union must be that of long-term, patient but firm and vigilant containment of Russian expansive tendencies.

Strategic crossroads pose great peril; there is danger coming from more than one direction. The Soviet Union did pose a great strategic threat, but the question of how to contain that threat presented its own set of hazards, as the Korean and Vietnam Wars amply demonstrate.

The Soviet Union in 1947 is not the only example of a former U.S. ally-turned-adversary. Prior to the Iranian revolution of 1979, which overthrew the Pahlavi dynasty, the United States and Iran were allies. Since 1979, the two countries have been at odds. The revolution was not only anti-Pahlavi but also anti-American, as demonstrated by the forcible capture of the U.S. embassy and the kidnapping of U.S. citizens, who were held hostage for 444 days. Ultimately, the revolution led to the formation of an Islamic republic, governed by Grand Ayatollah Ruhollah Khomeini. I visited Iran in 1976, just three years before the revolution, and demonstrated profound sagacity when I wrote to my parents to let them know Iran was not as stable as the U.S. government seemed to think, and that the Iranian students were anti-American and anti-Shah. Unfortunately, I brought my sagacity meter back to zero by telling them not to worry about me; I had been to the U.S. embassy and it was like a fortress, so I planned to go there at the first sign of trouble.

President Jimmy Carter imposed the first embargo against Iran in 1980. President Ronald Reagan imposed additional sanctions in 1987, and every U.S. President since then has enforced an embargo against Iran. And with what results? According to the Department of Defense in 2012:

> *During the past three decades Iran has methodically cultivated a network of sponsored terrorist surrogates capable of targeting U.S. and Israeli interests, . . . continues to develop technological capabilities applicable to nuclear weapons [including] . . . uranium enrichment and heavy-water nuclear reactor activities, . . . [and] continues to develop ballistic missiles that could be adapted to deliver nuclear weapons . . . that can range [sic] regional adversaries, Israel, and Eastern Europe.*

So, during a thirty-year period of a near-total U.S. embargo, the Iranians have managed to deliver a hat trick of threats to U.S. national security: support to terrorist organizations, nuclear weapon technology development, and a ballistic missile program. Here is how the Director of National Intelligence put it in 2013:

> *We assess Iran is developing nuclear capabilities to enhance its security, prestige, and regional influence and give it the ability to develop nuclear weapons. . . . Tehran has developed technical expertise in a number of areas—including uranium enrichment, nuclear reactors, and ballistic missiles—from which it could draw if it decided to build missile-deliverable nuclear weapons. These technical advancements strengthen our assessment that Iran has the scientific, technical, and*

industrial capacity to eventually produce nuclear weapons. . . . Iran's ballistic missiles are capable of delivering WMD [weapons of mass destruction]. In addition, Iran has demonstrated an ability to launch small satellites, and we grow increasingly concerned that these technical steps—along with a regime hostile toward the United States and our allies—provide Tehran with the means and motivation to develop larger space-launch vehicles and longer-range missiles, including an intercontinental ballistic missile (ICBM). Iran already has the largest inventory of ballistic missiles in the Middle East, and it is expanding the scale, reach, and sophistication of its ballistic missile arsenal.

It is difficult, in the face of this astonishing statement of Iranian military capability, to call the embargoes a success.

And what is the source of the failure? From what I have seen on the enforcement side of the embargo, the failure results from a lack of will. The Ardebili case served as an example of what the United States should be doing on a routine basis to enforce the embargo: luring Iranian arms dealers out of Iran to be arrested and prosecuted. But by standing out as the only example of this ever happening, the Ardebili case demonstrates more than anything what the U.S. government is not doing. The Department of Justice publishes a brag sheet announcing its export enforcement successes, including those relating to sanctions against Iran. There are some significant and worthwhile cases on that list, but overall it bears witness to the fast-food mentality: big cases, big problems; small cases, small problems.

Numerically too, the Justice Department's brag sheet fails to impress. The number of newly charged export offenses reported for 2013 is only eleven; of these, seven involved enforcing sanctions against Iran. The brag sheet is not exhaustive; in fact, my last indictment for the illegal export of arms—against a Russian arms dealer who was ultimately extradited through Lithuania to the United States for prosecution—was not listed in 2013 because it was under seal until 2014. But even if the numbers are off by 100 percent, these national-level statistics are underwhelming. The Drug Enforcement Administration (DEA) typically makes around thirty thousand arrests each year, meaning that it makes about three thousand times more drug-related arrests than the number of export-related arrests reportedly made by all agencies of the federal government. It might be true that drug investigations are three thousand times easier than export investigations. And reasonable minds might differ on where drug prosecutions should rank among the priorities of the Department of Justice. But I don't think a reasonable person would contend that drug arrests are three thousand times more important than export arrests.

Particularly galling are the reported cases where defendants are charged but not arrested because they are overseas. In one such case, eleven defendants were named in an indictment alleging a conspiracy to export to Iran components for F-14 and F-5 fighters, the Bell AH-1 Cobra attack helicopter, and CH-53 and UH-1 Huey helicopters. Only one defendant was arrested—the one who lived in California. The others are in the wind. What is the point of such an indictment? The pat answer from the government is: blame and shame. But does anyone really think an Iranian arms dealer operating with the blessing of his government will be shamed by the fact that the U.S. government has charged him with an export crime? To the contrary, he would probably wear that indictment as a badge of honor.

The same lackluster approach is on display in law enforcement efforts against Chinese cyber espionage and cyber piracy. Of the new export charges announced in 2013, only one involved illegal exports to China. In 2012, there were a few more, including an indictment of Chinese nationals involved in an elaborate scheme to export programmable logic devices from the United States to China. But no one was arrested—because they were in China. This theme continued with the announcement in May 2014 of the indictment of five officers in the PLA unit responsible for the widespread hacking of U.S. networks: five were charged and none were arrested. The U.S. government charged the following officers with offenses related to cyber intrusion, copyright infringement, and theft of trade secrets:

> Wang Dong, also known as "Jack Wang" and "UglyGorilla";
> Sun Kailiang, also known as "Sun Kai Liang" and "Jack Sun";
> Wen Xinyu, also known as "Wen Xin Yu," "WinXYHappy," "Win_XY," and "Lao Wen";
> Huang Zhenyu, also known as "Huang Zhen Yu" and "hzy_lhx"; and
> Gu Chunhui, also known as "Gu Chun Hui" and "KandyGoo"

This was the same unit that Mandiant had identified in its February 2013 report. I was heartened to see the government finally taking action, but disappointed to see that the indictment was unsealed only weeks after its return by the grand jury. This suggests that there was no serious effort to arrest any of the defendants. Such arrests would indeed be difficult, but certainly not impossible; at the very least, it would have been nice if the government had tried. Blame and shame is a paper tiger.

But some good did come of the indictment, primarily in the form of further information that filled in the gaps left after the 2013 revelations of massive Chinese hacking. The defendants were described as members of the PLA General Staff, Third Department (3PLA), a signals intelligence component of the PLA known as "Unit 61398" in Shanghai, China. Mandiant had described the unit in its February 2013 report:

> We believe that the PLA's strategic cyber command is situated in the PLA's General Staff Department (GSD,总参谋部), specifically its 3rd Department (总参三部). The GSD is the most senior PLA department. Similar to the U.S. Joint Chiefs of Staff, the GSD establishes doctrine and provides operational guidance for the PLA. Within the GSD, the

3rd Department has a combined focus on signals intelligence, foreign language proficiency, and defense information systems. It is estimated to have 130,000 personnel divided between 12 bureaus (局), three research institutes, and 16 regional and functional bureaus. We believe that the GSD 3rd Department, 2nd Bureau (总参三部二局), is the APT group that we are tracking as APT1.

The five defendants were charged with conspiring between 2006 and 2014 to hack into U.S. company computers to steal trade secrets and information advantageous to Chinese competitors, including state-owned enterprises. The method of intrusion was spear phishing, described in the indictment as follows:

The co-conspirators used e-mail messages known as "spear phishing" messages to trick unwitting recipients into giving the co-conspirators access to their computers. Spearphishing messages were typically designed to resemble e-mails from trustworthy senders, like colleagues, and encouraged the recipients to open attached files or click on hyperlinks in the messages. However, the attached or linked files, once opened, installed "malware", malicious code that provided unauthorized access to the recipient's computer (known as a "backdoor"), thereby allowing the co-conspirators to bypass normal authentication procedures in the future.

This is the oldest story in history: the weak point of any system is the human element. The victim companies were sophisticated international corporations that had most likely given some thought to cybersecurity, but even the best security systems can be defeated by one human who gets fooled.

Significantly, the indictment did not involve the Chinese hacking of defense contractors that Mandiant and others had reported, but rather the Chinese hacking of other commercial actors. Just as their targets were not defense contractors, the 3PLA's objective in the alleged cyber-theft conspiracy was not defense related: the goal was to provide maximum advantage to Chinese state-owned enterprises in direct economic competition with U.S. corporations. For example:

> *While a Pennsylvania nuclear power plant manufacturer was negotiating with a Chinese company over the construction and operation of four power plants in China, the conspirators stole, among other things, proprietary and confidential technical and design specifications for pipes, pipe supports, and pipe routing for those nuclear power plants that would enable any competitor looking to build a similar plant to save on research and development costs in the development of such designs. In the case of both of those American victims and others, the conspirators also stole sensitive, internal communications that would provide a competitor, or adversary in litigation, with insight into the strategy and vulnerabilities of the American entity.*

One of the more intriguing allegations in the indictment is that Chinese companies actually "hired" 3PLA to provide them with stolen U.S. proprietary information. "For example, one [state-owned enterprise] involved in trade litigation against some of the American victims . . . hired the Unit . . . to build a 'secret' database to hold corporate 'intelligence'."

The indictment was specific in its allegations of cyber theft from the victim companies. For example, in July 2007, Westinghouse Electric Company entered into an agreement with a Chinese state-owned nuclear power company labeled "SOE-1" to build and operate four Westinghouse AP1000 nuclear power plants—developed over a fifteen-year period with the investment of significant resources by Westinghouse. In 2010 and 2011, while Westinghouse negotiated with SOE-1 about building additional AP1000 nuclear power plants, 3PLA member Sun Kailiang hacked Westinghouse's network and stole "proprietary and confidential technical and design specifications for pipes, pipe supports, and pipe routing" within the AP1000 plants. The stolen information would "enable a competitor to build a plant similar to the AP1000 without incurring significant research and development costs." By stealing this information, the Chinese state-owned SOE-1 was able to bypass the time-consuming and costly development process and get Westinghouse's information for free.

To further solidify the Chinese government's advantage, 3PLA stole "internal Westinghouse communications concerning the company's strategy for doing business with SOE-1 in China and the potential that SOE-1 may eventually become a competitor." Included in the theft were e-mails from Westinghouse's chief executive officer. In total, 3PLA stole 1.4 gigabytes of data from Westinghouse, the equivalent of seven hundred thousand e-mails.

The 3PLA's motivation in hacking the United States Steel Corporation, the largest steel company in the United States, was also commercial. U.S. Steel had complained to the U.S. Department of Commerce that subsidized Chinese companies were dumping steel piping used by the oil and gas industries—known as oil country tubular goods (OCTGs) and seamless standard line pipes (SSLPs)—in the United States at below-market prices. In 2010, while this trade dispute was pending, 3PLA member Sun Kailiang sent multiple spear-phishing messages—one purportedly from the U.S. Steel chief executive officer—to U.S. Steel employees, including those in the division responsible for OCTGs and SSLPs. The e-mails contained a link that some recipients clicked open, installing malware on U.S. Steel computers, providing 3PLA with ongoing backdoor access to the U.S. Steel network. In the same time period, 3PLA member Wang Dong stole "hostnames and descriptions for more than 1,700 servers, including servers that controlled physical access to [U.S. Steel's] facilities and mobile device access to the company's networks."

The steel workers union—the United Steel, Paper and Forestry,

Rubber, Manufacturing, Energy, Allied Industrial and Service Workers International Union (USW)—was also a victim of 3PLA, according
to the indictment. One of the objectives of the USW was to oppose
unfair Chinese trade practices, and to this end, the USW represented
its members in international trade disputes, media campaigns, and
lobbying. In response to this activity, 3PLA hacked USW's computers,
as the indictment charged:

> *On at least four occasions between in or about 2010 and 2012 while
> USW was particularly vocal about China's trade practices Defendant
> WEN and an unidentified co-conspirator gained unauthorized access
> to USW's computers and stole e-mail messages and attachments from
> the accounts of six to eight USW employees who would be expected to
> have sensitive, non-public, and deliberative information about USW's
> trade strategy concerning China.*

For example, on January 30, 2012, the USW issued a press release
stating that a decision from the World Trade Organization on Chinese
trade practices was "a huge victory for American workers," along
with a statement encouraging further U.S. government action to protect the U.S. auto-parts industry from "China's predatory, protection-
ist and illegal trade practices." That same day, 3PLA member Wen
Xinyu stole e-mails from six senior USW employees, one of whom was
the USW's International President, as well as:

> *sensitive, non-public, and deliberative information about USW's strat-
> egy including, for example, USW's preparations for the January 31,
> 2012 news conference where it issued its "call to action" against Chi-
> nese trade practices in the auto parts sector; discussion of the merits of
> the January 31, 2012 WTO report on raw materials; and drafts of press
> releases announcing that report.*

Similarly, 3PLA member Wen Xinyu was charged with hacking USW's computers to steal e-mails in March 2012, after the International President of USW urged Congress to grant the U.S. Department of Commerce authority to impose countervailing duties on Chinese exports, stating that "it would be a travesty for Congress to stand idle while a country like China can provide lavish subsidies for exports."

Alcoa—the largest aluminum company in the United States—was another alleged victim of 3PLA. In 2008, Alcoa announced a partnership with a Chinese state-owned aluminum company labeled "SOE-3" to acquire a stake in a foreign mining company. According to the indictment, approximately three weeks later, 3PLA member Sun Kailiang initiated a spear-phishing campaign, impersonating a member of Alcoa's Board of Directors and attaching a file disguised as an agenda for Alcoa's annual shareholders' meeting. Once opened, that attachment installed malware on the recipients' computers. Thereafter, in June 2008, at least 2,907 e-mail messages were stolen from Alcoa's computers, including internal messages among Alcoa senior managers discussing the mining company acquisition.

If press reports from 2013 concerning widespread hacking of U.S. defense contractors by the Chinese are accurate, then a great deal was left out of the 3PLA indictment. It is not difficult to guess the reason: charging hacking of national security information risks the revelation of national security information. The government avoided that problem by choosing to charge instances of purely commercial hacking. But the indictment illustrates another point as well. By shining a light on 3PLA's commercial hacking, the indictment demonstrates that from the point of view of the PLA—and therefore the People's Republic of China as a whole—there is little difference between commercial and national security hacking: it is all of a single strategic piece. The Chinese goal is to steal U.S. proprietary information and technology to the strategic advantage of the Chinese government.

This suggests that China is not unlike the United States in that both nations understand that military power and commercial success are codependent. Thus, the Chinese government is just as focused on stealing commercially advantageous trade secrets as on stealing military technology. In the end, it is all about the market, regardless of which market: F-35 technology, rolled steel, missile defense, or mining. Whatever the commodity, the Chinese are looking for a market advantage anywhere they can find it. If they want the inside story on Alcoa's business strategy, they will steal Alcoa's e-mails. If they want STK, someone will steal it from AGI—or buy it from CRACK99 like we did.

In 2010, we didn't have the advantage of knowing the information about Chinese hacking that would be revealed in 2013 and 2014. But we did understand that CRACK99 was market based; Xiang Li had made this clear. This understanding was the fundamental premise to the plan we developed in Chicago to make ourselves important to CRACK99. The way to do that was for us to become an important source of current and future revenue, which is desirable in every business environment. To that end, we reinitiated contact with CRACK99 in November 2010. Xiang Li had previously responded to our request for the latest version of STK9.0, telling us:

> *good news*
> *STK 9.0 ----------------$USD 3000.00*
> *LATEST VERSION*

We followed up on this offer on November 8, 2010, but we wanted a bargain: 50 percent off.

> *Xiang,*
>   *We will buy STK 9.0 for $1,500 USD. Please remember we are returning customers. Thank you my friend.*

To our surprise, Xiang Li wrote back: "ok I agree." Then, realizing what we were up to, he quickly corrected his reply:

$ USD 1,500
NO . . .
ONLY
$USD 2000 FOR YOU
hi
sorry
Reason is very costly
The development cost

but . . .
GOOD NEWS
A GIFTS
Altera Quartus II latest version
Altera Quartus II v10.0(NOW) + stk 9 = $USD 2000

OK?
Good friends

He certainly was trying. His offer was to sell us the newest version of STK along with the newest version of QUARTUS for $2,000 total, allowing us to update two of the products we had previously purchased from CRACK99. He promptly followed up with another e-mail.

I will attach important our cooperation
Always trust my service

Shake hands!

He followed this up with another e-mail reminding us of the Western Union payment method and concluding with "waiting for your good news."

On November 9, we put him out of his misery: "Thank you. I will send payment. You are a friend." Nevertheless, on November 10, Xiang Li impatiently wrote:

HI
MY friend
YOU NO NEWS?
YOU PAY THE MONEY?

WAITING FOR YOUR GOOD NEWS

We sent the money from the Western Union at the Red Lion food store in Claymont, but then were surprised to hear nothing back from Xiang Li. So we wrote on November 15: "We still have not received the STK9.0 and all altera products." Xiang Li responded the next day with a list of downloadable links for Quartus II version 10, and the instruction "now download all files." We received a separate e-mail with a zip file labeled "STK921 Install," but it was empty. We let him know that: "Is there a problem?" we asked. Xiang Li wrote back:

Please be patient my E-MAIL
It takes a few days.
I'm in business Travel.

This was somewhat frustrating, but I considered it to be good news on the whole: if he was telling the truth, he was willing to travel, and traveling was exactly what we wanted him to do.

On November 23, Xiang Li sent a downloadable link for STK 9.2.1, and on November 29, he sent another link with video instructions on how to use the software. Once again, Xiang Li proved to be a man of his word, and a full-service software pirate at that. On December 2, we confirmed at AGI's office that the software was indeed fully functioning STK software. They did not seem pleased to learn that the latest version of their signature product was available at a discount on a Chinese piracy website.

AGI also determined that CRACK99 had changed its cracking methodology. In the past, the crack worked by enabling the user to change the host identification number of the license file to match the host identification number of his or her workstation. In the most recent iteration, the crack worked by enabling the user to change the media access control (MAC) identification address (a unique identifier) associated with the user's computer. The Maxalim licensing file that accompanied the STK 9.2.1 file matched the MAC address we were instructed to use. When the MAC addresses matched, the Maxalim licensing file allowed the user access to the STK 9.2.1 software, "thinking" it was actually authorized.

AGI estimated that the STK 9.2.1 software we bought for $2,000 was worth over $240,000. Furthermore, AGI pointed out that the version we acquired had just been released that month. This is why AGI was unhappy. CRACK99's inventory was very current.

The time had come for an end game. It was time to step things up.

8 | ONWARD THROUGH THE FOG

IN THE FALL OF 2012, I WAS on active duty with the U.S. Navy in Pyeongtaek, South Korea, standing on the bridge wing of the ROKS *Cheonan*, a South Korean Navy corvette. The view out toward the Yellow Sea was panoramic. Downward, the view was less uplifting: I could see the *Cheonan*'s savagely broken keel and her exposed, shattered aft compartments. On March 26, 2010, a torpedo fired by a North Korean submarine in the Yellow Sea had broken her in half. It was an act of unprovoked aggression, shocking in its cowardice and treachery. Forty-six unsuspecting sailors met their end in the cold depths of a dark sea, lost to their nation and their families, for no good reason.

The Mutual Defense Treaty between the United States and the Republic of Korea provides for U.S. assistance to South Korea in the event of an armed attack. Given this, one might have expected a military response from the United States to North Korea's unprovoked armed attack against the *Cheonan*. But there was none. The lost sailors of the *Cheonan* lie in their watery common grave unavenged, as if it had all been an unfortunate mistake. But the torpedoing of the *Cheonan* was no accident; it was a deliberate act of war by North Korea. It might very well be that the lack of a military response is for the best, considering the many awful implications of war with a nuclear-armed North Korea, a conflict that could escalate into war with China. However, it does call into question the parameters of the U.S. strategy on the Korean Peninsula. It became clear after the *Cheonan* incident that U.S. strategy is not to respond in kind to all acts of aggression by North Korea. The question remaining is, what exactly is the strategy?

So it is with the cyber strategy of the United States. Many words have been expended on the topic of U.S. cyber strategy without clarifying the essential question: What exactly is the strategy? America's senior military officer, General Martin E. Dempsey, Chairman of the Joint Chiefs of Staff, gave a troubling answer to this question in remarks to the Atlantic Council on May 14, 2014:

> *There's two issues that concern me with cyber. One is our lack of preparedness as a nation for a cyberattack. We have sectors within our nation that are more ready than others, but we don't have a coherent cyber strategy as a nation. And I understand why. There are some big—there are some big issues involved with achieving that kind of coherence—issues related to privacy and cost, information sharing and all of the liabilities that come in the absence of legislation to incentivize information sharing.*

The absence of a "coherent cyber strategy as a nation" is quite a strategic omission in 2014.

General Dempsey's comment drew a response from the White House: "Given that cyberspace permeates every aspect of the economy and national security, no single document can meaningfully capture our strategic direction. Instead, our efforts are informed by specific strategy and policy documents." Indeed, there are many documents that address the cyber threat: specifically, the International Strategy for Cybersecurity; the National Strategy for Trusted Identities in Cyberspace; the National Strategy for Information Sharing and Safeguarding; Executive Order 13286, titled "Assignment of National Security and Emergency Preparedness Communications Functions"; Executive Order 13587, titled "Structural Reforms to Improve the Security of Classified Networks and the Responsible Sharing and Safeguarding of Classified Information"; the Strategic Plan for the Federal Cybersecurity Research and Development Program; and the Cross Agency Priority Goal for Cybersecurity.

So, if you want documents with the word "Strategy" in the title, the White House has them. The question remains, though, if there is a strategy, what exactly is it? It is true, as the White House says, that there are many pieces to the cybersecurity strategic puzzle. It is also true that there is much more to cybersecurity strategy than federal law enforcement, although law enforcement is a key component. The problem is that there is no overarching strategy to guide the effort, and no demonstrated will to achieve any particular goal.

On March 13, 2013, the Department of Justice gave testimony to Congress on the timely and important topic "Investigating and Prosecuting 21st Century Cyber Threats." In this testimony, the Department provided Congress with recent highlights of its cyber prosecution efforts. Generally speaking, the highlighted cases were worthy of attention. One involved a conspiracy to steal and resell stolen credit card numbers on the web, and the execution of fifteen thousand fraudulent ATM transactions in 2008 by the notorious Russian "BadB." Another involved a gang of Romanian cyber thieves who hacked into the point-of-sale computer systems of retailers like Subway to steal credit card information, compromising fifty thousand accounts and making $10 million in fraudulent transactions between 2008 and 2011. An Estonian was prosecuted for hacking the networks of retail merchants such as Dave & Buster's to steal 110,000 credit card numbers in 2009. The Coreflood botnet was taken down in 2011, a significant achievement even though no one was arrested. The Russian operator of another botnet, known as "Mega-D," reportedly responsible for 32 percent of the world's spam, was arrested and convicted. The Department pointed to the takedown of a "scareware" operation that tricked consumers into buying fake antivirus software (although apparently only one person was arrested) and also to the arrests of six leaders of the "hacktivist" group Anonymous, which was responsible for illegally accessing the computer networks of HBGary, Fox Broadcasting, Sony Pictures Entertainment, and PBS.

The cases highlighted in the Department's congressional testimony were certainly worth pursuing. But they should not represent the vanguard in forward-leaning federal cyber law enforcement. Not one of the cases involved the theft of advanced technology. More astonishing still, notwithstanding the revelations by Mandiant only a month earlier, not one of the highlighted cases involved China. In fact, the testimony as a whole glossed over the cyber threat from China. The highlighted cases were not insignificant, especially to the victims, but they should not represent the frontier of the Department's efforts.

The problem is that for the Department of Justice, such cases do represent the frontier. When it comes to effective law enforcement action against Chinese cybercrime, the Department of Justice doesn't have much to say. By May 2014, the Department could boast of the 3PLA indictment, but given the fact that no one from 3PLA was arrested—and now that it has been publicized, no one is likely to be—that case is not so much a prosecution as a gesture in the general direction of a prosecution.

The Department's largest open case in terms of dollar value involves the audio and video piracy site Megaupload. The indictment charges Kim Dotcom and others with offenses related to the unlawful distribution of millions of copyrighted works, including audio recordings, video recordings, and electronic games, between 2005 and 2010. The way the scheme allegedly worked was that the website offered access to these copyrighted files in exchange for a subscription, resulting in $150 million in revenue for Megaupload. Subscribers were able to upload pirated files for pennies on the dollar by clicking on URLs for the titles they desired, without having to pay the copyright holders.

The Department of Justice should protect the rights of copyright owners, and in this sense the Megaupload case is certainly worthwhile. But even though some defendants have been arrested overseas, only one has appeared in a U.S. court to face charges. Even if Kim Dotcom and his codefendants are eventually brought to the United States, the Megaupload case—like the cases the Department highlighted in its March 2013 testimony—lacks strategic significance. Kim Dotcom's conspiracy to sell video and audio files without paying a fee to the copyright holders has little effect on the national security of the United States.

There is a serious disconnect between the national security threat from China and the efforts of the Department of Justice. On the occasion of the unsealing of the 3PLA indictment in May 2014, Attorney General Eric Holder said:

> In his 2013 State of the Union Address, President Obama called the theft of corporate secrets by foreign countries and companies a real threat to our security and our economy. . . . This Administration will not tolerate actions by any nation that seeks to illegally sabotage American companies and undermine the integrity of fair competition in the operation of the free market. This case should serve as a wake-up call to the seriousness of the ongoing cyberthreat. These criminal charges represent a groundbreaking step forward in addressing that threat. The indictment makes clear that state actors who engage in economic espionage, even over the Internet from faraway offices in Shanghai, will be exposed for their criminal conduct and sought for apprehension and prosecution in an American court of law.

A "groundbreaking step forward"? That characterization is difficult to square with the fact that no one was arrested, which leaves the strong impression that the purpose of the indictment was not law enforcement but diplomatic posturing. I don't necessarily object to diplomatic posturing, which is an essential part of diplomacy. And it is a positive development that after so many years of systematic Chinese cyber piracy, the U.S. government has finally pointed a finger at China. But it is hardly a "groundbreaking" step, and leaves open the question of what the next step will be, and the step after that. The fundamental problem is that the Department of Justice does not know the answer to that question because there is no strategy.

The IP Commission expressed a similar view in 2013:

> *American policy in this area has been limited mostly to attempts to talk foreign leaders into building more effective intellectual property rights (IPR) regimes. In addition, the U.S. Department of Justice has prosecuted individual employees of American companies who have been caught attempting to carry trade secrets with them to foreign companies and entities. This policy of jawboning and jailing a few individuals has produced no measurable effect on the problem.*

"Jawboning and jailing a few individuals" certainly does not comprise a strategy.

Suffice it to say, there were no calls in 2010 from Main Justice to the CRACK99 investigative team, urging us forward. So in the absence of any direction from the headquarters, we made our own strategy: onward through the fog. On November 23, 2010, we went to the grand jury and asked for an indictment of Xiang Li and Chun Yan Li.

Why November 23, 2010? The answer to that question is not deep: I wanted to move forward from investigation to arrest. With an indictment in hand, we would be able to make an arrest whenever and wherever we could lay our hands on Xiang Li. In particular, I anticipated that we would make an arrest in a foreign country—as we had with Amir Ardebili—and we would need charges in place to seek extradition. Where that arrest would take place, however, was unknown at the time of indictment.

Thanks to the e-mail search warrant, we had figured out that Xiang Li and Chun Yan Li were a married couple. We charged them with two conspiracies: to circumvent a technological measure that protects a copyrighted work (that is, the circumvention of the licensing files), and to commit criminal copyright infringement. Conspiracy is an abstract concept, and people shouldn't go to prison on the basis of abstractions. So we were required to prove the existence of the charged conspiracies by proving an overt act committed by the defendants: something concrete they did in order to achieve the objectives of the conspiracy. We charged quite a few overt acts, mostly relating to our undercover purchases of STK in January 2010, QUARTUS II in February 2010, and HyperSizer in March 2010.

We also charged Xiang Li and Chun Yan Li with substantive criminal copyright infringement, smuggling, and interstate transportation of stolen property in violation of the National Stolen Property Act (NSPA). The NSPA counts might surprise you if you recall the Supreme Court case about Elvis Presley, *Dowling v. United States*. In that case, the Supreme Court reversed Presley-bootlegger Paul Dowling's conviction for the interstate transportation of copyrighted Elvis Presley records. The Court held that the NSPA was not an appropriate enforcement mechanism for criminal copyright infringement because the stolen property—the copyright—is an intangible "bundle" of exclusive legal rights, not a physical good. You might wonder why, in light of *Dowling*, I would charge an NSPA violation. Part of my motivation was my persistent belief that the Supreme Court was wrong in its *Dowling* decision; I think stolen property is stolen property, regardless of whether it is tangible. In the spirit of helpfulness as a veteran public servant, I wanted to give the Supreme Court an opportunity to correct its mistake. The *Dowling* decision had invited such an effort in leaving open the possibility that the result might be different if the government could prove that the copyright infringer "obtained the source material through illicit means." I thought that we would be able to make that showing given the extremely "illicit means" on display in the global CRACK99 pirated software enterprise. Time would tell.

In the CRACK99 indictment, we alleged a number of transactions we had discovered as a result of the e-mail search warrants, such as the January 10, 2009, sale of Rockwell RSlogix5000 to a U.S. customer. Developed by Rockwell Automation, this design automation and configuration software retailed between $2,500 and $8,000. Xiang Li sold it for $200. In addition, we alleged that on February 5, 2009, Xiang Li sold an Indonesian customer a copy of Agilent Advance Design System (ADS), produced by Agilent Technologies. Its retail price was $229,000. Xiang Li's price: $60. Agilent describes ADS as:

> the world's leading electronic design automation software for RF, microwave, and high speed digital applications. In a powerful and easy-to-use interface, ADS pioneers the most innovative and commercially successful technologies, such as X-parameters and 3D EM simulators, used by leading companies in the wireless communication & networking and aerospace & defense industries. For WiMAXTM, LTE, multi-gigabit per second data links, radar, & satellite applications, ADS provides full, standards-based design and verification with Wireless Libraries and circuit-system-EM co-simulation in an integrated platform.

If you are having a hard time comprehending what this means, you are not alone: so did we. The software is not intuitive; just understanding its purpose requires substantial exposure to advanced engineering techniques—hence, the strategic significance of its theft and resale.

ADS, like so much of the software sold by CRACK99, is part of the high-technology infrastructure of the United States—and now of China.

We also alleged a $60 sale of NX Nastran on May 6, 2009, to a U.S. customer. NX Nastran is simulation software that provides modeling "solutions for structural (powered by NX Nastran), thermal, flow, motion, engineering optimization, multiphysics," and other design requirements. This software was manufactured by Siemens and sold at a retail price exceeding $25,000. We also charged that on June 2, 2009, Xiang Li sold another U.S. customer PC-DMIS 4.1 software, which provides users "the ability to effectively collect, evaluate, manage and present the information coming from the manufacturing operations." This software, manufactured by Wilcox Associates, retailed in the United States for $12,000. The CRACK99 price was $100. These software products provided state-of-the-art computing power in multiple manufacturing and design applications.

Finally, we charged that on October 16, 2009, Xiang Li sold a U.S. customer GibbsCAM 2009, software used in computer-aided manufacturing (CAM) for programming computer numerically controlled (CNC) machine tools, including five-axis machining. The software was manufactured by Gibbs and Associates, a U.S. company, and had a retail value of approximately $12,000. Xiang Li sold it for $150. The GibbsCAM software was especially concerning given the restrictions, based on the Wassenaar Arrangement and Nuclear Suppliers Group Agreement, on the export of precision machine tools capable of simultaneous, five-axis motion. Such tools—and the software that controls them—are necessary to modern weapons manufacturing, as explained by the U.S. Department of Commerce:

> *For example, turning, milling, and grinding machines are required for the fabrication of a range of items, from large aircraft structures, submarine and ship propellers (particularly quiet propellers), and turbine*

and compressor blades to small parts for gyroscopes, engine parts, and even nuclear weapons. . . . Grinding machines are used to produce parts for stealth applications, smart weapons, sensors, night vision devices, laser mirrors, molds for radar and sonar domes, and missile applications such as forward looking infrared (FLIR) capabilities, gyroscopes, inertial navigation, and high performance engine parts. Nearly every aircraft in service today requires precision-ground parts.

In the CRACK99 indictment, we alleged a total loss of more than $100 million. This number was based largely on the results from the e-mail search warrants on Xiang Li's china9981@gmail.com account, which revealed about five hundred illegal transactions between April 2008 and August 2010. We found another hundred or so sales when we explored the content of two other e-mail accounts used by Xiang Li in the CRACK99 enterprise, for a total of about six hundred illegal sales. After identifying these sales, we set about contacting the victims of the CRACK99 enterprise. But we had a problem: there were so many victims, we didn't know where to begin.

So, we took a sample. Cullen and the other agents discovered that most of the software products sold by CRACK99 fell into the categories of computer-aided design (CAD), computer-aided manufacturing (CAM), electronic design automation (EDA), structural engineering, and business systems including inventory control. Within these broad categories, the agents were able to identify subcategories such as antenna design, orbital trajectory, aircraft design, heat transfer, spatial analysis, oilfield design, shipbuilding, radio communications, and radar analysis.

Within this structure, the agents determined the retail prices of 144 out of the 600 pirated software programs sold by Xiang Li. The prices varied greatly depending on the complexity and sophistication of the software. For example, on the low end of the price spectrum was a jewelry design program valued at approximately $6,000. Some-

where in the middle was a software product used in electromechanical simulations, valued at approximately $50,000. At the high end was
a software program used in CAD/CAM applications ranging—as Cullen put it—"from the design of a soda can to the design of a military
aircraft," with an estimated retail value of over $1,400,000.

On this basis, the following sampling of retail value was prepared:

Software	Number of Sales	Individual Price	Total
Machining CAD/CAM	15	$100,000	$1,500,000
Digital Engineering	25	$250,000	$6,250,000
Project Portfolio	11	$30,000	$330,000
Measurement and Control	19	$8,600	$163,400
Electrical Engineering	15	$49,000	$750,000
General CAD/CAM	20	$1,400,000	$28,000,000
Electronic Design Automation	15	$230,000	$3,450,000
3D CAD and Data Management	24	$8,000	$192,000
Sample Total	144	N/A	$40,635,400

In total, we found over $40 million in losses from the 144 software
products sampled. Since the 144 software products represented 24 percent of the total number (600) of illicit sales we found on CRACK99,
we calculated a total loss figure of over $169 million.

You might well ask, Why rely on extrapolation? Why not just
total the retail prices of each software title unlawfully sold by Xiang
Li? One reason is that determining the retail pricing of software is

not as easy as determining the retail pricing for, say, a hammer; the prices vary depending on the type of customer, the number of modules purchased within each software title, the scale of network access (single-seat versus multiple workstations), and many other factors. In addition, some of the companies were not particularly enthusiastic about revealing their prices because they viewed such information as strategic and therefore proprietary. So we decided to estimate the loss for present purposes and wait until a later day to complete the task. Given that our estimate of more than $169 million was well over $100 million, I considered it conservative.

Indeed, the $169 million figure was itself but a fraction of the value of the software offered for sale on CRACK99. The total loss value we had calculated was based on the six hundred sales revealed through Xiang Li's e-mails, but there were thousands of software titles in the CRACK99 inventory, implying that the value of the pirated software offered by Xiang Li exceeded a billion dollars.

We had spent enough time on arithmetic and had other fish to fry: specifically, Xiang Li. The only means of putting Xiang Li in federal bracelets would be to meet with him face to face in a jurisdiction agreeable to his extradition back to the United States, along the lines of our plan in the Ardebili case. The best way to induce Xiang Li to agree to such a meeting was to become an important business partner—again, along the lines of what we had done in the Ardebili case. To do that, we needed to raise the ante.

Up until this point, most of the communications with Xiang Li had been by e-mail. But to take this next step, we needed the intimacy and immediacy of direct contact by Skype. And that meant introducing Xiang Li to the face of the man we fervently hoped he would one day meet in person: Robert (last name withheld). Robert was an undercover DCIS agent, and he was perfectly cast for the role. His shaved head and dark goatee belied an amiable nature; everyone liked Robert. This unassuming spokesman laid out our "business proposition" in a Skype session with Xiang Li on December 13, 2010. Robert told Xiang Li that he could get a better sale price for CRACK99 software in the United States, and gave the example of QUARTUS: CRACK99 sold it for about $100 but it was worth tens of thousands of dollars in the U.S. market. Robert said he could sell QUARTUS in the United States at a discount—for $5,000.

"In such case," said Robert, "we would give you a 50 percent kickback. [That] means you will get $2,500 for each."

Xiang Li was enthused: "That's fine. That's fine." But he had a concern: "Let me ask you a question. . . . It's that . . . I will keep it confidential . . . how will it be done?"

Robert told Xiang Li confidentiality would not be a problem because each sale would be private.

"I need to ask you another question," asked Xiang Li. "What's going to happen when there are differences in price? That means my price will be . . . different from his, from the price you guys have given him [the customer]. Not the same. Perhaps mine will be lower. What are you going to do then? Do I need to match it?"

Not a problem, said Robert, because "our customers trust us."

"I meant," Xiang Li persisted, "will he find out that my [price] is cheaper; cheaper than what you guys have given him."

It was a good question: Xiang Li had identified the flaw in our proposed business model. How did we know our customers wouldn't shop around and find a better deal, even on CRACK99 itself?

Brendan Cullen—not one to underestimate an adversary—had anticipated that Xiang Li might spot this flaw. We had prepared what I thought was a pretty good answer: our customers don't want to use Chinese piracy websites like CRACK99 due to their fear of being ripped off. But Robert took a simpler approach. Cleverly, he avoided the topic altogether by reminding Xiang Li of the 50 percent kickback. It is notable how greed dulls a person's inferential capacity.

"That's fine," said Xiang Li. "That's fine. No problem. We . . . can agree on all of these. I mean, I feel pretty good about our relationship. That's not a problem. . . . I will not bring up . . . the price. Okay?"

Robert agreed.

Then Xiang Li proposed an idea to prevent the disclosure of lower pricing to "our" customers: "You guys . . . will download my FTP. . . . Then, copy it to a CD and then give it to them." File transfer protocol (FTP) is a method of transferring files over the Internet, using sites that are like online storage lockers where the files are available for copying. Xiang Li was advocating that instead of providing URL links directly to the customer, Robert would obtain the software by FTP from Xiang Li and give it to the customer on a CD. This would reduce the chance of tipping off a customer that better deals might be available on the Internet.

During the conversation, Robert asked Xiang Li if he was interested in coming to the United States to talk. Xiang Li laughed and said, "Oh, thank you! Thank you! At this point, I am not." Robert persisted and Xiang Li said, "[I] am not able to come at this point. No problem. If there is anything, we can always communicate via the Internet. No problem. . . . Send me the list and I will reply back. . . . Okay?"

It was worth a try, but it was clear Xiang Li would not be willing to fly to the United States to be arrested. We would need to work on a place to do that. Meanwhile, we would push forward on the commercial end of things. On January 4, 2011, Robert sent Xiang Li a wish list of software products he wanted to buy. This was our breakout moment: our hope was that this long list would make us important customers.

How are you, my friend. I am sorry I have not been in contact. Our holidays are over and we are back to work. I have compiled a list of software programs we would like to purchase from you at a discount. Give us your best price. All the latest version.

Ansys 13.0

NI Labview

Agilent EMPro

Ansoft Nexxim

Antenna Magnus

CST Studio Suite

Ansoft Simplorer

Matlab

Catia

Vector Works

HyperWorks

Pronest

Ansoft Maxwell

Ansoft HFSS

Mastercam

As we discussed over Skype, we believe we could help re-sell these to our small businesses here. We look forward to doing more business together.

The response from Xiang Li was what we had come to expect. The same day, he replied with prices for each requested software title—between $50 and $150—totaling $1,630. Then he gave us a discount: "best price ---------- 1467.00 FOR YOU." Wasting no time, the agents went to the Red Lion Western Union in Claymont on January 7, 2011, and wired $1,467, confirming the transmission by e-mail. Xiang Li wrote back the same day, requesting a mailing address. "CD sent to you. The reason is too many files." We gave him an address in Philadelphia, where we eventually received the software.

We seemed to have succeeded in getting Xiang Li's attention, but I wasn't sure that he was taking the bait in terms of our ultimate objective: meeting in person. I thought our proposal to discuss a more evolved international business plan had real merit; surely, he realized that he did not have a clear idea of how to value his inventory for sale in the United States. We—the U.S. government—had found it difficult to determine the pricing of software; it must have been even more so for Xiang Li. And we were offering a solution to that problem. But Xiang Li was sending mixed signals. He had given us a reasonable discount on our latest purchase, but he probably would have done so anyway, regardless of his enthusiasm for the strategy of partnering with us to exploit the U.S. market.

My disquiet was soon assuaged. On January 8, 2011, Xiang Li sent us an e-mail in Mandarin. This took a day to translate, the agents and I having failed to pursue the study of Mandarin in school. Xiang Li became impatient, pinging us: "you no news? I am waiting for your reply message."

The translated e-mail was intriguing: Xiang Li was offering to sell us counterfeit design packaging for the software we had just purchased. It seemed to me that the only reason he was making this offer was his interest in a better penetration of the U.S. market. Counterfeit design packaging would be useful in reselling—as we said we would—the CRACK99 software in the United States. If the counterfeit packaging was good, U.S. customers would buy the pirated software thinking they were buying legitimate copies, thus enabling us to charge a price closer to the actual retail price. This was also a good way to address the problem Xiang Li had identified: the possibility of customers finding a better price online. We would not market the software as cracked but as legitimate. Our customers thus would be unlikely to go trolling around pirated-software sites like CRACK99. Xiang Li appeared to be nibbling at the bait.

We wrote back: "My friend, We are very interested in your design packaging. Could you please send demo and further explain? Screen shots?"

That same day, Xiang Li answered, listing all the software titles we had just purchased and saying, "All Software packing design fees

$USD 1500.00." We took this to mean he could provide counterfeit packaging for all the software we ordered for $1,500. Then, continuing in bold, he wrote:

> **More pleasant surprises**
> **I can gather some valuable information 20GB**
> **If you are interested**
> **Cost $USD 3000.00**
> **This is confidential. I do not have to sell to other customers**
> **ONLY FOR YOU**

He followed this up the same day with another e-mail attaching an image of counterfeit design packaging for ANSYS 13.0, and boasting, "This is my work. . . . All included CD printing, design, and exquisite box. . . . Your customers satisfied with your decision."

I was back to being perplexed. For one thing, I didn't have any idea what the twenty gigabytes of "valuable information" consisted of. But more than that, Xiang Li seemed to have gone completely off the rails. Whatever it was, the information didn't appear to have anything to do with our proposed business partnership in the U.S. market.

Or did it?

On January 15, 2011, Robert spoke to Xiang Li by Skype, where all was revealed: the twenty gigabytes of data was proprietary information hacked from a defense contractor (whom I will refer to as "Defense Contractor"). Defense Contractor is a U.S. company that develops engineering modeling software for use in military applications. We didn't know exactly what kind of proprietary data it was, but this was an important development for two reasons. First, it showed us that Xiang Li had access to data being hacked from U.S. defense contractors. Second, it showed that he was interested in our joint venture: he was offering this to us for cash, but also as a favor. He was warming up to us.

On January 20, the agents made the short drive to the Claymont, Delaware, Western Union and sent $4,350 to Xiang Li: $3,000 for the Defense Contractor proprietary data and $1,350 for the counterfeit packaging. (We drove a hard bargain, getting him to knock $150 off the price.) Five days later, Robert e-mailed Xiang Li: "My friend, please confirm that you have received our payment and that you have shipped our software products and [Defense Contractor] data. Thank you."

Xiang Li wrote back in Mandarin. And I was confused again. Why would Xiang Li do this? Xiang Li well knew that Robert could not read or speak Mandarin. And even though Robert had demonstrated the ability to obtain translations, the process took time. Xiang Li's English was not perfect, but it was certainly good enough to answer our simple question: have you shipped our products?

Was he stalling? Was a punk from Chengdu ripping us off for a few grand?

9 | PLEASANT SURPRISES

IN 1988, I WAS SENT TO Naval Air Station Brunswick in Maine for Arctic survival training. We had been given a briefing about our small arms and ammunition loadout—for use against polar bears—and I had some questions; evidently one too many, pressing a little too hard on the sufficiency of the planned ammunition allocation. In response, a grizzled commander closed down his facial apertures almost completely and said, "Lieutenant, maybe this will help. If you ditch, you're gonna die."

I did appreciate the commander's candor. This is one thing you can count on in the Navy, and it distinguishes the naval working environment from most others. But I did not agree with the assessment that if I ditched, I was going to die; my plan was otherwise. My plan was to survive. In fact, I was counting on it. This is known as optimism.

I am an optimist. You might not immediately recognize that aspect of my character if you were to meet me, because over the years I've become a bit grizzled myself. But I do, in the ordinary course of events, plan to overcome obstacles. If you're not an optimist, you cannot run with a case like CRACK99.

Xiang Li had promised in his January 11, 2011, e-mail that he had "**More pleasant surprises**" in the form of twenty gigabytes of valuable internal data hacked from the computer network of Defense Contractor. And we had taken the bait, paying him $3,000. But as January became February and February rolled into March, we didn't have what we'd paid for. Twenty gigabytes of data, a substantial quantity, can't be sent in a single e-mail, so some delay was to be expected. But this was getting to be extreme. Being an optimist does not mean forgoing altogether rational inference from empirical observation. I had to recognize something might be wrong: Xiang Li's reluctance to send us what we paid for made me suspect that we were not the predator but the prey. We might have spent ourselves into a corner with nothing to show for it.

Optimists, however, do not accept that end state without a fight; they recognize that there might be an unhappy ending but plan on the happy one. So it was with me and our merry band. We had a strategic objective: to get in front of Xiang Li, turn him around, and walk him into a U.S. courtroom. And we kept at it, Skyping at every opportunity, talking to him about our strategic vision for a profitable joint venture in the United States.

Robert, the amiable undercover DCIS agent with a gleaming pate, had suggested a face-to-face meeting in the United States, and Xiang Li had demurred. In March 2011, Robert again suggested a meeting, both to talk business and to accept delivery of the proprietary data we had paid for. How about the Philippines? They have gambling. Robert even sent Xiang Li a web link to a casino. Why the Philippines? Well, for one thing, there is the gambling and we thought Xiang Li might like that. But there was more: we had been told by our man on the ground in Manila that the Philippines might be amenable to the extradition of a Chinese national in a case like this.

The extradition treaty between the Philippines and the United States was ordinary on its face, providing for extradition for offenses that were "punishable under the laws of both" the United States and the Philippines. This is the standard dual criminality requirement of extradition: a nation will not extradite an accused for an offense that is not a crime under its own laws. The treaty also provided that neither nation would extradite for "political offenses," a term not defined with specificity. The terminology of such treaties tends to be broad—and therefore susceptible to a wide range of interpretations—making outcomes hard to predict. This had been recently demonstrated in the case of a Filipino national charged in California with murder-for-hire. His extradition from the Philippines to the United States was denied on the ground that the evidence against him was insufficient. It was not particularly surprising that a court in the Philippines exhibited reluctance to extradite one of its own, even though the case was serious and the evidence—such as was publicly available—appeared to be substantial. Xiang Li, a Chinese national, would not have the same home-field advantage as a Filipino national. Even so, I was not sanguine about our chances of successfully extraditing him from the Philippines.

Why then would our man in Manila suggest it? Because that is what his counterparts in the government of the Philippines were telling him. This is why you have a man on the ground in Manila: his job is to give you the inside track; he was there, and I was not. But still, it is a bit like reading tea leaves: Is that a flying bird—harbinger of good fortune—or a big blob of soggy tea?

Copyright infringement is not a crime in many countries, and so the dual criminality issue loomed large. This is one of the reasons why we had charged Xiang Li and his wife with other offenses, namely, interstate transportation of stolen property and smuggling. Receipt of stolen property and smuggling are universally understood criminal activities, so we hoped those charges would not be controversial. But we knew that they did not guarantee success. If what makes the property "stolen" in the first place is copyright infringement, a court in the

Philippines—like the U.S. Supreme Court in *Dowling*—might not treat the matter as a stolen property case, and might refuse to extradite.

Equally concerning was the question of whether a court in the Philippines would consider Xiang Li's copyright-infringement offenses to be "political" under the extradition treaty. Because the term "political" was undefined, it was up to the court to define it. And if the court decided that "political" means "geopolitical" and concluded that Xiang Li was caught up in a strategic Ping-Pong game between the United States and China, it might refuse to extradite him.

This is where optimism comes in: A pessimist would likely walk away from this mess. An optimist soldiers on. But optimism does not necessarily imply idiocy. I was actively considering alternatives. What about Thailand, which was generally considered a friendly law enforcement venue, reasonably proximate to China?

The problem with Thailand was Viktor Bout, a fellow who created problems wherever he went. Bout was a Russian arms dealer, reputedly the model for the protagonist, played by Nicolas Cage, in the 2005 film *Lord of War*. Bout was arrested in Thailand in March 2008 on the basis of U.S. charges that he had conspired to murder U.S. nationals, including U.S. officials; conspired to acquire and use antiaircraft missiles; and conspired to provide material support to a foreign terrorist organization, namely, the Fuerzas Armadas Revolucionarias de Colombia (FARC), a designated foreign terrorist organization based in Colombia. The U.S. government alleged—and ultimately proved—the following:

Between November 2007 and March 2008, Bout agreed to sell to the FARC millions of dollars' worth of weapons—including 800 surface-to-air missiles (SAMs), 30,000 AK-47 firearms, 10 million rounds of ammunition, five tons of C-4 plastic explosives, "ultralight" airplanes outfitted with grenade launchers and unmanned aerial vehicles. Bout agreed to sell the weapons to two confidential sources working with the DEA (the "CSs"), who represented that they were acquiring them for the FARC, with the specific understanding that the weapons were to be used to attack U.S. helicopters in Colombia. During a covertly recorded meeting in Thailand on March 6, 2008, Bout stated to the CSs that he could arrange to airdrop the arms to the FARC in Colombia, and offered to sell two cargo planes to the FARC that could be used for arms deliveries. He also provided a map of South America and asked the CSs to show him American radar locations in Colombia. Bout said that he understood that the CSs wanted the arms to use against American personnel in Colombia, and advised that, "we have the same enemy," referring to the United States.

Suffice to say, this case was not fast food. It was a serious case involving serious charges to be answered in the United States. And yet, in 2009, a Thai court denied extradition. One reason was that Thailand did not view FARC as a terrorist group, but as a political organization. So the case was "political," demonstrating how elusive that term can be. Another reason given for the denial was the extra-territorial nature of the charges: "One of the judges, Jitakorn Patana-siri, said, 'A Thai court cannot judge a case regarding aliens killing aliens outside of Thailand.'" This was an astonishing holding, as extradition cases commonly involve crimes committed outside the jurisdiction of the extraditing authority.

On appeal, this ruling was reversed, and Bout ultimately was extradited to the United States in 2010, where he was subsequently convicted and sentenced to twenty-five years in prison. But in 2011, the Bout proceedings illustrated the highly uncertain nature of extradition in general, and made me think that Thailand in particular was not an attractive option.

It's a big world, and there are more nations in it than Thailand

and the Philippines. I was giving careful consideration to a number of small island-nations in the Pacific, of which there are many, when I saw it on the map, beckoning.

Saipan.

Most likely, you haven't been there. It's a small (forty-four-and-a-half-square-mile) island in the western Pacific, continuously populated since before recorded history, punctuated by periods of foreign occupation. Spain sold the island to the German Empire in 1899, and the Japanese occupied it in 1914. By virtue of the Treaty of Versailles on June 28, 1919, and a League of Nations mandate on December 17, 1920, Saipan became the territory of the Empire of Japan.

This changed on June 15, 1944, when the U.S. military landed there, defeating a large and entrenched Japanese force. The United States held the island thereafter, first as a territory and then as part of the Commonwealth of the Northern Mariana Islands.

I started to wonder if it was too much—even for an optimist—to hope Xiang Li might consider a meeting in Saipan. From our point of view, the obvious advantage to Saipan was this: although not a state, it is part of the United States of America. It has federal courts and federal judges. No extradition is necessary: no need to worry about dual criminality or tea leaves or Viktor Bout.

At first, we kept the Saipan idea to ourselves and followed up on our invitation to meet in the Philippines: "My Friend, We have not heard back from you regarding our travel invitation to join us in the Philippines. Also we have not received the Defense Contractor proprietary data or the counterfeit packaging. Is everything okay?" And Xiang Li continued to shilly-shally:

I AM FINE
OKEY
This will soon be

I agree

But I work very busy now

Maybe, I thought, his reluctance to agree to the Philippines was an opportunity.

Our relationship with Xiang Li had grown beyond the bounds of e-mail, and by April we were Skyping on a regular basis. This gave me hope. If Xiang Li had no intention to meet us and was just keeping our money, why would he waste his time Skyping? Wouldn't e-mail be a better medium for stringing us along? I detected sincere interest, no doubt induced by the scent of money. Why not, I thought, just ask about Saipan?

And so we did. Robert told Xiang Li that he would be traveling to a number of Pacific Rim destinations, meeting with business partners. He listed several places, including Saipan, and asked if Xiang Li was interested in a meeting. When Xiang Li responded affirmatively, our spirits soared because—as Brendan Cullen pointed out—Xiang Li was usually true to his word. But we weren't sure which destination he had chosen. Eventually he clarified: he wanted to meet on Saipan, citing the island's visa-waiver program for Chinese nationals, making it more desirable than the other proffered destinations from his point of view. This was like a dream come true.

Just one caveat: we would have to pay his way.

Make that two: we were to pay for his family as well.

What sort of chumps did he take us for?

We answered that question on April 16, when Robert wrote, "I agree to the travel price for you and your family from Chengdu to Saipan. I want to discuss future business with you in person."

Xiang Li wrote back immediately: "Thank you very much, I am pleased."

As an optimist, I felt vindicated. Robert wrote back, "I am pleased also. . . . Book your travel and send me a scanned copy of the receipt. . . . Tell me your bank information where we can send you the reimbursement."

Xiang Li replied, "First of all need to pay 5,000 USD. . . . I am waiting for your good news."

Uh-oh. Not only did he expect us to fund his travel—and his family's—but now we're supposed to pay him cash up front? I recalled our first round of communication with Xiang Li more than a year before, in January 2010:

> Welcome
> Step 1 . . . .
> However, must be the payment. Do you understand?

Did he take us for complete chumps?

On April 19, Robert wrote, "Xiang, I sent the Western Union transaction today . . . $5,000 U.S."

If nothing else, we clarified exactly what sort of chumps we were. First, we sent him $4,350 for the Defense Contractor proprietary data and the counterfeit packaging. Then $5,000 to fund travel for Xiang Li and his family, which Xiang Li had clarified, did not include his wife, who was pregnant. Was Xiang Li patiently fleecing us for all we were worth? Would he use the $5,000 to travel to Saipan or to upgrade the living room furniture? I flashed back to that sickening feeling in the Tbilisi airport on October 1, 2007, awaiting the arrival of Amir Ardebili, John Malandra licking his ice cream cone and me wearing my fuzzy Georgian shepherd's hat. "That's nothing," Malandra had said, "compared to how ridiculous we're going to look if this bird doesn't show."

But I continued to be rewarded for my optimism. Xiang Li sent Robert dates for the meeting in Saipan: June 5 to 13, 2011. "I will contact you upon arrival Saipan," he wrote. As far as I was concerned, it was on.

Unfortunately, that meant I had to deal with Main Justice, that bastion of nonfeasance, and specifically the Office of International Affairs, the very organization that had failed to ensure the delivery of the diplomatic note to the Republic of Georgia in time for the undercover meeting with Amir Ardebili. I was not enthused about another interaction with that Office, but I had no choice, in consequence of the *United States Attorneys' Manual* and its section on lures:

> A lure involves using a subterfuge to entice a criminal defendant to leave a foreign country so that he or she can be arrested in the United States, in international waters or airspace, or in a third country for subsequent extradition, expulsion, or deportation to the United States. Lures can be complicated schemes or they can be as simple as inviting a fugitive by telephone to a party in the United States. . . . [S]ome countries may view a lure of a person from its territory as an infringement on its sovereignty. Consequently, a prosecutor must consult with the Office of International Affairs before undertaking a lure to the United States or a third country.

The bottom line is that I was required to "consult" with the Office of International Affairs. I looked the word up in a dictionary: to "consult" means to obtain information, advice, or counsel; it is not synonymous with obtaining approval or permission. So I sent an e-mail to someone in the Office of International Affairs who was assigned to China. He had the title "Trial Attorney," although I'm pretty sure he was not—in point of actual fact—a trial attorney. I did not ask for approval, but instead summarized the case and the arrest plan for Saipan, pursuant to the consultation requirement of the *United States Attorneys' Manual*. And as far as I was concerned, I had satisfied that requirement just by sending the e-mail.

Not so fast. He responded, asking for more information, specifically in the form of a "lure memo" describing the case and the need for the lure. Well, I thought, this is a waste of time, but I sent him the lure memo anyway. I had once again, in my opinion, satisfied the *United States Attorneys' Manual* consultation requirement.

Not so fast. He got back to me, demanding more information; specifically, he wanted to know if I had obtained approval from the U.S. ambassador to China. I was surprised by the question, as there is no such requirement. If there were, it would be quite a significant encumbrance, as foreign nationals are routinely arrested inside U.S. territory.

I replied in the negative, keeping my editorial thoughts to myself, thus yet again satisfying the consultation requirement.

But the attorney in the Office of International Affairs persisted, earning him a phone call from me. "Why," I asked, "are you insisting on pre-arrest approval from the ambassador?"

"Because he is the one who will have to deal with the Chinese government when they complain about the arrest."

"Maybe so, but isn't that just his job?" I asked.

"The ambassador needs to know in advance so he is not blind-sided."

I said I was happy to advise the U.S. ambassador promptly after the arrest. But the trial attorney wanted to give him advance notice. We went around this circle for too long before I realized this was a conversation with no destination. I decided the better part of valor was to suspend communications. I said I would check with HSI to see what their attaché in China could do.

I called Ronayne, embarrassed that I had to waste his time with this task for the sole reason that I was unable to handle a bureaucrat in my own agency.

"Let me see what I can do," he said.

Meanwhile, the undercover Skype calls with Xiang Li continued. On April 27, 2011, Xiang Li said he would come to Saipan with his mother-in-law and son. "I will probably leave on June fifth," he said.

"My suggestion is," he continued, "I will block out a day or two to spend time with [you] during the trip and will spend the rest of the time with my family. Is that okay? What do you think?"

Robert agreed to the plan but pressed Xiang Li to send his itinerary, which would provide some reassurance that Xiang Li would actually show up. Evidence that he had spent our money to buy airline tickets (as opposed to a really nice plasma television) would help ease our worried minds.

Xiang Li kept repeating that he would leave on June 5. Robert asked what hotel he would be staying in. Xiang Li said he hadn't decided. This conversation about logistics ended when Xiang Li said, "After I've arrived in Saipan, I'll send you guys the e-mail. Once you reply back to me, I'll then know where you are at."

This was not perfect. However, we did have his assurance that we would meet "either on the sixth or the seventh." Xiang Li said that he "will definitely be there. Do you understand?"

Before hanging up, he asked for some customs advice: "Will I be able to bring food products through the customs?" Robert strongly advised against it. But Xiang Li, as was his practice, persisted: "I was thinking of bringing over some of the delicious foods from here."

The next day, Xiang Li did something surprising even to me, the optimist: he e-mailed a photo of himself and his son. This was both welcome and perplexing. It is not the sort of thing criminals ordinarily do while negotiating the expansion of their criminal empires. But I had to think it was a good sign, suggesting he was comfortable with Robert. And it begged a question: Shouldn't we return the favor and send a picture of Robert's son?

Literally sending a photo of Robert's actual son, of course, was out of the question. Instead, we sent what Robert described as "a photo of my daughter meeting her favorite Princess during our last trip to Walt Disney World." The "daughter" was not Robert's real daughter but a photoshopped version of a picture Robert had taken at Cinderella's Castle during a family vacation. "Very beautiful," Xiang Li replied.

I found the whole exchange a little creepy, and so did everyone else, particularly Robert.

Meanwhile, Ronayne got back to me on the China situation. He spoke with the HSI attaché on a hypothetical basis, meaning he gave no names or dates or details. The attaché said he had never been asked to do that, and that it was a bad idea given the extent to which the Chinese were able to intercept U.S. communications.

"Thank you," I said, before calling the trial attorney at the Office of International Affairs.

"No can do," I said, explaining the situation and adding that I would be more than happy to provide the ambassador whatever information he needs at the time of the arrest.

"I won't approve this request," said the trial attorney flatly, "until you get the ambassador's concurrence."

"I am not asking for your approval," I said. "I am consulting with you, as required. I don't need more than that."

This had him a bit flummoxed.

"You can look it up," I added.

"And besides," I said, "I'm not even sure this is a lure; he's the one who picked Saipan as the place to meet."

"I'll get back to you," he said.

Through the phone line, I could smell the stench of smoldering defeat. Ultimately, the trial attorney told me that the Office of International Affairs had decided it wasn't a lure after all. I think it was more likely that they wanted to make me go away. This was fine with me.

Victory.

It takes a long time to fly to Saipan. And it's fourteen hours ahead of Eastern Daylight Time. So I was pretty discombobulated when we arrived there at night the weekend before the planned meeting with Xiang Li. I took a nice relaxing shower and went to bed, longing for coma-like repose. I woke up a few hours later without any hope of getting back to sleep. Then I did what I always do under such circumstances: I went to the gym. And there was Mike Ronayne, as he always was under similar circumstances.

"Hey," he said.

"Hey," I said.

"You notice anything unusual," he asked, "in the lobby just now?"

"You mean the perverts?" I asked.

"Yeah," he said. "They look like pedophiles."

And indeed they did. It was a very strange scene in the hotel lobby at three o'clock in the morning: Individual middle-aged men, pasty looking in that pedophile way, were lurking around; no one was talking, and eye contact was fleeting. No one was actually doing anything; it was like they were waiting for something. Something bad. So it is with lurkers. That scene—unfortunately—would be repeated every night we were there, since Mike and I never synced with the time difference. Even more unfortunate, the lurkers probably thought we were among their number, given that we were keeping the same hours.

Mike and I had a similar experience in Bangkok. We were there to recruit an informant, but everywhere we went we saw predatory Western males in the company of young Thai women—and sometimes Thai children. It was sickening. Mike summed it up well: "You know, we haven't done anything wrong. And yet, I feel guilty." Somehow, it felt wrong just to be there.

First thing the next morning, we met with the other agents: Robert, Brendan Cullen, Dave Battalico, and Brian (last name withheld)— all from Philadelphia—along with a Mandarin-speaking agent from Seattle and a female Mandarin-speaking agent from San Diego. Then we headed to the HSI office, which was manned by agents from Honolulu who rotate through on ninety-day tours. Particularly because they were on temporary duty, I expected an island attitude from these guys—and maybe a little hostility as we were cluttering up their island

and making them work on the weekend when they could be playing on the beach. I was dead wrong: These guys were true professionals, and selfless ones at that. They had no skin in the game; it wasn't their case, they didn't know us, and they weren't going to share in the glory if it worked. And yet, all they wanted to do was help.

Xiang Li was booked at the grandly named Saipan World Resort. The agents on Saipan reserved a room under Robert's name for the undercover meeting at the nearby Fiesta Hotel. Both hotels were just a short distance from the hotel where we were staying. We jumped into HSI G-rides to get the lay of the land, which didn't take very long, as the island is only about twelve by six miles and there is only one town: Garapan.

We spent that day and the next one preparing for the undercover meeting. This probably sounds like more fun than it was, given that the venue was a tropical island in the Pacific Ocean. Saipan does offer more than one panoramic vista, but on the whole the island is somewhat shabby. Many of the buildings needed a fresh coat of paint. And it would be a significant improvement if someone would restrain the ladies of Garapan from jumping out at you on the street asking if you want a massage.

Crime on the island was a persistent problem, one that kept the Honolulu agents busy on their ninety-day rotations. I was standing on a corner in Garapan waiting for Ronayne when a Honda pulled up across the street and a shockingly large number of Asian girls jumped out and ran into a building. I say "girls" because they looked very young, although I had no way to confirm their ages. They were crammed into the Honda like the old circus clown car routine. The difference is, it wasn't funny. The girls were probably victims of the human-trafficking trade, sold into sex slavery, sleeping on filthy mattresses in a warehouse somewhere, and delivered to a brothel for their twelve-hour shift of having sex with strangers. This explained the lurkers in the hotel lobby. I told the agents about it, and they were not surprised. They raid these brothels continually, deporting foreign nationals back to their countries of origin, only to find the brothels back in business with the next shipment of smuggled girls. After seeing that, I found it difficult to view Saipan as an island paradise.

And then there were the pregame jitters. My athletic career peaked when I played high school football more than forty years ago, but I well remember the slightly queasy pregame state when your body is humming and your head is buzzing and you are pacing around the locker room more or less at random, trapped like a caged animal. I really loved playing football, but I really hated that time just before the game. So it was on Saipan: there was a lot of pacing and hand wringing, particularly over the looming question of whether, in Malandra's turn of phrase, the bird would show up. Financially, we had started this case on the cheap, spending only $1,000 to buy a $150,000 STK software program. But since then, we had spent many more thousands of dollars in public money, including flying a squad to a remote island and leasing a Gulfstream IV private jet to take our bird off the island in the event he showed up. That would be hard to justify if Xiang Li decided to keep the money and pass on the meeting.

Ronayne in particular suffered at times like these. He didn't look like a worrier, and for the most part he did not outwardly manifest his anxiety; he appeared cool and relaxed, almost indifferent. But inside he was a cauldron of boiling anxiety.

What was not troubling Ronayne—or any other member of the team—was Xiang Li's impending ruination. After all, he was a husband and the father of a growing family, winging his way to sunny Saipan for what he thought—based on our misrepresentations—would be a tremendous business opportunity. As a fellow optimist, I could well imagine how his spirits must have soared on the very eve of his downfall.

But no, this concern did not occupy our thoughts. For one thing, we had spent the preceding year and a half actively evaluating whether Xiang Li was an appropriate law enforcement target. I had harbored serious doubts the first time I saw the CRACK99 website with its inanely bright colors and overblown promises of honesty and dependability. But since then, I had come to realize that there was a reason Xiang Li did not present as a terrifying Dr. No on his website: that was no way to sell a product. And judging from his success with CRACK99, I would have to say inanely bright colors and overblown promises of honesty and dependability might be the way to go. Having had a long and careful look at Xiang Li's illegal piracy, Ronayne, Cullen, and I had no doubt about whether we were targeting the right guy, or were right to do so. Our thoughts were only on how to put him in cuffs.

The day before the undercover meeting, Ronayne and I gathered as usual in the gym at three in the morning. I told him I had a plan for the morning: I wanted to try to retrace my father's footsteps. He knew what I meant. On the long flight to Saipan, I showed him my late father's worn copy of the red-bound Marine Corps after-action report on Saipan, where my father had been decorated for valor in 1944. I didn't want to distract Ronayne and the others if there was more work to do, but I thought we were about ready for Xiang Li and I wondered if they'd like to come along. This way we wouldn't spend the entire day pacing the locker room like caged animals. He agreed.

We all met in the lobby later that morning. I unfolded the center map of the Marine Corps report. The landing beaches were labeled by color and regimental assignment: "Green Beach" was marked with a printed "X8," which represented the Eighth Marine Regiment, my father's. I saw a hand-penciled arrow pointing to Green Beach, as if my father was confirming it for me from beyond the veil. The penciled arrow went across the southern plain of Saipan, up Mount Tapochau, the height of land held by the Japanese, down the other side of Mount Tapochau, and then northward to the northern end of the island. I held a tourist map of Saipan next to the Marine Corps map and figured out where Green Beach was on modern Saipan.

We drove down the aptly named Beach Road to get there. The sea was perfectly still, like highly polished turquoise, bordered by a white sand beach. I could see a rusting tank offshore, its gun still at the ready, covered in gull droppings, abandoned to time and the elements. I walked to the southern flank of Green Beach, Afetna Point, where the after-action report said the marines from the Eighth Regiment came ashore. This was where my father made his third combat landing in June 1944, already a battle-tested warrior at the age of twenty-five, having fought at Guadalcanal and Tarawa. It was difficult to fully comprehend, particularly given the morning's tranquillity, that this was the very beach my father had crossed under enfilading fire some sixty-seven years before. So many men had lost their lives here: over three thousand marines were killed in action fighting an entrenched force of approximately thirty thousand Japanese soldiers, most of whom also died in combat. The fact that my father survived Saipan—and the rest of the war—made my existence a statistical anomaly. He was, as his fellow officers described him, "one helluva marine."

I was startled by a loud splash. It was Robert, who had swum out to the tank to dive off the turret. He was grinning like a schoolboy. I grinned back, and walked to Afetna Point, trying to divine where my father's landing craft made shore. When I looked up from the after-action report, I realized I was standing in water up to my knees. And that's when I saw it: Framed in palm trees before me was the Saipan World Resort, the very place Xiang Li would be staying, or more accurately, the very place Xiang Li would be leaving in handcuffs, if we succeeded.

The Eighth Marines fought from Green Beach to Mount Tapochau, Saipan's height of land, over a period of ten days. We followed that route in about forty minutes by car, and stood at the summit where my father stood, looking back to Green Beach and the heavy jungle the marines fought through to take the 1,550-foot mountain. The agents and I could also see the airport where Xiang Li would be landing the next morning, and I could see that that fact was weighing heavily on Ronayne's mind.

"You good?"

"Yeah," he said. "We're ready."

We headed back toward Garapan, as my father had. There were a number of differences though, most notably the absence of a banzai attack, like the one the marines repulsed on July 7, 1944. After that last Japanese gasp, the marines pushed northward and saw—to their horror—Japanese soldiers and civilians jumping off cliffs into the sea at a place now called Banzai Cliff. My father didn't talk much about the war, except to praise the courage of others, but he did say one thing about Banzai Cliff: "After three combat landings, you'd think I couldn't be shocked. But I was."

It is a somber place. The agents and I stood for a while on the edge, staring into the dark sea. Nearby was the Japanese command post, located in a cave. My father had described this cavern to me, and now, bent over to avoid the low ceiling, I explored it, dripping sweat. This was one thing my experience on Saipan had in common with my father's: my shirt was soaked through. I suppose there was another commonality as well: both my father and I went to Saipan in the interests of U.S. national security. He was fighting the Japanese, and I was fighting the Chinese effort to steal U.S. technology. But my fighting was highly abstract. There was some chance that things would go wrong and Xiang Li would decide to go out in a blazing firefight. But that probability was very low. When my father landed on Saipan, the probability of a firefight was 100 percent. That is a big difference.

It was a sobering day on the whole, and accomplished the goal of distracting us from concerns about the next day's events. But once we were back at our hotel, the worrying resumed in full force. The agents and I met to talk, yet again, about what information we wanted to elicit from Xiang Li during the undercover meeting, and how best to draw it out of him.

Looming over us was the one question too important to ask and too elusive to answer: Would Xiang Li show up?

10 | UNPLEASANT SURPRISES

THE HOURS BEFORE SUNRISE WERE TENSE. We met in the lobby, under intense scrutiny by the perverts lurking in the potted foliage, casting sidelong glances in our direction. We didn't say much, and there wasn't much to say.

"You good?" I asked Ronayne.

"Good as I'll ever be," he said, voluble as ever.

We got into the G-rides and caravaned down to the airport in the dark. I sat in the passenger seat as Ronayne drove. At a stoplight, I noticed his knee jiggling, the only outward manifestation of the enormous stress he was feeling. We'd had a call that a male named Xiang Li was on the airline passenger manifest. This was good news, but the name "Xiang Li" is a bit like "John Smith." As Ronayne said, "Great; the odds are up from one in a billion to one in a million."

The airport's exterior lighting cast a sickly amber glow into the dark, humid air. Inside, the air conditioning was humming. Customs and Border Protection showed us the manifest, and we briefed them on what we hoped would happen. We asked that a CBP officer give us a heads up when Xiang Li passed immigration. Brendan Cullen was stationed in the immigration bay for that purpose. Then, we went back outside for the long wait in the car: Mike, me, and Mike's jiggling knee. I was really wishing we had coffee, although I don't know that would have improved the knee situation.

I thought I'd be funny, so I asked, "Remind you of anything?"

"Yeah," he said, knowing I was referring to the wait for Amir Ardebili at the Tbilisi airport. He laughed a little, but not with real mirth.

"That turned out well," I reminded him.

"Yeah," he said, "that would be good." Then after a pause: "If this guy doesn't show . . . "

"I know," I assured him. And I really did know. As far as the United States Attorney for the District of Delaware was concerned, I was on an adventure of my own. He was a new United States Attorney, having been sworn in just six months before. When I briefed him on the case—naively hoping to win his undying support—his only reaction was, "Neat." His only follow-up question over the next several months was "What does any of this have to do with Delaware?"

I made sure he wasn't joking before answering, "Delaware is part of the United States, so the Chinese cyber threat to U.S. national security is a threat to Delaware." This seemed to satisfy him.

I tried to be patient. This United States Attorney, like the vast majority I have known, had no federal law enforcement experience prior to his appointment. As a result, he tended to think of the United States Attorney's Office as an adjunct to the Delaware Attorney General's Office. This is a profoundly flawed construct in a number of ways, starting with the fact that our salaries were paid for by taxpayers nationwide, not just those in Delaware. Even more importantly, the circumscribed construct of the United States Attorney's Office as a support mechanism for state law enforcement erases the important constitutional distinction between federal and state crimes.

The U.S. Supreme Court recently dealt with a case that demonstrates what happens when a United States Attorney's Office loses sight of that distinction—and its core mission as a federal law enforcement agency. The origins of the case were inauspicious: Carol Anne Bond learned that her best friend, Myrlinda Hayes, was pregnant, and Bond was happy to hear about it until she learned that the father was her husband of fourteen years. Vowing revenge, Bond mixed a chemical compound that she put on the doorknob of Hayes's home, intending to give Hayes a bad rash. She used the compound about two dozen times, ultimately managing to cause a minor burn on Hayes's thumb by placing the mixture on the handle of Hayes's car door. After that injury, Hayes asked the local police for help. They told her to wash her car.

When Bond came back again, this time putting the substance on Hayes's mailbox, Hayes told her mail carrier, who advised the U.S. Postal Service. Postal inspectors put the mailbox under video surveillance and recorded Bond stealing a letter and applying the chemical mixture again on Hayes's car. In a move the Supreme Court generously called "surprising," federal prosecutors in Philadelphia charged Bond with two counts of using a chemical weapon, in violation of the Chemical Weapons Convention Implementation Act. That Act, as its name suggests, implements the 1997 Chemical Weapons Convention, which seeks to "verify the destruction of chemical weapons worldwide as well as ensure the non-proliferation of these weapons and the toxic chemicals used in their manufacture." The Convention targets chemical weapons such as sarin gas, mustard gas, and chlorine gas, and its framework has been used to destroy stockpiles of chemical weapons in places like Syria and Iraq.

Bond pled guilty and appealed on the ground that her conviction violated the Tenth Amendment because the federal prosecution usurped the police power reserved to the states. The appellate court affirmed her conviction, even while commenting that "Bond's prosecution seems a questionable exercise of prosecutorial discretion." The U.S. Supreme Court, unanimously reversing the appellate court's decision, found that the application to Bond's lover's triangle of a statute enacted to address chemical warfare violated fundamental principles of federalism. Stating that it was "reluctant to ignore the ordinary meaning of 'chemical weapon' when doing so would transform a statute passed to implement the international Convention on Chemical Weapons into one that also makes it a federal offense to poison goldfish," the Supreme Court found that the federal government had intruded unlawfully into the police powers reserved for the state alone. For Bond, this vindication came too late: she had already served a six-year sentence for a federal crime that turned out not to be a federal crime.

The federal government should leave to the states what belongs to the states—state offenses—and utilize its resources to investigate and prosecute true federal offenses, like, say, $100 million international conspiracies to steal U.S. technology. But the United States Attorney's focus did not extend beyond the boundaries of Delaware, and he had already complained about the amount of time I was spending outside the state. A failure on Saipan would not be forgiven; it would validate the United States Attorney's view of federal law enforcement and condemn me to serve out the remainder of my federal career within the confines of Delaware, prosecuting cases that affected Delaware and only Delaware.

Ronayne's phone rang.

"Okay, Brendan has eyes on," said Ronayne.

Mike and I swiveled our heads back and forth, sweeping the airport exits, now swarming with Chinese nationals who had deplaned and were headed for waiting buses. That's when we saw him: Xiang Li, the pudgy dude in a Hawaiian shirt chasing a kid.

"Got him," said Ronayne.

"So he brought the kid," I said. "Great."

"Yeah, that's all we need."

The bus carrying the new arrivals started moving, and so did we, driving to the Saipan World Resort. From the parking lot, we saw Xiang Li alight and enter the lobby. Several agents were waiting in the hotel to follow him to his room. They watched as Xiang Li, his five-year-old son, and his mother-in-law moved luggage into their room.

I ran across the street for coffee, and we resumed surveillance.

"Let's just make sure we put him to bed," said Ronayne.

While we sipped our coffee in silence, I thought about what had happened sixty-seven years earlier in this very place, now a parking lot where we sat in comfort. In 1944, it was a scene of indescribable chaos and horror: artillery shells exploding, automatic weapons rattling, rifles firing, men yelling, and men dying. And in that place, I was now quietly sipping coffee, waiting for the sun to come up. I really wished my father were still alive so we could compare notes, but on the whole I saw more to contrast than compare.

In many ways, war has changed since 1944. For one thing, no one back then was thinking about cyber battle space. But, in other ways, nothing has changed. The United States was not prepared for war with Japan in 1941. Today, the United States—having spent the years since 9/11 focused exclusively on the Middle East—is not prepared for cyber war with China.

In contrast, China's preparations are in high gear. As we were getting ready to meet with Xiang Li, PLA hackers stole software for the F-35, the Black Hawk helicopter, missile defense systems—and drones. "I believe this is the largest campaign we've seen that has been focused on drone technology," said Darien Kindlund of the cybersecurity company FireEye. "It seems to align pretty well with the focus of the Chinese government to build up their own drone technology capabilities." FireEye's finding on China's interest in UAVs is consistent with that of the Defense Department's Defense Science Board in 2012: "The military significance of China's move into unmanned systems is alarming." The Defense Science Board continued:

In a worrisome trend, China has ramped up research in recent years faster than any other country. It displayed its first unmanned system model at the Zhuhai air show five years ago, and now every major manufacturer for the Chinese military has a research center devoted to unmanned systems.

And, further, the Defense Science Board found that the People's Republic of China was using Western technology to accomplish its unmanned system goals:

In this defense-dominated field, China cannot look (openly) to the West for technical expertise and experienced suppliers, as it has done in the commercial airliner sector, and therefore it is evident the Chinese are copying other successful designs to speed their development of unmanned systems and rapidly apply lessons learned. The scope and speed of unmanned-aircraft development in China is a wakeup call that has both industrial and military implications.

As a result of this extraordinary effort, the Chinese UAV order of battle now numbers in the thousands. And the Chinese plan on using their growing UAV fleet. On September 9, 2013, the People's Liberation Navy launched a BZK-005 surveillance drone toward the uninhabited Diaoyu Islands in the East China Sea. The island chain is claimed by both China and Japan. China's purpose in flying the drone over the island was to assert its claim of sovereignty. To the same end, the Japanese Air Self-Defense Force launched F-15 fighters to intercept the drone over the East China Sea. Cooler heads prevailed and armed conflict was averted, but no one knows what will happen next time.

Among the many applications of AGI's Satellite Tool Kit—the software we purchased from Xiang Li in 2010—is the tracking of UAVs. This software would be useful to the Chinese government in both the development and the employment of drones. We didn't know if the Chinese were using STK in their UAV program, but we did know it was available to them through Xiang Li.

Eventually, Ronayne and I left the Saipan World Resort parking lot on Afetna Point and drove back to our hotel, leaving others to cover the hotel in the event that Xiang Li unexpectedly left. That seemed highly unlikely, however, given that he was traveling with his family and had just gotten off a long red-eye flight from China. We had just returned to our hotel when Ronayne's phone rang.

"You gotta be shittin' me," he said.

The news was bad. Xiang Li had suddenly exited the hotel, jumped into a waiting jeep, and sped off through Garapan and into the hills beyond. What was this about? Did he have a confederate on Saipan? Was he engaged with Chinese intelligence? And if he didn't want to nap, why wasn't he calling his American new best friend, Robert, to set up a meeting? As an ambitious Chinese businessman, wouldn't that be his priority? Had the Chinese government played us all along?

The relief we felt at the airport only hours before, as we watched Xiang Li get on the bus, was now a distant memory. With our target now missing, we faced once again the prospect of failure on a grand scale. The question was what to do next. It is not easy to follow someone on a small island; in doing so, we ran the risk of exposing the tail, and thereby blowing the undercover meeting.

Cullen and Ronayne weren't going to sit around talking about it. They found Xiang Li's jeep and followed it northward into a remote part of the island, until a cow and two large shirtless dudes blocked the road. Wisely, Cullen and Ronayne backed off and turned the jeep over to other members of the surveillance team, who followed it up Mount Tapochau, then to Banzai Cliff and the Japanese command post, pretty much tracing our steps from the previous day. Was Xiang Li seeing the sights, or riding around with a Chinese handler pretending to see the sights? As the hours ticked by in miserably slow motion, Robert continued trying to contact Xiang by phone and e-mail:

Hello Xiang,
Are you in Saipan?

After all the effort to avoid pacing around the locker room, trying to manage pregame jitters, we spent the day doing just that.

At the end of the day, we finally heard from Xiang Li. Robert wrote back, a bit frostily:

I got your message.
I am at the Fiesta Hotel room 871.
Please meet at 9am. Call my cell phone when arriving.

Xiang Li's response was lackluster to say the least.

ok
I see

What did all this mean? Rather than contacting us after his arrival, Xiang Li had disappeared, and then just as suddenly he reappeared. And when he did, instead of enthusiastically setting up a meeting, he was vague and noncommittal, like the meeting was not really a priority for him. What was going on? Was he gallivanting around the island seeing the sights—after we had paid his way? Or were we being played, perhaps by Chinese intelligence?

As I was thinking through these possibilities, Xiang Li suddenly called Robert and firmly set a meeting time; he was commanding, even downright bossy. We found this perplexing; he was indifferent one minute, demanding the next. It didn't seem consistent with his behavior over the past year and a half on e-mail and Skype. Then it hit me:

he's a Chinese businessman; he needs to control the conversation and set the terms. We were being played, but not by Chinese intelligence.

"Whatever," I thought. "He can be as bossy as he wants now; tomorrow, he'll be in the lockup."

Early the next morning, we headed down to the Fiesta Hotel to prepare. Brian—the tech agent—set up all the recording devices in the room. The rest of us poured into a nearby room, ready for the arrest. All we needed was Xiang Li.

Then he called: "Can you pick me up?"

Robert, of course, agreed.

This might not seem like a significant change in plan, but it was. Brian now had to wire Robert for a meeting in a car. This was necessary for a number of reasons, primarily Robert's safety, but also because we didn't want to miss any opportunity to collect evidence against Xiang Li. And further to the goal of protecting Robert, we had to divert agents from the Fiesta Hotel to follow Robert in the car.

After getting Robert wired, Brian shut off all the recording devices in the Fiesta Hotel room so the batteries didn't run out while Robert was picking up Xiang Li.

I e-mailed Ed McAndrew to let him know what was going on. Although already a member of the Pennsylvania and District of Columbia bars, Ed had decided to become a member of the Delaware bar, and was sitting at that moment in a bar review class in Wilmington.

----- *Original Message* ----- *From: Hall, David L. (USADE) Sent: Monday, June 06, 2011 08:00 PM To: McAndrew, Ed (USADE) Subject: Status Uc picked up tgt. On route to hotel for meet.*

----- *Original Message* ----- *From: McAndrew, Ed (USADE) Sent: Monday, June 06, 2011 08:10 PM To: Hall, David L. (USADE) Subject: Re: Status Very good*

On the ride from the Saipan World Resort to the Fiesta Hotel, Robert and Xiang Li chatted like old friends. Back at the Fiesta, we were peering out the window awaiting their arrival. We saw them pull into the parking lot, get out of the car, and head into the hotel. Over the monitor, we could hear them enter the hotel room. Ronayne, looking around the monitoring room, said to Cullen, "Hey, where's Brian?" Cullen, preoccupied, said in an uncharacteristically absent way, "I don't know."

That's when Ronayne got the e-mail from Brian:

Do not shit yourself, but I am still in the room. All is well. Please start the recording on the non phone receiver. Do this by pressing and holding the Rec button and then pushing the play button.

"You gotta be shittin' me," said Mike, ably summing up the situation.

This is when it pays to have a tech agent like Brian, a former Special Forces operator unfazed by surprise. We hadn't given Brian a heads up that Xiang Li and Robert were heading to the room, where Brian was busy turning the recording devices back on. When he heard someone at the hotel room door, he slipped into one of the suite's two bathrooms.

Mike did as instructed and recorded the meeting from our monitoring room. It was a crowded place. Brendan Cullen was sitting in a chair by the window, Mike was sitting on the bed, and the arrest team was milling about putting on raid gear. I was on my knees on the floor with my ear to a monitoring cell phone on the bedside table. Robert was introducing Xiang Li to the second undercover agent, a female Mandarin speaker who would be interpreting.

----- Original Message ----- From: Hall, David L. (USADE) Sent: Monday, June 06, 2011 08:16 PM To: McAndrew, Ed (USADE) Subject: Re: Status
*   In hotel room*

----- *Original Message* ----- *From: McAndrew, Ed (USADE) Sent: Monday, June 06, 2011 08:19 PM To: Hall, David L. (USADE) Subject: Re: Status I'm in torts lecture. I might be willing to trade places with Li.*

As Xiang Li sat abruptly on the couch with Robert, there was very little small talk; he was all business, continually grabbing Robert's knee for emphasis. He was almost spasmodic in his excitement. Robert gave him a small gift, which he all but ignored, instead unwrapping the counterfeit labels he brought with him: "This is the packaging," Xiang Li said breathlessly, referring to the labels for the fifteen titles of software he had sold us in January. Once he had the packaging unwrapped, Li started unwrapping something else.

"It's the database," explained Xiang Li, meaning it was the twenty gigabytes of proprietary data hacked from Defense Contractor. Then he asked Robert, "What is the rest of your itinerary after this? . . . I was thinking [it] would be difficult to pass through the custom."

Xiang Li was referring to the many discs containing the twenty gigabytes of data. We would later learn that this proprietary data included military and civilian aircraft image models, a software module containing data associated with the International Space Station, and a high-resolution, three-dimensional imaging program. Xiang Li was concerned—justifiably—that U.S. Customs would be suspicious of so many discs in a traveler's luggage. So he had some advice on how to smuggle them into the United States: "I wanted to make sure there will be no problem with the custom. . . . [I] have packed separately. . . . You should just do the same as I did. Pack them separately. . . . Let several different individuals bring them over."

Evidently doubting Robert's ability to understand just how illegal this enterprise was, Xiang Li added, "This . . . is not allowed to bring this. . . . The custom will not let [you]. Do you understand?"

Seizing the opportunity, Robert asked, "It's not okay in the United States?"

Said Xiang Li: "Correct."

If you are asked, he continued, "You can just say, [these] are the study materials."

Robert asked Xiang Li if any companies had ever contacted him about his sale of their products. This was an important point and something we talked about prior to the undercover meeting. A jury will want to know that the defendant—particularly a foreign national conducting business in his native land—understands that what he is doing is a violation of U.S. law. Xiang Li's lecture on smuggling showed that he had a highly nuanced understanding of the illegality of his actions.

We already knew from Xiang Li's e-mails that U.S. companies had contacted him, directing him to cease and desist the illegal distribution of their software. This too was strong evidence that Xiang Li knew he was violating U.S. law. We wanted to know if Xiang Li would admit it to Robert. And he certainly did. When Robert asked how he responded to such e-mails, Xiang Li said, "I just deleted it."

I let Ed know.

----- *Original Message* ----- *From: Hall, David L. (USADE) Sent: Monday, June 06, 2011 08:24 PM To: McAndrew, Ed (USADE) Subject: Re: Status Says cos have contacted him saying you're stealing our stuffff*

Further demonstrating his willfulness, Xiang Li offered advice to Robert on not getting caught:

Don't just sell it . . . randomly! That's what I mean. . . . Only the familiar and reliable customers. . . . The products . . . are pretty . . . um . . . like confidential. [Don't] . . . go and tell other people.

Xiang Li was at pains to let us know that he could get us more counterfeit packaging or "anything else." He assured us: "I will be able to handle it." This gave Robert a good opening to ask Xiang Li how he obtained his software—the question that had burned at the front of our minds since 2009.

People have different ways of being evasive: some tell fully formed premeditated lies, some act like they don't understand the question, some tell half-truths. Xiang Li's method was to serve up a word salad: a towering helping of words too immense to consume and too disparate to reassemble in any coherent form. Sensing Robert's frustration, Xiang Li protested: "However, you must believe that what I have are real. *Real!* Real! . . . Not a lie."

Robert asked if Xiang Li could get software in addition to what he had listed on CRACK99. "I mean as long as [you] can tell me the name," Xiang Li said, "I could find a way to get it. . . . "

I gave Ed—still sitting in a classroom in Delaware—an update:

----- *Original Message* ----- *From: Hall, David L. (USADE) Sent: Monday, June 06, 2011 08:48 PM To: McAndrew, Ed (USADE) Subject: Re: Status*
He can get whatever we want

----- *Original Message* ----- *From: McAndrew, Ed (USADE) Sent: Monday, June 06, 2011 08:50 PM To: Hall, David L. (USADE) Subject: Re: Status*
I want a passing grade on the bar.

----- *Original Message* ----- *From: Hall, David L. (USADE) Sent: Monday, June 06, 2011 08:51 PM To: McAndrew, Ed (USADE) Subject: Re: Status*
Ill ask later

Robert pressed one last time on the question of where Xiang Li was getting the software: "Do you . . . have to ask someone else for this software?"

The answer was particularly unhelpful: "Some of them yes, some of them no." Xiang Li was not going to reveal his sources.

One of the lessons of the Ardebili case was the importance of seizing a defendant's electronic data at the time of arrest. We thought there was a good chance Xiang Li had data—maybe pirated software—in his hotel room, and we didn't want to miss the opportunity to seize it. So Robert subtly asked Xiang Li if he had brought any other software to Saipan. Xiang Li said he had: "Probably few hundreds G [gigabytes]."

"So your hotel has this?" asked Robert.

"Yes, yes," said Xiang Li.

I let Ed know.

----- *Original Message* ----- *From: Hall, David L. (USADE) Sent: Monday, June 06, 2011 08:51 PM To: McAndrew, Ed (USADE) Subject: Re: Status Has external hard drive at hotel*

An agent was sent to secure Xiang Li's hotel room. On the whole, things were going well, and I started to feel confident. That is when it always happens.

"I need to go to the bathroom," said the female undercover agent.

What? I looked up at Ronayne, who had stopped breathing. I felt my stomach tie up into a square knot. The female agent didn't know that Brian was stuck in one of the two bathrooms. And I didn't know which of the two she was headed for. This was a fifty-fifty proposition: If she walked into the wrong bathroom, she would get quite a shock. Would she manage to keep it to herself, and avoid alarming Xiang Li? The arrest team, aware that something was amiss, started stacking at the door in case they had to bring down the undercover meeting on short notice.

Then the female undercover agent asked Xiang Li, "Do you need to go to the bathroom also?"

My stomach was now in a double square knot. This had the potential to get very bad, very fast.

"No," said Xiang Li, to my enormous relief.

"There is another one over there," she said helpfully.

"No, no, no," said Xiang Li emphatically.

It seemed like an eternity until she returned. As it turned out, she used the bathroom not occupied by Brian.

Although Xiang Li seemed unable to form a coherent sentence when he was discussing the source of the software sold on CRACK99, he was very coherent indeed when it came to reviewing the mechanics of the new business enterprise with his new American partner. He discussed in detail the process by which he would supply the software: he would use the file transfer protocol (FTP) to send the software to Robert, who would copy it to discs and pack the discs in the counterfeit packaging provided by Xiang Li.

"You will download the data onto the discs. So, you will do it yourself. No need to mail it. This will save a lot of time. . . . Do you understand?"

The counterfeit packaging was for the U.S. distribution plan Robert and Xiang Li had discussed and agreed to earlier. As Xiang Li explained, "All of my customers . . . they all want the data only. . . . [They] don't want the packaging." This is because they are "individuals . . . not companies." Therefore, they have no interest in appearing legitimate. But the U.S. distribution plan did require the appearance of legitimacy so that Robert could command a higher price than Xiang Li was charging on CRACK99.

Once again, Xiang Li questioned Robert about how he would protect his source, namely, CRACK99.

"I want to ask a question. . . . Will [your] customers be able to find me? Will [they] be also contacting me? Is it possible? [Pause] Will [the customers] be able to locate me?"

Robert assured him that was not possible.

"Then, that's okay."

The conversation then turned to the question of how to install the cracked software. Both Robert and Xiang Li were keenly aware that installing cracked software is often difficult and that on multiple occasions in the past we had asked Xiang Li's help in executing the installation. How would that work in this new enterprise?

"If there's such a circumstance," said Xiang Li, "where [your] customers do not know how to install [it] . . . under such circumstance, I will then show [you, Robert] how to do it."

Xiang Li amplified: "*So*, [you] can show it to . . . customers, demonstrate to them. . . . Yes, yes, yes. It's safer. Yes. Because among all these . . . I'm the only one who knows how."

His point was clear: he was a necessary part of this operation; Robert would not be able to go it alone.

Robert then went through the discs Xiang Li had brought with him, confirming that everything we had ordered was there. Xiang Li told Robert he would find "[all] I have promised." He repeated that he was delivering them in person "because I was concerned about mailing [them]. . . . Do you understand?" The face-to-face meeting provided an "opportunity" to "bring them over." Apparently regretting the delay, Xiang Li said, "I'm sorry!"

Robert said Xiang Li could make it up to him with a discount on the next purchase.

"I agree," said Xiang Li. "I agree with this."

Then Xiang Li started bestowing gifts on Robert: Chinese tea and a number of food items, including dried seasoned tofu. Robert had warned Xiang Li not to bring food items, but apparently Xiang Li did not consider Robert particularly sage when it came to customs matters. "Eat it here," Xiang Li advised.

There was a package of chocolates too, but that was not for Robert. "That's for my son, that's for my son," said Xiang Li. A sad moment to be sure, because we all knew Xiang Li would not be giving the chocolates to his son.

In the monitoring room, we knew the meeting was coming to an end. The arrest team, clad in raid gear, was stacked at the door, Ronayne and Cullen in front, ready to make entry. They were waiting for Robert's prearranged signal: "Our business here has come to an end." I let Ed know.

----- *Original Message* ----- *From: Hall, David L. (USADE) Sent: Monday, June 06, 2011 08:53 PM To: McAndrew, Ed (USADE) Subject: Re: Status Going down in 30 sec*

Then Xiang Li asked, "Do you have anything scheduled after this? We can go . . . and hang out together."

But Xiang Li's hanging-out days were about to be put on hold. Robert suggested they set a time for tomorrow and then uttered the code words—"Our business here is over"—to summon the arrest team. Almost instantly, I could hear the room filling with large men giving clear commands. Xiang Li was shocked, the kind of shock that can transform a highly intelligent global entrepreneur into a mouth breather. It must have been highly incongruous from his point of view: one minute you're making plans to hang out with your new best friend; the next, you're staring at the carpet following directions from strangers. Cullen put the cuffs on. Ronayne said to Xiang Li, in a very low, calm voice, "Stay down." Xiang Li did as he was told; he wasn't calling the shots anymore.

Xiang Li had been at the epicenter of a hacking and cracking ring that stole American technology and then sold it back to Americans. The scale of his enterprise was enormous: $100 million by our count, but that included only what we knew he sold. Thousands more software titles—conceivably worth more than a billion dollars—were still advertised on his website. His CRACK99 enterprise was no more, but as Xiang Li was being cuffed, I wondered, "How many Chinese hackers are out there right now, stealing American technology for use by the Chinese military? How many Xiang Lis are there, selling hacked and cracked U.S. technology back to American customers?"

Will America be funding its own demise?

11 | DEAD OR ALIVE

IN FEBRUARY 1998, I WAS CHARGED by a wounded elephant. I didn't have much sympathy for him at the time, but I do now. He was old.

I was in South Africa with a fellow AUSA, Bob Goldman, investigating a conspiracy to evade the arms embargo of South Africa during the apartheid era. An American company had been actively supplying South Africa with military components in violation of U.S. law, and the South Africans were providing us with evidence of those crimes. The criminal activity had been vast in scope, involving the sale of U.S. technology and munitions to South Africa throughout the 1980s. The case demonstrated the recurring theme that once American technology and munitions have been exported, they can end up anywhere. In 1991, during Operation Desert Storm, U.S. forces found components manufactured by this very American company in Saddam Hussein's artillery stores—for use against U.S. forces. This foreshadowed the dynamic we would observe in the Amir Ardebili case: components procured for the Iranian government could go anywhere, to be used against the U.S. military. While the South Africans were collecting documents, Goldman and I had a break in the action. We were invited to the ambassador's residence for a barbecue. But his secretary had a better idea: "You should go on a safari." So we headed for the Bushveld.

Our jeep was navigating a rutted road. A man with a rifle was seated on the front hood, bouncing and smiling amiably. He became less sanguine when he saw the jackalberry trees suddenly start to sway back and forth. It was a strange sight, a great wave of foliage undulating for no apparent reason, accompanied by the startling popping sound of cracking wood. Then the source of the commotion was revealed: two bull elephants were locked in pitched battle, crashing into each other, heedless of all around them, including large hardwood trees. We watched in awed silence until one of them—the elder—glanced in our direction, as if to say, "What're you lookin' at?" Then he decided he liked us even less than the younger bull, and charged.

The driver threw the jeep into gear and floored it. That's about when I noticed the bull's broken tusk. Shortly thereafter, I realized that the bull was faster than the jeep. He was gaining on us, and of the two objects hurtling through space, he was much larger.

It's funny what you do in circumstances like that; I found myself leaning toward the front of the jeep, as if that would help it go faster, all the while keeping my eyes fixed on the bull, as if I could slow him down telepathically. Just before he reached us, he stopped abruptly. It turns out that bull elephants can run fast, but not for long. He stood in the track with his broken tusk, watching us flee, with an expression of unadulterated disdain.

You never know what's going to happen next. When you're an optimist, you hope for the best. But that doesn't mean you actually believe the best will automatically happen. If you start doing that, you complete the transition from optimist to nitwit.

We had a concern. It was not something we considered likely to occur; I would go so far as to say it was a low-probability contingency. But if it manifested into a reality, the consequences could be significant. Our concern was that the Chinese government would intervene to obtain the release of Xiang Li once he was arrested.

There are about 1.3 billion Chinese nationals. Even for a government experienced in totalitarianism, that is a large number of people to keep track of. I have no doubt the People's Republic of China spends more effort spying on some individuals than others. The question I could not answer was where Xiang Li ranked in terms of this totalitarian tracking: Would the Chinese make a point of keeping tabs on him? This is what caused us such acute concern when Xiang Li went missing shortly before our undercover meeting. Was he in communication with the Chinese intelligence services? Did he have a minder?

Our worries persisted after Xiang Li's arrest. Would the Chinese notice his arrest, and would they care enough to intervene? We had no evidence indicating he was a government officer. But at the same time, we had ample reason to believe the Chinese government could benefit from his piracy activities. As the IP Commission would later report, "National industrial policy goals in China encourage IP theft, and an extraordinary number of Chinese in business and government entities are engaged in this practice." The question was, how much did the Chinese government encourage Xiang Li personally? And was that enough for the government to be particularly concerned about his arrest?

On balance, we thought it prudent to get Xiang Li off the island as soon as possible after he was arrested. That way, we reasoned, if the Chinese lodged a protest, we could fight it from home, instead of Saipan. This is the reason HSI had chartered the Gulfstream IV— demonstrating in concrete terms that Ronayne had by now convinced his agency of the importance of the case, even if I had not convinced mine. But there was one important step between Xiang Li's arrest and our departure on the Gulfstream IV: the judge. Every defendant— including Xiang Li—is entitled to an initial appearance before a judicial officer "without unnecessary delay" following his arrest. When a defendant is arrested in a district other than the one issuing the arrest warrant, the defendant is also entitled to a removal hearing, at which the government must prove the defendant is the person named in the warrant. In addition, the defendant is entitled to a detention hearing, at which the judge determines whether the defendant will remain in custody pending his transfer to the district issuing the warrant.

This process takes time. It is common for a defendant to make an initial appearance in court without a lawyer, for the simple reason that none can be summoned "without unnecessary delay." So, in the normal course of events, judges hold initial appearances for recently arrested defendants and then schedule removal and detention hearings for another date, days or even a week later so the defense lawyer can be present. We wanted to move faster than that.

No federal judge is permanently assigned to Saipan, but federal judges do stop in from time to time, riding circuit, just like in the Old West, except that instead of riding horseback, they ride on airplanes. I made contact with the court and learned that a circuit-riding judge— from the Eastern District of Washington—was on the island. I advised the court of the arrest and requested an initial appearance. I let the court know Xiang Li would need a Mandarin interpreter and would be requesting an appointed lawyer. They set the hearing for the next morning, when both would be available.

While I was doing that, Brendan Cullen was busy with Xiang Li. Speaking through a Mandarin interpreter, Brendan advised Xiang Li of his Miranda rights in English and Mandarin:

You have the right to remain silent. Anything you say can and will be used against you in a court of law. You have the right to an attorney. . . .

Xiang Li waived his right to remain silent and said he wanted to make a statement. He seemed to have recovered from the shock of the

arrest. I'm sure it helped that he no longer lay face down on the carpet, surrounded by hulking men. He was now seated comfortably at a
table with Brendan, who was respectful and businesslike. An equable
demeanor gives rise to the most productive questioning: give a fellow
who's having a bad day a chance to explain himself, ask reasonable
questions, and you might get reasonable answers. That doesn't always
result in the truth, but it's a good first step. And the approach seemed
to work in the case of Xiang Li, who became reanimated as he told his
side of the story.

He lived, he said, in Chengdu with his wife, Chun Yan Li. He was
the one who operated the CRACK99 website; his wife was only responsible for collecting the money sent to CRACK99; he insisted she had
no other role. He was the only person who had access to the e-mail
accounts we had searched, including the main one: china9981@
gmail.com.

He said he maintained a large inventory of software for sale on
CRACK99, but would find software not in his inventory upon customer request. Most of his U.S. customers were individuals who used
the software for their businesses. For the most part, he interacted
with his customers through the Internet, although he did admit meeting one customer from Hong Kong and one from California. He confirmed using two websites in addition to CRACK99 to distribute the
pirated software. Why did he use three different sites? Because, he
said, sometimes a customer could not access CRACK99 and the others
served as an alternative. He used other sites as well, but he did not
advertise content on them; rather, he used them exclusively to access
FTP space on the hosting servers.

Xiang Li described himself as an "opportunist." His access to specific cracked software market sectors came through his participation
in Internet "fans" or "fan groups." The market for cracked software,
he said, was a niche market, and he was the "middleman." He said
that the people in the fan groups were knowledgeable about hack-

ing software, but they didn't necessarily know how to distribute what they had hacked, except to post it online. Likewise, consumers frequently did not know where to find this hacked software, and even if they did find it, they did not know how to install it. Xiang Li described himself as a middleman, occupying the space between the hacker and the consumer, making the pirated software available and helping to install it—just as he did with us. Xiang Li said he specializes in the installation process and considers this a significant part of what he offers consumers.

Cullen pressed Xiang Li on the big question: Where did he obtain the software? Xiang Li said he obtained it on websites, based mostly in China and Russia. For the most part, he said, he could obtain a download at no cost—although in some cases he had to pay. Xiang Li also told Cullen he participated in web forums about hacking software as a way to find out what software was available. Cullen asked Xiang Li how he found software that customers specifically requested. The answer was simple: by running the title through search engines, mostly in China. Cullen asked to see the website where Xiang Li obtained STK software, and Xiang Li complied. He claimed to have received it at no charge.

At the conclusion of the interview, Cullen called Special Agent Alex Zuchman, back in Philadelphia, who executed seizure warrants on six domains utilized by Xiang Li.

Early in the interview, Xiang Li granted permission to search his hotel room, so Ronayne, Special Agent Chuck Akeo, and I drove down to the Saipan World Resort. There, we encountered Xiang Li's mother-in-law and five-year-old son. We explained to the mother-in-law that Xiang Li had been arrested. To my immense surprise, her only question was "What about my airline ticket?" She never asked a single question about Xiang Li. Not "Why was he arrested?" Not even "How's he doing?" She didn't seem particularly surprised or concerned. Her only focus was the flight home. Plenty of people don't get along with their in-laws, but this was just cold.

We didn't think it was the best idea to be searching the room in front of Xiang Li's son, so I took him to get an ice cream cone—using Ronayne's money. We sat amiably together in the hotel lobby while he enjoyed the cone. Then he did what any five-year-old would do after eating an ice cream cone: he ran around the lobby in circles. I felt sorry for the boy, who was guilty of nothing but would soon be paying a price for his father's crimes. Likewise, Xiang Li's unborn child. There was no telling what Xiang Li's future held in the United States, except that he would be away from his family for some period of time. It is commonplace that the defendant is not the only one punished for his crimes: the whole family is. Defendants frequently beg judges for mercy on the ground that a long period of incarceration will harm innocent family members. Judges just as frequently tell defendants, "You should have thought of that before committing your crimes." So it was with Xiang Li; still, it is sad to separate an innocent child from his father. I can only hope that the separation will spare the children their father's bad example.

We seized quite a lot of evidence that day. In their search of the hotel room, Ronayne and Akeo found a laptop computer, four DVDs, a thumb drive, and an external hard drive. The laptop was hidden behind a window curtain, and the external hard drive was tucked in a glove on top of the refrigerator, raising an important question: Who needs a glove on Saipan? At the Fiesta Hotel, the arrest team seized twenty-eight DVDs containing software, Defense Contractor's proprietary data, and numerous DVD cases containing counterfeit design labeling for the software products Xiang Li had sold us in January 2011. And, of course, the seasoned tofu.

Subsequent forensic analysis of the computer equipment and removable digital media confirmed that it contained pirated copies of the software sold to Robert, counterfeit packaging for that software, and approximately twenty gigabytes of proprietary data obtained from Defense Contractor. And there was more: the forensic analysis answered a question we had not been able to answer: Did Xiang Li have access to hackers? The answer was a resounding yes: the proprietary data from Defense Contractor had been hacked. There was more than one forensic finding supporting this conclusion, but the most intuitive was this: included in the proprietary data were music files that Defense Contractor employees had uploaded to the company server. The music files had nothing to do with the proprietary data itself; most likely, the employees had uploaded the music to listen to during the workday. One does what one must do to get to the closing whistle. This led to the conclusion that the hacker had indiscriminately copied everything he found in Defense Contractor's server—including the music files—and exfiltrated it. The other possibility was that the hacker was a music lover who was smart enough to penetrate Defense Contractor's server but too dumb to realize there are easier ways to get free music.

We finished our work at the Saipan World Resort about the time Brendan finished taking Xiang Li's statement. The next stop was the HSI office, where Xiang Li was fingerprinted. Gone was the animated businessman slapping Robert on the knee to emphasize his "True deal" guarantee. He was very serious, as the very serious circumstances warranted, and highly compliant. Everything about him—including his voluntary statement—was fully consistent with a defendant who wanted to cooperate. We sincerely hoped to accommodate this interest, after he made his initial appearance in court the next morning.

That night was not entirely pleasant. The U.S. Marshal maintains a holding cell on Saipan, but only one deputy. Back home, we were accustomed to leaving prisoners with the U.S. Marshal and calling it a day. Not on Saipan. We would be responsible for securing the prisoner for the night in the holding cell. So the agents took shifts, in pairs, watching over Xiang Li.

There is a deadening finality to the metallic clang of a jail cell door. I have experienced it many times while interviewing prisoners; that sound invariably caused a deep visceral tug somewhere deep inside me, even though I knew I could go home at the end of the day. Xiang Li seemed to feel it too. As the door closed behind him, he stood staring at the rear cell wall with his back to us. Then he sat down and stared at the floor. It was all sinking in.

We asked him what he'd like for dinner, and he continued looking at the ground, shaking his head. We told him we could get Chinese food. He said no. I asked if he was sure. He said, "Nothing." Everyone else was hungry, so Ronayne and I drove to McDonald's, returning to the holding cell with bags of burgers and fries. We gave Xiang Li a meal, but he declined it, preferring to roll up in his blanket on the hard bed. He was very still, but I doubt he slept much. His bubble had well and truly burst. The rest of us ate fast food and talked about what we needed to accomplish the next day: Ideally, Xiang Li would agree to detention and removal to Delaware. If he didn't, it could take days—or even longer—to get the detention and removal order.

The next morning, I collared Xiang Li's appointed lawyer, an amiable white guy who lived on Saipan for reasons he never explained. I regretted this because I thought his story might be interesting. He was extremely windblown, like he had taken a few tumbles in an industrial dryer. Would he talk to Xiang Li about stipulating to pretrial detention? There was no compelling argument against detention, particularly since he was a foreign national; he was likely to be detained whether or not he objected. Likewise, there was no question about whether the court would order Xiang Li removed from Saipan to answer charges in Delaware. Brendan would be able to testify that the Xiang Li in court was the Xiang Li who was wanted in Delaware; the man on Saipan was the same man from the Skype sessions. Oh, and there was one more thing: "He says he wants to cooperate. We'd like to talk to him on the flight home. Will you agree?"

"I'll see what I can do," the windblown lawyer said.

A wily defense lawyer never promises anything. So when we walked into court, I had no idea what Xiang Li would do. It really is up to him in the end, and even if the windblown defense lawyer had agreed to all my requests, Xiang Li was free to say the opposite to the judge. Predicting courtroom behavior is always difficult, and particularly so when the defendant is a foreign national unfamiliar with American law. I tried to imagine how all this looked from Xiang Li's point of view: in a foreign country, represented by a stranger, sitting in a forbidding courtroom governed by rules totally unlike those of China. In an initial appearance, a large number of constitutional rights are explained to the defendant; it really is a short and substantive lesson in American jurisprudence. This is a good thing. But if everything you're hearing is new, it has to be overwhelming. I imagined the questions running through Xiang Li's mind. Right to remain silent? What does that mean? Right to counsel? Is this the guy next to me? Is he my guy? Who's the other guy over there? The bald one. Right to a detention hearing? Is that good? Or bad? Removal? To Delaware? What is a Delaware?

Xiang Li maintained a serious expression throughout the hearing and for the most part looked at his feet, except for his frequent glances at Brendan and me. I don't know what was behind those glances, and it might have simply been that we were the only two familiar faces in the room. But he might also have been experiencing some sense of disbelief. Who are those guys? How had it come to this? Xiang Li had traveled to Saipan to meet his new business partner, Robert, and the next thing he knows he's being led in handcuffs to a courtroom where an American judge is explaining his right to a detention hearing and a removal hearing. In the end, he waived both, to our enormous relief: it meant we could launch the next day. And in fact, by the time we got back to our hotel, the Gulfstream IV flight crew was checking in. If you didn't know how random and chaotic federal law enforcement is, you'd think we were operating a well-oiled machine.

There was one hiccup. I asked Xiang Li's appointed lawyer about talking to him on the flight home. Now that Xiang Li was a represented party, we would need his lawyer's approval to do that. My argument in favor was that it was a good way for Xiang Li to begin his cooperation: "He can hit the ground running in Delaware," I said, employing a hackneyed cliché I hoped would nevertheless inspire. I try to avoid hackneyed clichés, except for the inspiring ones.

But for Xiang Li, going along with my plan carried some risk. He had not agreed to plead guilty, and the windswept lawyer on Saipan didn't want to assume he would. He was just representing Xiang Li for his initial appearance on Saipan, and didn't want to do anything to limit Xiang Li's options in the future.

"Best to leave the cooperation question to his lawyer in Delaware," said the windswept lawyer.

Disappointing, to be sure, but on balance not surprising.

Our work on Saipan was done. So, we thought maybe we'd have a beer to celebrate. Hypothetically, if someone were to suggest that one thing led to another, and certain individuals ended up singing the Bon Jovi anthem "Wanted Dead or Alive" at a karaoke bar, would you be scandalized?

Generally speaking, I recommend against narrating your life to the tune of rock lyrics. It is a short step from there to tattooing fatuous slogans on your chest next to the Aztec symbol some dude at the bus station told you means "Warrior." That said, a song about a cowboy looking at cold faces in a new place that's just like the last one is bound to appeal to veteran Federales at the lonely end of a long tether held by an indifferent employer—especially veteran Federales who push the envelope hard in overcoming that indifference. Everybody likes a cowboy. And besides, it's a great tune. If the Chinese intelligence services, hypothetically, were to have a video of that episode, what would be your reaction? Mine would be: post it on YouTube, and spice up my reputation. When we hit that chorus, we hit it hard. We were that good. Hypothetically.

The next morning, we picked Xiang Li up at the holding cell and, in a convoy of Chevy Tahoes, drove him to the airport. When we took him out of the car, he blinked a couple of times against the bright sunlight and turned toward the tarmac, where a gleaming Gulfstream IV awaited. He took an involuntary step backward and looked up at Brendan, who seemed almost twice his height. Xiang Li did not seem particularly enthused about leaving with us.

"Come on, Xiang," Brendan said flatly.

As the aircraft lifted off and made a leisurely northward turn over the Pacific, we offered Xiang Li sandwiches in silence.

"Where going?" Xiang Li wanted to know.

I decided this one could be answered: "Delaware."

Xiang Li looked confused.

"It's a state."

He still looked confused, so Brendan drew him a map of the United States and pointed to Delaware.

"I want talk."

"No," I said, "not until we get to Delaware."

"What is Delaware?"

So we showed him the map again, gave him an overview of the fifty states, and a short summary on federalism.

"I want talk."

"Not until we're in Delaware."

We landed in Honolulu at night. To save money, HSI had decided not to fly us all the way home on the Gulfstream IV. The goal was to get Xiang Li off Saipan, and we did. We would fly a commercial airline from Honolulu. HSI agents met us at the airport and took the prisoner, which I considered an act of high professionalism, since they could have left that responsibility to us. Again, I was impressed by the work ethic of the HSI agents from Honolulu. Then they took us to our hotel. On Waikiki Beach. Sometimes you luck out, validating one's innate optimism. We had time for a swim and lunch on the beach the next day, before the final leg of our journey home. Better lucky than good.

We boarded the jet in a group, having placed a shirt over Xiang Li's handcuffs to avoid alarming the other passengers. Then we wedged him into the window seat. It was a long flight home. Once we got back, we brought Xiang Li to federal court in Delaware, and a federal defender was appointed to represent him. I provided the defense lawyer with investigative reports summarizing the evidence against his client. His response was to request a proffer, a meeting at which Xiang Li would answer questions with the understanding that his answers could not be used against him at trial. Over the course of the summer of 2011, we had a number of proffers in the federal building in Philadelphia. We tried to be sympathetic to his plight; he was in a strange land far from home. We brought him Chinese food—real Chinese food from his region, Sichuan Province—procured by Malandra, who seemingly knows everybody in Philadelphia, including Chinatown.

But if Xiang Li appreciated the gesture, he didn't say it out loud. He refused to eat in front of us, eyeing the food warily. Maybe he preferred the cheese sandwiches they served in the U.S. Marshal's lockup. We had encountered many versions of Xiang Li on Saipan, and now we faced a new one: a dark and sullen Xiang Li. This is not hard to understand. No one likes to be arrested and taken away from his family, particularly just months before the birth of a child. We gave him a phone so he could call home and talk to his wife, but he declined. We were being kind, but with the benefit of hindsight, I wonder if Xiang Li thought we were being cruel.

Despite our best efforts, the proffer sessions did not go particularly well. We continued bringing food, and he continued to refuse it. We gave him more opportunities to call home, and these too he declined. He answered direct questions but made no effort to explain his answers. He remained within the four corners of his statement to Brendan Cullen on Saipan, but added nothing. Consistency is a good thing, and is generally viewed as an indication of veracity, but it is unusual for an unrehearsed statement made after the shock of an arrest to be so complete as to require no subsequent amplification or correction. If it was unrehearsed.

Xiang Li continued to insist that his only means of obtaining hacked software was through Internet search engines and fan groups and that he didn't know any hacked software providers personally. This was a plausible statement on its face, because the Internet abounds with such providers, who can be located through the search methodology he described. And he did corroborate his version of events somewhat by showing us the websites where he obtained software.

If Xiang Li's story was a lie, it was difficult to falsify. But I found it too pat, and I suspected that Xiang Li was reluctant to reveal his sources—or a connection to the Chinese government. And there were tidbits at odds with his story, such as his instant-messaging chats with a hacker from Taiwan bragging about how much money he had made from his exploits.

But cooperation is often a work in progress. With this in mind—and thinking we could win him over in time—we offered Xiang Li a plea agreement with a cooperation provision. The deal was that Xiang Li would plead guilty to every charge in the indictment, and we would agree to file a motion with the court to reduce his sentence—if we were satisfied with his cooperation by the time of sentencing. We emphasized that our willingness to file such a motion would depend on whether we concluded he was honest with us, and that at that moment we did not think he was being honest. This troubled him. Understandably, he did not like the fact that he was theoretically exposed to more than one hundred years of incarceration. Notwithstanding these concerns, he agreed to the deal.

On the day of the plea hearing, however, Xiang Li balked. Now we saw the angry and fiery Xiang Li. He refused to plead guilty and fired the federal defender in favor of a privately engaged lawyer in New York. How did that happen? Who was paying for the New York lawyer? Was it his family? Or, say, the People's Republic of China?

These questions were never answered to my satisfaction, mainly because the circumstances of a criminal defendants' representation are not ordinarily a proper focus of a prosecutor's inquiries. Xiang Li had every right to fire his lawyer and to hire a new one. I had no evidence to indicate there was anything untoward about this new arrangement. I had only my suspicions.

After changing horses in midstream, Xiang Li expressed no interest in a guilty plea. So we prepared for trial. But trials often represent the failure of negotiation. To avoid wasting resources, I always made a point of exhausting non-trial alternatives. To this end, I asked the new lawyer if there was anything to be gained by discussing a plea agreement. He said yes, that he had a proposal, and asked to meet. Brendan Cullen, Alex Zuchman, Ed McAndrew, and I gathered in the Wilmington courthouse for this momentous event. The lawyer kept us waiting for more than an hour, which we spent wondering what he would propose. When he finally arrived, he sat down and carefully unpacked his briefcase, which contained one thin file. Oddly, the file was covered with Dole banana stickers. From this file, he removed a single sheet of paper on which were written Chinese characters. He looked at each of us and said with great gravity, "I have discussed this matter with my client at length. And we have a proposal to resolve this matter."

He looked soberly at each of us in turn, prompting me to ask, "And what is it?"

"You will drop all charges against my client. And my client agrees to leave the United States and never return."

Brendan Cullen is a patient man. He did not say anything. His only response was to slowly turn a shade of red that I did not know existed in nature. On the whole, it was a remarkable display of self-discipline.

"Thanks for the offer," I said, "but no thanks."

I added that we were willing to dismiss some of the charges in exchange for Xiang Li's guilty plea to those remaining.

Xiang Li's New York lawyer said, "No, my client will not consider this."

We parted amiably. And then we raised the stakes. The plea deal Xiang Li had originally accepted required guilty pleas to the offenses we charged in the November 2010 indictment, which did not include Xiang Li's criminal conduct between November 2010 and the time of his arrest in June 2011. We filled that gap by presenting to a grand jury a superseding indictment for the entire period, charging four conspiracies (to circumvent a measure that protects copyrighted work, to traffic in access control circumvention services, to commit criminal copyright infringement, and to commit wire fraud). We also charged Xiang Li with the substantive counts of circumvention of a measure that protects copyrighted work, trafficking in access control circumvention services, criminal copyright infringement, interstate transportation of stolen property, smuggling, and wire fraud, as well as trafficking in counterfeit labels and packaging. With respect to the charges of interstate transportation of stolen property, I was still graciously willing to give the U.S. Supreme Court a chance to correct its holding in the *Dowling* case, the one involving the bootlegged recordings of Elvis Presley.

The superseding indictment returned by the grand jury in April 2012 covered a lot of ground. When we first indicted Xiang Li in November 2010, we had estimated the value of the cracked software sold by CRACK99 at over $100 million. The number was higher now by virtue of the software—worth over $5 million—that Xiang Li sold us in January 2011.

The software products we bought in January 2011, like the majority of CRACK99's software titles, were advanced and state-of-the-art, with a wide range of industrial applications. CST Studio Suite, for example, is electromagnetic simulation software, described by its manufacturer as "the culmination of many years of research and development into the most accurate and efficient computational solutions for electromagnetic designs." The software includes CST Microwave Studio, which is "the leading edge tool for the fast and accurate 3D simulation of high frequency devices and market leader in Time Domain simulation. It enables the fast and accurate analysis of antennas, filters, couplers, planar and multi-layer structures and SI and EMC effects etc." CST Studio Suite also includes CST EM Studio, which is a "tool for the design and analysis of static and low frequency EM applications such as motors, sensors, actuators, transformers, and shielding enclosures." CST Particle Studio "has been developed for the fully consistent simulation of free moving charged particles. Applications include electron guns, cathode ray tubes, magnetrons, and wake fields." This software is not for amateurs.

Among the software products we bought in January 2011 were ANSYS titles. One of them, ANSYS Multiphysics, is a product suite that:

> *allows engineers and designers to create virtual prototypes of their designs operating under real-world multiphysics conditions. As the range of need for simulation expands, companies must be able to accurately predict how complex products will behave in real-world environments, where multiple types of coupled physics interact. ANSYS multiphysics software enables engineers and scientists to simulate the interactions between structural mechanics, heat transfer, fluid flow and electromagnetics all within a single, unified engineering simulation environment.*

The National Institute of Standards and Technology used ANSYS simulation software in its analysis of the collapse of World Trade Center

Building 7 on September 11, 2001. It sells for around $58,000 to legiti-
mate buyers; Xiang Li sold it for about $100.

Another ANSYS product we bought from Xiang Li was HFSS,
which is described as:

> the industry-standard simulation tool for 3-D full-wave electromag-
> netic field simulation and is essential for the design of high-frequency
> and high-speed component design. HFSS offers multiple state-of-the-art
> solver technologies based on either the proven finite element method
> or the well-established integral equation method. . . . Engineers rely
> on the accuracy, capacity, and performance of HFSS to design high-
> speed components including on-chip embedded passives, IC packages,
> PCB interconnects and high-frequency components such as antennas,
> RF/microwave components and biomedical devices. With HFSS, engi-
> neers can extract scattering matrix parameters (S, Y, Z parameters),
> visualize 3-D electromagnetic fields (near- and far-field) and generate
> ANSYS Full-Wave SPICE models that link to circuit simulations. Signal
> integrity engineers use HFSS within established EDA design flows to
> evaluate signal quality, including transmission path losses, reflection
> loss due to impedance mismatches, parasitic coupling and radiation.

Unless you have a lot of experience in extracting scattering matrix
parameters or designing on-chip embedded passives, the usefulness
of HFSS software might not resonate. Suffice it to say, it is highly
advanced and didn't grow on a tree; HFSS is the result of the concerted labor of many innovators over many years. Xiang Li sold HFSS,
worth $49,000, for under $100.

Following the same pattern, Xiang Li sold Ansoft Designer 3.5, a
software product worth $25,000, for $40; Agilent Advanced Design
System 2008, worth $229,000, for $60; Matlab R2009B, Agilent System Vue2009.05, and OPNET Modeler 14.0, worth $150,000, $45,000,
and $25,000, respectively, for a total of $210. Comsol Multiphysics 4.0,

worth $270,000, went for $120. We continued to be stunned by the CRACK99 price discount—more than 99 percent. If Xiang Li was to be believed, he was able to sell at such steep discounts because of his low overhead: he claimed to obtain some software products at no cost, others at low cost. These valuable, proprietary, powerful software tools were plucked by Xiang Li from the Internet and then cast back in, ending up anywhere and everywhere.

With the superseding indictment in hand, we asked the court for a trial date, telling the judge we thought the trial would last three months. The judge scheduled it for March 2013. In a last-ditch effort, in December 2012, we gave Xiang Li one final chance: we would accept his guilty plea to one count each of conspiracy to commit criminal copyright infringement and conspiracy to commit wire fraud, with no credit for cooperation, exposing him to a maximum of twenty-five years of incarceration. We told his lawyer that if we didn't have a plea agreement by the end of December 2012, we would not be willing to consider any plea agreement at all. We were not about to go through the enormous effort of preparing for a three-month trial, only to give him a deal at the last minute.

In late December, I was in Baghdad on an unrelated matter, listening to the occasional report of distant small-arms fire on the far side of the T-walls surrounding the compound. During a long and active life, I have learned many things, and one of them is this: it is generally preferable for small-arms fire to be on the far side of T-walls. Unable to sleep, I checked my e-mail at about two in the morning. Through tired eyes, I read one message with particular interest. It was from Xiang Li's lawyer. There was a great deal of lawyerly blather but the bottom line was clear: Xiang Li had capitulated.

I forwarded the news to the United States Attorney. The next day, I received another e-mail, assigning me a payroll tax case against a businessman named Smith who didn't like paying payroll taxes. Many people feel this way. The difference between Smith and the others is that Smith didn't pay them. The case was not exactly an epic challenge of monumental consequence. But it was easy.

On January 7, 2013, Xiang Li went to court to enter his guilty plea. A guilty plea hearing normally lasts an hour at most. This one went on for three hours. We had filed a written statement of facts beforehand, with the idea that it would expedite matters. We were wrong. As Ed McAndrew and I took turns reading from the statement of facts, we outpaced the Mandarin interpreter. This was not a good thing inasmuch as the central purpose of the hearing was to ensure Xiang Li's guilty plea was knowing, voluntary, and intelligent. In order to be certain he understood everything we were saying, we had to stop repeatedly to let the interpreter catch up.

Then there were the interpreter's questions. I would say, "In February 2008, Defendant registered the domain names for www.crack99 .com, www.cad100.net, and www.dongle-crack-download.com," and the interpreter would ask, "Excuse me, what is dongle?" Interestingly, Xiang Li explained this one to the interpreter. Ed would say, "In January 2010, undercover agents purchased a pirated copy of Satellite Tool Kit 8.0 . . . ," and the interpreter would ask, "Satellite Tool Kit?" Xiang Li explained this one to him as well, demonstrating that Xiang Li's plea was knowing, voluntary, and intelligent.

A guilty plea hearing is always something of a letdown; after the thrill of the chase, the defendant throws in the towel and says, in effect, Yup, I did it.

This is the way the world ends
Not with a bang but a whimper.

But our work was not yet done.

12 | THE AMERICANS

DUBAI'S OLD SOUK IS LIKE AN organic being: it has its own pulse
and rhythm, its own set of permissions and demands; it has decided
moods and mores. Its location at the junction of the Khor Dubai and
Port Rashid is no accident. You can stand anywhere in the vast port
and watch through the haze as cargo ships come and go and dhows
set out for Iran across the Persian Gulf, which Arabs call the Ara-
bian Gulf. It's a complicated place, but commerce is fairly straightfor-
ward: supply moves to demand. The dhows are filled with everything
from spices and textiles to GE microwaves and U.S. military avionics.
Dubai is a transshipment point, a port where cargo changes direction and becomes invisible to its country of origin. For this reason,
Iranian importers—including arms dealers—use Dubai for transship-
ping U.S.-origin goods. The export declaration in the United States
will identify the cargo's destination as Dubai, which is true in so far
as it goes; but the ultimate destination is actually Bandar Abbas. Utilizing Dubai in this way gives cover to U.S. suppliers and exporters;
they can say they didn't know. Sometimes that's true and sometimes
it's not. As a result, Dubai is a monument to the failure of the United
States to control the proliferation of its own goods and technology.

Western progress from mechanical to digital technology, and the accompanying miniaturization of digital components, has compounded the problem. Amir Ardebili's enterprise was a case in point. He trans-shipped U.S. weapons components through an Emirati front company, utilizing the port of Dubai. Among the components he procured for the Iranian government was the phase shifter, a tiny microchip—smaller than a fingernail—that is a critical component in phased array radar. The U.S. Navy's Aegis system employs phased array radar to acquire multiple targets simultaneously. This is an example of technology acting as a combat force multiplier: a ship freed of the constraint of one missile per fire-control radar becomes a fleet. It doesn't take much imagination to see why Iran would desire such technology: in combat against the U.S. Fifth Fleet in the Persian Gulf, phased array radar would improve the warfare capabilities of Iranian forces, diminishing the U.S. technological advantage. All the products procured by Arde-bili went to Iran, but there is nothing about Dubai as a transshipment point that is limited to Iran. Once goods are in the port of Dubai, they can go anywhere: Iran, North Korea, China, or any other adversary of the United States.

Intangible technology like software doesn't even require a trans-shipment point. It can go anywhere at any time without regard to ports, shipping routes, or export paperwork. And it can end up in very strange places, as we saw when we pursued Xiang Li's cus-tomers, hundreds of them all over the world. The mysterious acqui-sition by Nasir in Syria of the simulation software ANSYS Ansoft Simplorer is just one example. It might be that Nasir's intentions were benign and he was just looking for a bargain; it might be his intentions were nefarious and that simulation software is now in the hands of al-Qaeda—which is known to have utilized flight simula-tion software in preparing for the 9/11 attacks. Or perhaps Nasir was running his own Syrian version of CRACK99 and sold the Ansoft Simplorer software to a third party, beginning the proliferation cycle anew. This is the nature of technology proliferation: when control is lost, it is lost forever.

Although CRACK99's customers were seemingly everywhere, Xiang Li's e-mails showed that a large proportion of customers were in the United States. This struck me as strangely circular: a Chinese national in China acquires stolen U.S. technology and sells it back to customers in the United States. Why was this? Why would consumers in the United States be acquiring such high-technology industrial-grade software from CRACK99 when it is readily available in the legitimate marketplace?

One obvious answer is price: CRACK99 sold its products at pennies on the dollar, a true bargain, if an illegal one. But that did not solve the mystery. The kind of software CRACK99 sold was not ordinary consumer software, such as Microsoft Word or Adobe Reader, or software used for entertainment, like video games. CRACK99's software did not have wide demographic appeal. To the contrary, it was useful only in a narrow and rarified bandwidth of the market, in cutting-edge engineering applications in advanced industries, such as the aerospace and aviation sectors. People who are employed by large companies like Boeing and Lockheed and their many subcontractors and suppliers have access to advanced software in the ordinary course of business; they do not need to buy pirated software from CRACK99. And they have a particular incentive not to do so: it is well known that pirated software contains malware that not only can cause the software to malfunction, but also can infect entire networks. The cost savings resulting from buying cracked software from CRACK99 is not worth the risk to a big company.

This was our operating assumption, but could we be wrong? Having identified hundreds of U.S. customers who had purchased software from CRACK99, we were now in a position to answer this question. Who, after all, were the U.S. customers of CRACK99? As a first step, Brendan Cullen sent leads to HSI offices all over the country, provid-

ing the information we had and requesting further investigation. Each
lead represented a potential prosecution, depending on where the evidence led. It might be that some of the people who bought pirated
software from CRACK99 had innocent explanations, but it was hard to
imagine that was true for the majority. For one thing, they bought the
software from a website called CRACK99. That is called a clue. And
as we had seen from his e-mails, Xiang Li was open about explaining
the cracking process to his customers. More than that, many of the
customers had required Xiang Li's personal attention in applying the
crack, as we had. When you spend that much time applying a crack,
the claim that you didn't know you were dealing with cracked software is not particularly credible. As a result, I expected Cullen's leads
to result in a large number of arrests across the United States.

Like me, Cullen is an optimistic person. But he was not naive.
He knew that collateral leads are usually not assigned to the busiest
agents, who are already occupied with their own investigations. The
leads tend to go to the less busy agents, who might be less busy for a
reason. So, to increase the probability that these leads would actually
be pursued, Cullen did something astonishing: he wrote up search
warrant affidavits and sent them to the agents assigned the leads. In
other words, Cullen did the heavy lifting for them.

The problem with being an optimist is you are frequently disappointed. The response to Cullen's CRACK99 leads replicated the
results from the leads generated after Ardebili's arrest: nothing. There
were no new arrests, only the ones we made. I don't know the reason
for this. It could be lazy agents on the receiving end of the leads, or it
could be lazy AUSAs turning down referrals from enthusiastic agents.
What I do know is that no one on the receiving end of the leads was
being encouraged to pursue them. And in the end, only the CRACK99
team itself developed spin-off cases resulting from the investigation.

Xiang Li's e-mails revealed that one of his best customers was an
American named Wronald Scott Best, a resident of Owensboro, Ken-

tucky. In case you are wondering about the name Wronald, Best contended that "Wronald" is the correct spelling for the name the rest of us spell "Ronald." This tells you something about Best: he is right and the rest of us are wrong.

Between November 2008 and June 2009, Best exchanged over 260 e-mails with Xiang Li and acquired ten pirated software programs, used in electric engineering, aerospace engineering, telecommunications design, and electronic design automation. Best communicated with Xiang Li using the e-mail account mister.peabody1@gmail.com. I had to explain to the younger agents who "Mister Peabody" was. If you don't know, Mister Peabody was a cartoon beagle featured on *The Bullwinkle Show* in the early 1960s. Mister Peabody was the most intelligent being in the known universe. No doubt like Mr. Best.

Best's first communication with Xiang Li was a request for assistance. Best had acquired a cracked version of CST Studio Suite 2008 from Shooters, an Internet group involved in the theft and distribution of stolen software. It was an earlier version of the software we bought from CRACK99 in January 2011. But Best couldn't get his version of CST Studio Suite to operate properly. In his e-mail to Xiang Li, Best attached a fourteen-page document explaining in a methodical, step-by-step manner—including "screen shot" images—how he had tried to install the pirated software provided to him by Shooters. Best wanted to know where he was going wrong in the installation.

The screen shots benefitted us greatly, showing us the directory structure of Best's personal computer, which featured folders with names like "DFAS Letters" and "NATO Specialist Meeting." "DFAS" stands for Defense Finance and Accounting Service—the component of the U.S. Defense Department in charge of payroll. Like the website name CRACK99, these folder names qualified as clues, and they led us to the conclusion that we might be dealing with someone in the defense industry. And this turned out to be the case: Best was an engineer who had been employed by the U.S. Navy's Surface Warfare Center in Indiana until 2008. After that, he was employed by MPD, a conglomerate of five companies providing military and law enforcement customers with services relating to communications and radar.

There were other clues too, such as a folder called "New House in Owensboro" and "W. Scott Best's Documents." These latter folders were like finding a fingerprint; it would be hard for W. Scott Best, resident of Owensboro, to deny he was the author of the e-mail to Xiang Li after including these screen shots. I was wondering if the Mister Peabody analogy was apt.

Best ended up solving his problem with CST Studio Suite 2008 by buying a cracked copy of the same software from Xiang Li in November 2008. This one worked. In addition, Best bought six other cracked software products: ADS 2008, ANSYS Multiphysics, Mathematica 6.0.3, Autodesk Investor 2008, ANSYS Service Pack I, Genesys Eagleware 2008.07. He asked Xiang Li to deliver the software files via FTP.

Xiang Li said he would prefer to mail a "DVD-R" containing the software, and he requested Best's mailing address. Best replied:

Mailing a DVD-R is not a secure method for transfering these programs, and it violates a number of international laws. A FTP transfer is much easier and faster, and provides some level of security for both of us. Lets do it by FTP one program at a time, OK?

Best's desire to use FTP as the transfer medium to avoid detection by law enforcement told us that Best—like Xiang Li—knew he was involved in an illegal transaction. This would, I thought, be a useful fact to emphasize at his future trial.

On November 24, 2008, Xiang Li told Best that the FTP method would not be possible because the software files were too large, and sought to pacify Best thus: "Please be assured that I have chosen the method is safe." Best asked Xiang Li what shipping service he would use, and Xiang Li said he would use China Post. Best then asked Xiang Li, "And how do you avoid problems? . . . How many times have you done this without problems?" Xiang Li assured him, "Believe me. I at least once a week." Best ended the discussion by writing, "OK, so lets try it."

Best paid by means of a Western Union transfer to Chengdu, China, just as we had. He provided Xiang Li with his home address, and on December 3, 2008, wrote that a package of seven DVDs arrived in the mail the day before. In the same e-mail, Best asked technical questions about the software programs. Xiang Li promptly answered the questions. You have to hand it to Xiang Li: he was all about customer service.

Best was a satisfied customer, and the day after receiving the package of eight cracked software programs, he wrote to Xiang Li requesting more: this time, cracked versions of the ANSYS HFSS and Maxwell software programs. ANSYS HFSS was one of the software programs we bought from Xiang Li in January 2011. ANSYS describes it as "the industry-standard simulation tool for 3-D full-wave electromagnetic field simulation . . . essential for the design of high-frequency and high-speed component design." Given the nature of the HFSS software, we wondered if Best was using it in the course of his employment with MPD. Likewise, we wondered how he was using ANSYS's Maxwell program, which the manufacturer describes as follows:

ANSYS Maxwell is the premier electromagnetic field simulation software for engineers tasked with designing and analyzing 3-D and 2-D electromagnetic and electromechanical devices, including motors, actuators, transformers, sensors and coils. Maxwell uses the accurate finite element method to solve static, frequency-domain, and time-varying electromagnetic and electric fields. A key benefit of ANSYS Maxwell is its automated solution process, for which you are required to specify only geometry, material properties and the desired output. From this point, Maxwell automatically generates an appropriate, efficient and accurate mesh for solving the problem.

Since MPD was a defense contractor, we were concerned about the use of these cracked software products in developing military components. Compounding this concern was evidence that Best had been buying pirated software for a long time. He told Xiang Li, "I have used these codes for over 10 years, so I have a lot of work that I cannot access without the codes. This is why I have patiently been looking for a solution. I have paid people for solutions and received nothing in return, so I have lost both money and time." This statement assured us we were not catching Best on a bad day; his involvement with pirated software was sustained and systematic—and apparently related to his engineering work. But it begged the question, why did he have to buy software from CRACK99, rather than having his employer buy it legitimately from ANSYS?

Further to his December request for ANSYS HFSS and Maxwell software, Best wrote a series of e-mails to Xiang Li starting on January 15, 2009, about how to acquire the most current versions: HFSS 11.1.3 and Maxwell 12.1. Best seemed to be taunting Xiang Li, saying he had communicated with other pirated software suppliers who claimed to be able to crack the most recent editions. Xiang Li wrote back, telling Best that the other software vendors were deceiving him. According to Xiang Li, cracks of the most current versions were not available anywhere. Best responded by sending Xiang Li web links to several different Chinese websites offering the cracked Maxwell 12.1 software and requested Xiang Li's help in acquiring it. This, I thought, was an interesting move on Best's part: there was no reason why Best could not deal with these Chinese vendors directly, and Xiang Li had no particular advantage in acquiring the cracked software just because he was in China. Best was trying to transfer the risk of acquisition to Xiang Li. If Xiang Li got burned by his fellow Chinese pirates, it would be sad indeed; but Best would be unharmed.

Xiang Li was not fooled. When Best asked Xiang Li if he had any experience working with the Chinese cracked software vendors he had identified, Xiang Li responded that Best should not trust these companies. Evidently sensing that Best was playing one Chinese vendor against the other, Xiang Li asked Best not to share information about CRACK99 with anyone else. Best agreed: "I trust you, so you are my sounding board concerning honesty and integrity for others in your business. I will not share your information with others since we have had a good working relationship." So far as we could tell, Best kept his word.

In the end, Xiang Li managed to supply Best's needs, providing him with current cracked versions of HFSS 11.1.1 and Maxwell 12.0, as well as an updated CST Studio Suite 2009.

Over time, Best seemed to warm up to Xiang Li. On April 23, 2009, he sent Xiang Li an e-mail attaching a seventeen-page document providing a detailed account—once again including screen shots—of how he had installed his newly acquired cracked CST Studio Suite 2009 software. Best did not charge for this information, apparently providing it to Xiang Li as a professional courtesy.

The screen shots in Best's installation instructions contained CST's copyright warning: "This program is protected by copyright law and international treaties." Part of the procedure outlined by Best required clicking a button entitled "I accept the terms in the license agreement," which followed this statement:

This software and documentation may not be copied, reproduced, disclosed, transferred, or reduced to any form, including electronic medium or machine-readable form, or transmitted or publicly performed by any means, electronic or otherwise, unless CST consents in writing. It is strictly prohibited to reverse engineer, decompile, or disassemble the software.

This was a powerful fact for us. In the face of this evidence, Best would be hard-pressed to convince a jury he didn't understand he was buying pirated software.

The screen shots in the April 23, 2009, e-mail offered another benefit to us as well. Like the screen shots Best had sent Xiang Li in 2008, these showed Best's desktop screen, including folders with titles relating to software programs such as ADS, Agilent, Ansoft, Autodesk, MATLAB, CST, Cadence, Genesys, and HFSS. Best also had folders with titles such as "XIANG LI krak" and "Shooters." I can't imagine the real Mister Peabody being so careless.

In total, Best bought the following cracked software from CRACK99, valued at $609,000:

Date	Program	Retail Value
November 21, 2008	CST Studio Suite 2008	$75,000
November 23, 2008	ADS 2008	$228,000
November 23, 2008	ANSYS Multiphysics	$58,000
November 23, 2008	Mathematica 6.0.3	$5,000
November 23, 2008	Autodesk Inventor 2008	$7,000
December 19, 2008	ANSYS Service Pack I	$48,000
January 5, 2009	Genesys Eagleware 2008.07	$29,000
January 21, 2009	Ansoft HFSS 11.1.1	$49,000
February 28, 2009	Maxwell 12.0	$35,000
April 23, 2009	CST Studio Suite 2009	$75,000
Total		$609,000

All of this, we discerned from reviewing Xiang Li's e-mails. The next step was to obtain a search warrant for Best's Mister Peabody e-mail account. We did so on June 1, 2011, the day before departing for Saipan. And when I say "we," I mean Ed McAndrew. The results were significant. Here is a summary prepared by Brendan Cullen of what the Best e-mail search warrant ultimately showed:

- *BEST communicated with individuals at over thirty-five different e-mail addresses about cracked software.*

- *In total, BEST purchased or received over sixty (60) pirated software programs from various Chinese, Russian and Ukrainian sources of cracked software.*

- *BEST made financial transfers totaling over $6,000 to these foreign-based cracked software vendors for software products and technical software installation instructions.*

- *BEST also provided legitimate software and software licenses to his cracked software sources and requested that they crack the license files associated with these software programs.*

- *Several of the software license files that BEST provided to his illegitimate Russian sources were derived from his employer MPD, Inc. BEST did this to assist these foreign-based software hackers in the cracking or disabling of these legitimate software license files.*

- *BEST mostly obtained cracked software over shared access to FTP sites. In these cases, BEST made payments to his illegitimate software source and was given a logon and password allowing him access to the foreign controlled FTP space containing the stored cracked software files.*

- *BEST also obtained cracked software programs from various vendors through downloads from file sharing websites. . . . These download links generally require passwords to access the files.*

- *In total, the cracked software illegally acquired by BEST from 2008 through May 2011, has an estimated retail value exceeding $2,000,000.*

Best's e-mails revealed extensive communication with a Russian cracker who will be referred to as "Russian Cracker" because his real name cannot be used here. Russian Cracker was connected to a global network of other international cybercriminals. His communications—like those with Xiang Li—struck us as peer-to-peer communications between fellow professionals. For example, on March 26, 2009, Best coached Russian Cracker about how to avoid detection when cracking software. Best specifically warned Russian Cracker that a particular simulation software product had an access control feature that could alert the manufacturer to unauthorized use. "Be very careful when using [the] software. The program likes to send e-mail messages to [the manufacturer] regarding your simulations. . . . They are provided with your IP address and e-mail address using this subroutine . . . [which] allows [them] to keep track of kraked software as well as legitimate versions of the software. Be cautious."

Best was a true team player when it came to the global software-cracking enterprise. On April 6, 2009, he e-mailed Russian Cracker his instructions for installing the cracked version of CST Studio Suite 2009 that he had acquired from Xiang Li. Best told Russian Cracker he could forward the instructions on to his other cracked software customers: "Feel free to use this Installation Procedure document for distribution to others who need to know how to install the code. My name should be removed from the last file that I sent to you." Best didn't charge for this service; consistent with his dealings with Xiang Li, he provided these instructions to aid the cause of software cracking. Best appeared to feel he was part of a movement to free software from the constraints of private ownership. As Ed McAndrew would later put it, Best's communications with Russian Cracker were "infused with tones of seemingly philosophical devotion to the crime of cracking."

Best provided Russian Cracker with software to which he had legitimate access—through his employer—so it could be cracked. We could not tell from the e-mails exactly why he was doing this, but he probably wanted to be free of the license file restrictions. Typically, license files have set parameters, including date limits and a single assigned IP address where the software can be used. Best might have been eliminating these limitations to make it easier to use the software whenever and wherever he wanted to, for example, so he could work from home. Or he might have wanted the license files disabled so he could distribute the software to others. We really couldn't tell.

But we did know that Best provided Russian Cracker with licensed software for the purpose of cracking the licensing file. In May 2009, Best uploaded a number of advanced engineering and simulation software programs to an FTP site controlled by Russian Cracker for this purpose. Best did the same in April and May 2011, when he legitimately acquired three-dimensional analysis and visualization software through his employer and sent it to Russian Cracker to be cracked. Best's conduct answered one of the questions that had long troubled us in the CRACK99 investigation: How do crackers get access to licensing software to crack? The answer is that it comes from a wide range of sources, including users like Best who have access to legitimate versions.

Best was only too happy to provide Russian Cracker with the raw material to ply his trade, leaving further distribution entirely to Russian Cracker. All, however, was not perfect between Best and Russian Cracker. They had some squabbles. In November 2010, Best complained about Russian Cracker's request that he be paid $100 for his cracking efforts. Russian Cracker responded by reminding Best of the actual estimated retail value of the cracked HFSS software Russian Cracker had given Best for free: "For info : HFSS by ANSYS-ANSOFT 75 000 USD and more."

Best was very specific about his software requirements. He repeatedly requested that Russian Cracker provide him with a cracked version of ATK Magic 2D or 3D software, which is used in the design of electromagnetic devices for both military and civilian purposes. On July 29, 2009, Russian Cracker e-mailed Best a download link to a cracked version, commenting that bypassing the licensing file of ATK Magic was "a hard job."

Best could be demanding. Even after receiving ATK Magic 7.43 software, he pressed Russian Cracker for updated versions of ATK Magic 2D or 3D. Russian Cracker expressed his reluctance to transfer the updated software to Best because it "has limitations for the export." This was true: some modules of ATK Magic required a license for export. Best complained that Russian Cracker was being too fussy: "It is used around the world." But Russian Cracker continued to resist: "Magic is the export-controlled program and cannot be officially set in Russia." Best was unimpressed: "Magik is used in both Russia and China, so it exists at several universities and national labs." Of course, Russian Cracker had the better argument. The fact that ATK Magic had been illegally disseminated to Russia and China did not mean he and Best were immune from prosecution for illegally trafficking in it.

There were other problems between Best and Russian Cracker as well. Several cracked programs that Russian Cracker transmitted to Best contained malicious code. On May 29, 2009, for instance, after receiving a pirated Ansoft program from Russian Cracker, Best complained, "You are distributing a virus in every .exe file. Who wrote these patches?" On September 22, 2009, after receiving cracking software from Russian Cracker, Best wrote, "There is a Trojan Horse virus in the keygen.exe file. Can you remove or disable the Trojan Horse so I can use the keygen.exe file?" (A "keygen" is a program used to generate a license key to operate licensed software.) On April 13, 2010, Russian Cracker sent Best another corrupted file included in links to the Adobe Creative Suite 5 Master Collection. Best wrote back, "There is a really nasty Trojan in these DVD ISO files. Why did you install a Trojan?" But none of this stopped Best from continuing to deal with Russian Cracker.

Best's e-mails were damning. They demonstrated that he was one of the best customers of CRACK99 and that he was actively involved in trafficking cracked software with others on a global scale. The next step was to utilize this evidence to obtain search warrants for Best's home and workplace, with the objective of seizing his computers and storage devices. Once we obtained the evidence showing Best logging on to the mister.peabody1@gmail.com e-mail account at an IP address assigned to his home address in Owensboro, Kentucky, Brendan Cullen went to Kentucky and obtained a search warrant.

In addition to the home address, Brendan obtained a warrant for Best's workplace. The workplace situation was disturbing. We had determined that Best was employed as "Chief Scientist" at MPD, whose customers included the U.S. military, avionics manufacturers, and law enforcement organizations. MPD develops and manufactures microwave transmitters and transceivers, vacuum electron devices, precision ceramic/metal and metal components, and sensors, as well as radar equipment for law enforcement agencies. The company states that it "has been a leader in the law enforcement radar market for more than twenty-five years . . . pioneer[ing] many of the features that have become standard on modern radars, including three-window displays, dual antennas, and directional radar technology." One of the military platforms MPD supported was the U.S. Army's Black Hawk helicopter. Another was Marine One, the helicopter that transports the President. Best could do a lot of damage in a place like MPD.

Ed McAndrew and I contacted MPD. We were concerned about the intersection of Best's illegal activities and his professional life. MPD's answer was short and sweet: whatever Best was doing in the area of software piracy was not authorized by MPD. To the contrary, it was expressly forbidden. The company provided us with documentation showing that as an MPD employee, Best executed a "Software Code of Ethics" on July 28, 2008, which required him to "use software only in accordance with the license agreement." It can safely be said that Best violated that standard. The MPD Software Code of Ethics also states:

> *MPD will not tolerate the use of any unauthorized copies of software at the company. Any person illegally reproducing software can be subject to civil and criminal penalties including fines and imprisonment. MPD does not condone illegal copying of software under any circumstances and anyone who makes, uses, or otherwise acquires unauthorized software shall be appropriately disciplined.*

Best had been warned.

Although we were satisfied that Best was conducting his illegal activities without the knowledge or approval of MPD, we were nevertheless concerned. Cracked software is not reliable and puts computer networks at high risk of malware infection. We had no doubt, based on Best's e-mails, that he was using cracked software in connection with his work, and we wondered how this might have affected the quality of MPD's products. Given the nature of the company's work, this was troubling to say the least. So we wanted to get access to Best's computer at MPD.

On November 15, 2011, at approximately 6:15 a.m., Cullen and other HSI special agents, accompanied by Owensboro police officers, executed a search warrant at MPD. They thought they would be getting there before Best, but Best—an early riser—was sitting at his desk. The agents seized his work devices (two computers, one external hard drive, and five flash drives), and fifteen minutes after arriving, Cullen verbally advised Best of his constitutional rights. Best waived his right to remain silent and said he would like to make a statement. Cullen then asked Best if he understood why the agents were searching his office, and Best said he did. Cullen told Best they would be searching his home next and asked if he would like to accompany them. He said he would.

At Best's house, HSI agents seized four computers, four external hard drives, one computer server, one flash drive, and 179 CD/DVDs. While Cullen's fellow agents conducted the search, Cullen and Best resumed their conversation. Best said he had worked for several different companies as an electrical engineer, including DuPont and the Naval Surface Warfare Center in Crane, Indiana, before working for MPD, starting in 2008. He said that when he worked for the Navy, he had a secret security clearance and worked as a "microwave engineer." During that employment, Best used $500,000 worth of computer software programs, including Ansoft Designer and ANSYS HFSS, Ephysics, and Multiphysics. Best said his career with the Navy ended when his security clearance was revoked because he married a foreign national.

At MPD, Best said, he worked on a number of different projects, including revamping MPD's magnetron product line, Patriot missile components, police radars, and police breath-analysis equipment. Best admitted to using cracked software for many years, including during his time at MPD. He said—oddly—that he used the illegal software to stay abreast of technological advances. He also used it in connection with his work at MPD, including redesigning the cathode for the Black Hawk helicopter. Best said he used cracked software due to constraints MPD had imposed on him. For example, he said that MPD did not believe in computer-aided modeling when designing its products, preferring a trial-and-error approach. Consequently, Best claimed, MPD did not provide him enough server space to conduct computer software simulation at work, so he downloaded the pirated software to perform these functions at home, a claim MPD would emphatically deny. There was a glimmer of good news in Best's claim: he wasn't using the illegally obtained software at the MPD facility, thus reducing the chance of malware infection of the company's network. On the other hand, he was using the software for work-related purposes, which made us concerned about the reliability of Best's output. Ultimately, we did not find evidence that Best's use of cracked software affected MPD's products.

Cullen showed Best printouts of his e-mails with Xiang Li and Russian Cracker. Best confirmed that the Mister Peabody e-mail account was his, and that he was the person who sent the e-mails. He admitted to receiving cracked software from foreign-based vendors, usually by FTP. Best said he no longer dealt with Xiang Li. We already knew this, of course, because Xiang Li had been in custody since June.

As for Russian Cracker, Best said he did not know if he did the cracking himself or had someone else do it for him. Cullen showed Best an e-mail exchange with Russian Cracker about cracking a software program. Best explained that he had obtained a legitimate trial license of the software through MPD, and sent it to Russian Cracker for cracking. Best said he wanted to use the software on a modeling project to optimize a design for an antenna that he was working on for MPD. His goal was to eliminate the trial license's time limitation. But he never did provide a satisfactory explanation as to why he didn't just acquire a licensed version of the software legitimately through MPD, suggesting again his seeming "philosophical" devotion to cracking.

Cullen asked Best about the export-controlled ATK Magic software he obtained from Russian Cracker: Why was he so interested? Best said he wanted it because it is the best software on the market, describing it as the "gold standard" in the field of microwave tube simulation. Again, Best claimed his focus was on obtaining the software he needed to perform his engineering work at MPD. But we had to wonder. He seemed to prefer cracked software to licensed software.

After executing the search warrants, Brendan advised Best to have a lawyer call Ed and me about the case. Best did so promptly, and we soon had a plea agreement in place. We charged Best with conspiring with Xiang Li to commit criminal copyright infringement, and he pled guilty on March 30, 2012. It was all very cordial.

That changed as we approached sentencing. That's when things started to go sideways. Gone was the contrite Best who admitted his crimes to the agents. Confronted with the likelihood of a prison sentence, Best became defiant. His crime, he contended, had caused no harm; it was victimless, if you really thought about it. This is what they all say: I didn't really cause any harm because the software company didn't lose a sale; I never would have purchased a legitimate licensed version of the software. It is a laughably self-serving argument because it is impossible to prove or disprove. But more than that, it is irrelevant. By purchasing cracked software from CRACK99, Best was supporting an illegal enterprise that was dispensing U.S. software programs globally at pennies on the dollar, an activity clearly harmful to the owners of the copyrights. The software belonged to others and had been taken without permission. Best knew this, and bought the pirated software anyway. And the stolen property Best purchased was worth quite a bit of money: $2.3 million in total, $609,000 from Xiang Li alone. Aggravating Best's offense was the fact that he used the pirated software to work on computer simulations involving military helicopters, Patriot missile components, and radar equipment.

More than that, Best was not only a consumer of cracked software. He was also an active participant in international software-cracking schemes, interacting with thirty-five different crackers throughout the world by our count. He provided software he had obtained from MPD to Russian Cracker, who would then crack it and distribute it as he saw fit. The effect of this activity was to release technology, developed by U.S. companies at great expense, into what Ed McAndrew described as the "wilds" of the Internet, a domain untamed, for good or ill, a place where information can be used by anyone at any time for any purpose whatever.

Best's work on Marine One illustrates the point: no one is safe from software piracy, not even the President of the United States.

The pernicious effects of software piracy were illustrated not only

by the Best case but also by that of another American customer of
Xiang Li: Cosburn Wedderburn, an electrical engineer for NASA with
a computer engineering business on the side. From 2008 through
2010, Wedderburn purchased twelve different high-end pirated software programs from Xiang Li worth over $1 million. Like the case
against Best, our evidence against Wedderburn came primarily from
Xiang Li's e-mails.

It all started on September 3, 2008, when Wedderburn sent an
e-mail to Xiang Li: "I need Ansoft designer/nexium. . . . How much
does it cost? Will it come with the license or key generator? Do you
take credit cards American express?" The e-mail was signed, "Cosburn." This is the sort of slipup that interests me. Wedderburn is one
of those fifty-pound-brain engineering types, and yet he used his real
name in communicating with a software pirate in China. It goes to
prove two points: first, even fifty-pound brains can do dumb things,
and second, no one is afraid of getting caught when they're buying
pirated software.

The software Wedderburn wanted was Ansoft Designer 3.5, a complex telecommunications simulation software program that allows
users to precisely model and simulate highly accurate radio frequen-
cies and to create radio signal integrity. It is manufactured by ANSYS
and retailed for approximately $25,000. Xiang Li charged only $40.
He e-mailed instructions to Wedderburn on how to send the money
via Western Union, just like the instructions he had sent us. Once
the money was received, Xiang Li provided Wedderburn with web
links to download the software. One of the links included the word
"Crack," another useful tidbit from my point of view as a prosecutor
weighing how this would look to a jury. After successfully download-
ing the software, Wedderburn sent Xiang Li an e-mail: "Thanks! You
are my Friends for ever."

Wedderburn was a satisfied customer, like Best and so many other
purchasers of CRACK99 products. On September 11, 2008, friend-

for-life Wedderburn sent another e-mail: "I need Agilent Advanced Design System 2008 update 1 for windows/pc $60 [and] Modelsim SE 6.3d for windows/pc $80. . . . Can you send all example files and manuals for both software packages?" The first requested software, Agilent Advanced Design System 2008, is electronic design automation software for radio frequency, microwave, and signal integrity applications. Developed by Agilent Technologies, the software program retailed for approximately $229,000. The second requested software, ModelSim SE 6.3d, is simulation software for circuit board design and debugging design blocks. It is manufactured by Mentor Graphics, with a retail price of approximately $19,000.

Xiang Li did as requested and provided both software programs—after receiving Wedderburn's money.

On September 20, 2008, Wedderburn sent another e-mail requesting "Ansoft HFSS 10 Electromagnetic simulation for windows/pc $80 . . . [and] Ansoft SiWave 3.0 for windows/pc $50." Wedderburn asked, "Can you send me all example files and manuals for both software packages?" These two software products—Ansoft SIwave 3.0 and HFSS—are made by ANSYS. HFSS, which Best and the undercover agent Robert had also purchased, is used for "3-D full-wave electromagnetic field simulation." SIwave 3.0 is used for "power integrity, signal integrity and [electro-magnetic interference] analysis of electronic packages and [printed circuit boards]" and is employed in the defense, aerospace, telecommunications, energy, and electronics industries. SIwave 3.0 retailed for about $10,000. Xiang Li was happy to oblige Wedderburn upon payment, and promptly sent the links to download both software programs.

Wedderburn was really on a roll that month. On September 21—the day after he ordered the two other ANSYS products—Wedderburn placed an order for Ansoft Nexxim for $50, sending the money by Western Union. Ansoft Nexxim is a circuit simulation engine and analysis software program for microprocessors and advanced communications systems. The program was manufactured by ANSYS, and its retail value was approximately $25,000.

Wedderburn was so happy with CRACK99 that on October 27, he referred a friend: "I told my friend about your software products and he is interested in buying some of your products." Strangely, however, after the flurry of activity in September, Wedderburn waited until September 2009 to make his next purchase. On September 16, he e-mailed Xiang Li: "I need Agilent Systemvue 2009.5." Apparently, Xiang Li forgot they were "Friends for ever," because he did not respond immediately. After not hearing from Xiang Li for two days, on September 18, Wedderburn plaintively asked, "What happened, you are not responding to any of my messages. Did I do something wrong to you? I really need your products. Please contact me. I have the money." Feelings apparently get hurt in the cracked software business, like any other.

Agilent SystemVue 2009.05 is an electronic design automation software program that aids in the development of wireless, defense, and aerospace communications systems. It sells for approximately $45,000 in the legitimate market. Xiang Li replied to Wedderburn's request for SystemVue software by asking for Wedderburn's mailing address, explaining that the files were large and promising to mail a DVD containing seven gigabytes of data. Wedderburn replied that he needed not only the Agilent SystemVue software but also two more: OPNET Modeler 14.0 and Matlab R2009b.

OPNET Modeler 14.0 is a program for the analysis and design of communication networks, frequently used in military applications. Produced by OPNET Technologies, it had a retail value of approximately $25,000. Matlab R2009b is a program widely utilized in technical computing, system modeling, data analysis, algorithm development, and digital signal processing. Used in the defense, energy, and aerospace industries, it was developed by MathWorks and sold for approximately $130,000.

Wedderburn wired $210 to pay for the three pirated software programs. On September 19, Wedderburn provided Xiang Li with a post office box in Hanover, Maryland, and asked imploringly how long he would have to wait: "When i receive it I buy more software from you. I trust you please dont let me down." Xiang Li was reassuring: "need 1–2 weeks to your hands Please be patient. And always trust in our services." It sounded somehow familiar.

On September 22, Wedderburn placed an order with Xiang Li for Analytical Graphics STK 8.1.1 and wired $1,000 in payment. I continued to be impressed by the widespread demand for STK software; everyone seemed to want it. On September 23, Xiang Li sent the links to download those files. On September 24, Wedderburn complained that "the crack does not work." Xiang Li promised to help him, and on September 28, he provided a link that appeared to solve the problem.

Using this information from the Xiang Li e-mails, we obtained an e-mail search warrant for Cosburn Wedderburn's account. We saw a great deal of activity in the account that appeared to relate to an engineering services business he was running on the side. For example, Wedderburn received an e-mail from a company regarding a future project, asking if he had experience working with COMSOL software. Subsequently, on October 25, 2010, Wedderburn contacted CRACK99 to request COMSOL Multiphysics 4.0 software, sending $120 on October 27. The same day, Xiang Li sent five links to access the COMSOL software. We concluded that Wedderburn was using cracked software in his side business, but continued to wonder if he was using it with his primary employer, NASA. We were also concerned about whether Wedderburn's communications with Xiang Li—some of which were conducted from his NASA workstation—might have infected NASA's network with malware. Ultimately, NASA told us that its network had not been infected.

We discerned from Wedderburn's e-mails that the project for

which he would need COMSOL related to the Chinese company Huawei Technologies, which had requested a "thermal simulation." Wedderburn was not hired directly by Huawei but by an intermediate Canadian company. On November 8, Wedderburn e-mailed his customer in Canada to say he would need to obtain "INVENTOR 3D files" to complete this project, and on November 19, he sent Xiang Li $110 via Western Union for that software. On November 21, Xiang Li sent Wedderburn the links.

On November 29, Wedderburn advised his customer that the project was taking longer than expected because of the slow process of importing files into COMSOL and Inventor, complaining that the 32-bit version of COMSOL was too slow. He then e-mailed Xiang Li to ask if he could provide him with a 64-bit version of COMSOL software, which would be faster.

The project for Huawei eventually fizzled out. But the indirect link between Wedderburn and Huawei was troubling. Huawei is a large Chinese telecommunications firm—earning almost $40 billion in revenue in 2013—that has been linked with Chinese government cyber intrusion, specifically through the introduction of malware. The Permanent Select Committee on Intelligence of the U.S. House of Representatives reported in 2012 that:

> Huawei . . . provide[s] a wealth of opportunities for Chinese intelligence agencies to insert malicious hardware or software implants into critical telecommunications components and systems. . . . Further, it appears that under Chinese law, . . . Huawei would be obligated to cooperate with any request by the Chinese government to use their systems or access them for malicious purposes under the guise of state security.

The potential harm to U.S. interests from this scheme was assessed as significant:

The capacity to maliciously modify or steal information from gov-
ernment and corporate entities provides China access to expensive
and time-consuming research and development that advances Chi-
na's economic place in the world. Access to U.S. telecommunications
infrastructure also allows China to engage in undetected espionage
against the United States government and private sector interests.
China's military and intelligence services, recognizing the technolog-
ical superiority of the U.S. military, are actively searching for asym-
metrical advantages that could be exploited in any future conflict
with the United States.

Even more concerning, the Permanent Select Committee reported that
Huawei had connections with the PLA unit conducting cyber attacks
on U.S. interests:

The Committee also received internal Huawei documentation from for-
mer Huawei employees showing that Huawei provides special network
services to an entity the employee believes to be an elite cyber-warfare
unit within the PLA. The documents appear authentic and official
Huawei material, and the former employee stated that he received the
material as a Huawei employee.

As if that was not enough, the U.S.-China Economic and Security
Review Commission reported to Congress that Huawei was engaged
in espionage against the United States:

During an interview with the Australian Financial Review *in July*
2013, former director of the Central Intelligence Agency and NSA, Gen-
eral Michael Hayden (Retd.), confirmed and augmented the HPSCI's
findings regarding Huawei. When asked to verify whether he believed
"it is reasonable to assume that hard evidence exists that Huawei

has engaged in espionage on behalf of the Chinese state," General Hayden said, "Yes, that's right." He then added, "At a minimum, Huawei would have shared with the Chinese state intimate and extensive knowledge of the foreign telecommunications systems it is involved with. I think that goes without saying."

Wedderburn was not employed directly by Huawei. And we found no evidence that Wedderburn was personally aware of Huawei's involvement in cyber espionage. But the episode demonstrated the pernicious nature of Chinese cyber intrusion; it is coming at the United States from all directions.

In the end, Wedderburn bought a dozen software titles from Xiang Li, totaling $1.51 million in value.

Date	Program	Retail Value
September 3, 2008	Ansoft Designer 3.5	$25,000
September 11, 2008	Agilent Advanced Design System 2008	$229,000
September 11, 2008	ModelSim SE 6.3d	$19,000
September 20, 2008	Ansoft HFSS 10	$200,000
September 20, 2008	Ansoft SIwave 3.0	$10,000
September 21, 2008	Ansoft Nexxim	$25,000
September 16, 2009	Agilent SystemVue 2009.05	$45,000
September 16, 2009	OPNET Modeler 14.0	$25,000
September 16, 2009	Matlab R2009b	$130,000
September 22, 2009	Satellite Tool Kit 8.1	$150,000
October 25, 2010	COMSOL Multiphysics 4.0	$185,000
November 19, 2010	Autodesk Inventor 2011	$8,000

We charged Wedderburn with conspiring with Xiang Li to commit criminal copyright infringement, and he entered a guilty plea on April 18, 2012.

Xiang Li's two best American customers had been brought to the bar of the court. The question now was, what would the court make of all this?

13 | SLAYING THE DRAGON

I WAS A PRETTY GOOD DEFENSIVE END by the time I was a senior in high school. But it didn't start out that way. In my freshman year, Coach Gaylord Quandt was giving me a try at middle linebacker. He stood nearby, hands on his knees, watching me intently. This was my big chance. The quarterback barked out signals from a Power-I formation as I watched the offensive linemen for any hint of where the ball was going. When the ball was snapped, I could see the play form: it was a draw, coming right toward me. This was my moment: I was going to be the Dick Butkus of San Rafael High; the fullback would never forget this day. I dug in my cleats and prepared to deliver a legendary blow.

The fullback probably does still remember that day because he was absolutely destroyed. But not by me. By a kid named Kyle playing outside linebacker to my right. He too saw the play form. The difference between Kyle and me is that he didn't dig in his cleats and prepare to deliver the blow; he ran forward from his position and delivered the blow. Coach Quandt put his arm around me as we both admired Kyle's work.

"Good hit," said Coach.

"Yes, sir," I said.

"Came all the way from over there to make that hit, didn't he?"

"Yes, sir."

"What did we learn?"

"Don't wait," I said.

"Go to the play, son," said Coach. "Don't wait for the play to come to you."

Forgive the football analogy, but there are lessons in sports, and this is one of them: go to the play.

Generally speaking, the government doesn't do that. Instead, it waits for fast food to be delivered—fast food in the form of easy, small cases. This is why prosecutors are under constant pressure from United States Attorneys to prosecute rural mail carriers and small-time drug dealers and payroll tax violators. But law enforcement is a zero-sum game, and every hour spent feeding on fast food is an hour lost by not going to the play.

I often told young prosecutors to get out from behind their desks because they weren't likely to find any criminals there. It was my way of saying, Go to the play. Transnational criminals like Xiang Li don't set up shop in convenient locations to await arrest. They are in China for a reason, and it is difficult to get them to leave. It is true that some will never leave, but that's no reason not to try. In the case of Xiang Li, we tried and it worked.

As 2013 arrived, Xiang Li was sitting in the Federal Detention Center in Philadelphia, having meekly admitted guilt, awaiting sentencing. His top American customers, Best and Wedderburn, also awaited sentencing. All the cases were assigned to Leonard P. Stark, a young judge without much experience. But he did have two things going for him: a high intelligence quotient and a strong work ethic. No cyber case of this magnitude had ever been brought in the District of Delaware; in fact, no cyber case of this magnitude had ever been brought in any district. So Judge Stark was in uncharted waters; he could do anything he desired with the defendants. If we failed to make our point with the judge, Xiang Li might get what he wanted: an immediate return trip home to China.

The sentencing of Wronald Scott Best on March 18, 2013, was a warm-up for Xiang Li's sentencing. Best's position at sentencing boiled down to: What he did is no big deal; piracy is just part of modern life, and who can be surprised when someone buys a software product for pennies on the dollar? No one was really harmed, Best contended, because Best never would have paid retail prices for these products, so there were no lost sales. In short, it's not so much that Best was involved in criminal cyber piracy; it's more like he was a really good shopper.

Our position differed somewhat. Well, entirely. We contended that theft is theft; that buying a stolen car is not acceptable even if it's a good deal. We emphasized the broad effects of Best's crimes in economic terms, quoting the U.S. Department of Commerce's report on intellectual property:

> *Innovation—the process through which new ideas are generated and successfully introduced in the marketplace—is a primary driver of U.S. economic growth and national competitiveness. . . . The granting and protection of intellectual property rights is vital to promoting innovation and creativity and is an essential element of our free enterprise, market-based system.*

Best's trafficking in cracked software involved not only stolen property but also stolen ideas. U.S. companies spent billions of dollars to develop sophisticated, industrial-grade software only to have it pilfered by Chinese and Russian cybercriminals, who then released it into the "wilds" of the Internet, ending up who-knows-where being used for who-knows-what. Best's case illustrated both sides of the technology proliferation equation. On the supply side of the equation, he was the one releasing MPD's software into the "wilds" of the Internet by providing it to Russian Cracker, and assisting Xiang Li by providing detailed installation instructions. On the demand side of the equation, as a consumer, Best used stolen, cracked software to design and manufacture products for the military and law enforcement, without payment to the companies that created the software in the first place.

The National Intellectual Property Rights Coordination Center estimates that online piracy "currently accounts for between 6.5 and 12 percent of the total value of infringing goods" and estimates the value of online piracy as reaching $240 billion globally by 2015. The CRACK99 operation alone, from which Best purchased $609,000 worth of pirated software, was responsible for illegally distributing software valued at over $100 million in just over two years. For many of the companies involved in the CRACK99 caper, the stolen software amounted to what Ed McAndrew aptly called "digital crown jewels."

We let Judge Stark know about the pernicious second-order effects of cracked software: the introduction of malware that can compromise the integrity and security of data, which in turn can lead to the malfunctioning of computer operations, fraud, and cyber espionage. The malfunctioning of the cracked software was a particular concern in Best's case because of the nature of his work. We contended that his use of cracked software put MPD's products at risk, although we did not allege that they had malfunctioned.

Best fought back. He claimed he bought the software just because he was "curious" about it. This of course flew in the face of his admissions to Brendan Cullen: that he used the illegally obtained software in connection with his employment at MPD, including his work on redesigning the cathode for the Black Hawk helicopter. He also claimed that he was forced to buy the cracked software because MPD refused to purchase it for him. This was untrue: MPD officials told us they had a program under which employees could request the purchase of software needed to perform company work, and that Best made only one such request—and not for the software at issue in the prosecution.

We made the most of Best's e-mails. He wasn't just trolling the Internet looking for cheap, cracked software. He was—again in Ed McAndrew's words—"an acolyte of software piracy." Best's e-mails demonstrated that he was an enthusiastic member of a global cracking team, supplying written instructions on how to install cracked software products, and encouraging his compatriot Russian Cracker to "feel free to use this Installation Procedure document for distribution to others who need to know how to install the code."

There were a number of other factors at work in the sentencing that were unrelated to the seriousness of the offense, including Best's lack of criminal history. Judge Stark took them all into account and rejected Best's plea for a probationary sentence. He also rejected our request for three years in prison and gave Best one year instead.

What did this mean for us in terms of predicting an outcome for Xiang Li, who was scheduled for sentencing in a matter of months?* On the one hand, the judge rejected Best's categorical minimization of the crime and sentenced him to prison. On the other hand, he didn't give him as much time as we wanted. On balance, based on the record of Delaware's district court in meting out light sentences in white-collar cases, I was satisfied with the result. While one year is quite a bit shorter than three years, it is one year in prison, something few of us would like to experience.

The question now was, what would the judge make of Xiang Li?

When the time came for Xiang Li's sentencing, on June 11, 2013,

---

* Cosburn Wedderburn wouldn't be sentenced until September 4, 2013, after Xiang Li's sentencing, by which time I had retired from the government. Wedderburn received a probationary sentence after the judge granted him credit for assisting the government's investigation of Xiang Li. Randall Chase, "Ex-NASA Engineer Gets Probation in Software Piracy," AP: The Big Story, September 4, 2013, at http://bigstory.ap.org/article/ex-nasa-engineer-gets-probation-software-piracy.

we were surprised to hear Xiang Li's lawyer making many of the arguments Best had made. Viewed from my perspective—given that Best did not receive the probationary sentence he had sought—the Best sentencing demonstrated that minimizing the crime was not the optimal approach. But Xiang Li's lawyer had a different point of view. Xiang Li had been in custody for two years by the time of his sentencing hearing. If the court imposed a sentence on Xiang Li twice that imposed on Best, it would equal time served. That would amount to a ticket home to China.

And, sure enough, that is exactly what Xiang Li's lawyer asked for: time served. He claimed that we were exaggerating the seriousness of his offense by using the value of the software stolen: over $100 million. Xiang Li didn't get anything like $100 million in criminal proceeds, said his lawyer, so this number should be ignored. Instead, he proposed a loss figure of $2.5 million. We countered with an analogy to the Hope Diamond. We asked Judge Stark to imagine that Xiang Li had stolen the Hope Diamond, which was insured in 2011 for $250 million, and sold it for $25. What is the nature of the crime: the theft of a $25 rock or the theft of the $250 million Hope Diamond? We contended the latter was the right answer.

One unfortunate fact about a sentencing hearing is that the judge does not necessarily address in detail each and every argument made; there simply isn't time. So you rarely get the satisfaction of a judge pounding on the bench, exclaiming, "That Hope Diamond bit really puts it in perspective, and you, sir, are the victor!" Instead, the judge sits impassively, staring at you indifferently, like he would rather be somewhere else. So, my enthusiasm for it notwithstanding, I don't really know how far that analogy actually got us.

But generally speaking, judges don't like defendants who minimize. And this was a classic case of minimizing. Not only did Xiang Li claim the $100 million loss figure was exaggerated, he also had the brass to contend he should get a time-served sentence because cyber theft of American intellectual property is culturally acceptable in China. Xiang Li had been interviewed by the probation office prior to sentencing, and had explained his conduct thus:

> *I was learning about computer software. There were forums online. Many people were interested in acquiring certain software, and many people put it online for free. In Chinese culture, sometimes this is "fine and normal" and sometimes people don't look at it as a violation.*

Xiang Li added that software piracy was "prevalent" in China, opining that "probably ten million people in China are doing things illegally with software." It was the old everyone-is-doing-it defense, which I well remembered from elementary school.

In the sentencing memo we filed prior to the hearing, we conceded the point that cyber theft is prevalent in China, quoting from a *New York Times* article:

> *The culture of hacking in China is not confined to top-secret military compounds where hackers carry out orders to pilfer data from foreign governments and corporations. Hacking thrives across official, corporate and criminal worlds. Whether it is used to break into private networks, track online dissent back to its course or to steal trade secrets, hacking is openly discussed and even promoted at trade shows, inside university classrooms and on Internet forums.*

We pointed the judge to a report estimating China's illegal software market as reaching $9 billion in 2011, out of a total market of nearly $12 billion, thus setting a piracy rate of 77 percent. Where we differed with Xiang Li was in our contention that the prevalence of Chinese cyber theft was no reason to condone it.

Of course, Xiang Li well understood that his cyber piracy activities, prevalent or not, were illegal, as demonstrated by his e-mails. We

provided these to the court as well as the "cease and desist" demands
he received from software manufacturers, such as this one:

> *You are illegally selling an old version of TraumaCad on your website.*
> *You are ordered to cease and desist and to immediately remove the*
> *product from your website. Failure to comply will result in full prosecu-*
> *tion through the United States Department of Justice, Computer Crime*
> *& Intellectual Property [Section].*

When Robert had asked him in Saipan about receiving such notices,
Xiang Li had said he simply deleted them.

Prior to the sentencing, we also directed the court's attention to
the powerful nature of the software Xiang Li trafficked. We focused
on STK in particular, given the many nefarious potential uses by an
adversary of the United States. We let AGI do the talking by providing
the court with an AGI videotape explaining the many military and
intelligence uses of STK. The video showed how STK allows the military to engage in "battlespace management" by creating "the ability to fuse geospatial intelligence with real-time operations to provide
decision-makers with the opportunity to comprehensively understand
the activities of friendly, hostile and neutral forces." STK software
supports the "mission planning, real-time operations, and post-mis-
sion analysis necessary to maintain decision superiority" in battle.

We also provided the court with an AGI video of STK Simulation
of the Intercontinental Missile Defense System, contending that it was
difficult to perceive a legitimate reason for a person outside the U.S.
military or intelligence sectors to require such software. Particularly
disconcerting was the fact that Xiang Li obtained the STK software as
part of an international cybercrime organization. Once hacked and
cracked, the software was available to anyone in the world, to use for
any purpose.

Paradoxically, of course, the cracked software often came back to the United States. We reminded Judge Stark of the case of Best—as if he needed reminding—who obtained ten pirated software programs from Xiang Li worth $609,000. Unsurprisingly, we gave particular emphasis to the fact that Best used this software in military applications, including the radar system employed in the presidential helicopter, Marine One. Likewise, Cosburn Wedderburn, the NASA engineer who bought twelve cracked software programs from Xiang Li, risked the exposure of NASA's network to infection by malware.

I had been wondering which Xiang Li would show up for the sentencing hearing. Would it be the enthusiastic and upbeat Xiang Li, or the sullen and vanquished Xiang Li? The earnest Xiang Li who had explained his side of the story to Brendan Cullen on Saipan, or the dark and angry Xiang Li who ultimately refused to cooperate in the United States?

The answer was not revealed until Xiang Li was given a chance to speak to the court. A humble and beseeching Xiang Li held up his hands in supplication as he asked for mercy:

I didn't [have] . . . an evil intention to violate the law in the United States. All I hope is to be able to return to China to reunite with my family. I believe if I have to stay a long time in the jail in the United States, my family will fall apart. I will only see a broken family. My wife and my kids, they will be hurt. I'm sorry. I'm not, not a bad person.

Xiang Li's plea was sincere. And there is something seriously wrong with you if a plaintive invocation of children suffering doesn't touch you just a little bit. Xiang Li was counting on that chord resonating with the judge, and played it hard.

At sentencing, Xiang Li barely resembled the disconsolate brooder we had encountered in proffer sessions. He appeared to have moved past all that, evidently deciding to play every card, as demonstrated by his direct appeal to Brendan Cullen: "Brendan can prove I'm not,

not a bad person. I'm an honest person. I want Brendan to be able to speak for me, please."

This was an unusual move; defendants do not ordinarily call on the government to speak on their behalf, particularly when they did not cooperate. I had to wonder what was motivating Xiang Li. I was reminded of the initial hearing on Saipan when he kept looking at Brendan and me at the counsel table. Xiang Li must have felt a strong bond with Brendan, which made me wonder—and not for the first time—why Xiang Li did not elect to cooperate.

Brendan turned to me with an expression of concern as Xiang Li stood staring at us. I told him, *sotto voce*, "You won't be doing that." As if to confirm it, Judge Stark intervened: "Mr. Li, this is your time to speak. Do you have anything else you want to say?"

Xiang Li summed up thus: "I believe everyone in their life would have a chance to make a mistake. . . . I didn't really hurting any real person, nor any real corporation. . . . I just wish the Court will give me a lighter sentence and give me a second chance." Xiang Li stood blinking for a minute and then said, "That's all, your honor."

I was given an opportunity to respond. I started out by reminding the court that Xiang Li "presents to this Court as the biggest cyber-criminal in terms of copyright infringement ever prosecuted. The scale is something we're asking the Court to consider." I also asked the court "to consider that . . . the defendant enabled [the] software to flow without restriction throughout the world, including to places where it cannot legally be transferred, and to places that are hostile to the United States."

And I couldn't let Xiang Li's remark about making a "mistake" go.

This is someone who is a very enthusiastic participant in this criminal activity. It was a sustained criminal activity. He calls it a mistake, but that makes it sound like it's shoplifting, that it was just a quick deci-

sion that he made that he regrets. This was his business. . . . This is
what he did for a living for many years until he was finally arrested.

Xiang Li stared at the floor as I spoke, shifting his weight from side to side. He seemed less than pleased.

Judge Stark was unmoved by Xiang Li's entreaty. Noting "the extensive amount of crime that the defendant was engaged in," he found, "This was nothing less than a crime spree, and it was brazen." He added that the software was "highly sophisticated" and "ended up with individuals and sometimes in countries that are not authorized to have those software materials." Judge Stark addressed head-on Xiang Li's plea to have mercy on his family:

> There is no doubt that the situation for Mr. Li and his family but par-
> ticularly for his family is quite sad. It may well be that this family will
> fall apart over the years that he will be serving the sentence I will be
> imposing, and certainly that would be regrettable. But it is ultimately
> traceable solely and entirely to the conduct of Mr. Li which brings him
> here today.

Xiang Li asked Judge Stark for mercy, but he wasn't handing out mercy that day. Instead, he sentenced Xiang Li to twelve years in prison. Xiang Li stared blankly at the judge. Recovering himself, he said a few words quietly to his lawyer, and then walked toward the deputy marshals to be taken down to the holding cell. He did not look at Brendan or Ed or me.

Judge Stark is no rubber stamp for the government. Through that long sentencing hearing, it was obvious he had carefully reviewed the voluminous submissions by both the government and the defendant. The judge had thought about Xiang Li long and hard. And then he handed out the longest sentence ever imposed in a criminal copyright prosecution. After the judge and Xiang Li left the courtroom, I shook hands with Ed, Mike, and Brendan, thanking them for a job well done. And then I walked out of the courtroom. It was my last court appearance on behalf of the government. Never again would I say, "Good afternoon, your honor. David Hall for the United States." It was a good way to finish.

. . .

We did not solve all of CRACK99's mysteries, but we did answer some questions. We were able to determine one process by which international cybercriminals obtain, crack, and distribute software via the Internet. Stolen software can get into the hands of crackers from a multitude of sources: from hackers who steal it from corporate networks, like those of Defense Contractor; from users like Best who get a trial copy and send it to confederates like Russian Cracker for cracking; and from rogue employees or distributors, my failed theory about the Maxalim rogue employee notwithstanding.

This is far from a well-defined supply chain or hierarchical procurement system. It is more like an amorphous electronic blob where relationships are anonymous and diaphanous: this fan group, that website, some dude with no name. At one level, it makes perfect sense because this is what the Internet hath wrought, for good or ill. But Xiang Li's story is also too pat, particularly when you consider the scale of the CRACK99 operation. I think there is more to it, especially in light of Xiang Li's refusal to cooperate, but I can't prove it. I would like to know if something more systematic was going on—for example, to what extent software piracy is coordinated or directed by the Chinese government.

The question of foreign government sponsorship is one the U.S. government dwells on. The answer has significant geopolitical implications and has much to do with which U.S. agency will investigate and what charges can be brought. But which is worse for the United

States: a piracy program sponsored by the Chinese government or one that is free market based? It is certainly unfavorable to U.S. national security for the considerable resources of the Chinese government to be invested in hacking and cracking U.S. technology. But is the People's Republic of China the monument to competence we assume it is? During the Cold War, there were many pictures published of the Soviet army marching flawlessly in formation, seemingly super-human in its perfection. Even the soldiers' eyesight appeared to be perfect—an important advantage in combat—given that not a single one of them was wearing eyeglasses. But how rigorous is that conclusion? Maybe they told the soldiers not to wear their glasses for picture day. It is hard to know when you are on the outside looking in.

Even if the Chinese government is as competent as feared, are nongovernmental market-based attacks better for the United States? I don't think so. They can be harder to thwart because they are numerous, highly motivated, and omnidirectional. They go after whatever they can, which ends up being pretty much everything. It might not seem like the end of the world if one software product ends up in the wrong hands, but that one technology transfer could become significant if a Chinese company uses the stolen software in connection with its penetration of U.S. communications systems on behalf of the Chinese government. Multiply that one technology-transfer scenario by thousands, and you approximate the scale of the threat. In the end, whether Chinese hacking and cracking is state sponsored or not, the "onslaught" of Chinese cyber attacks is bad for the United States.

Whatever the source of the stolen software, pirates like Xiang Li both obtain it and release it into the "wilds" of the Internet, including to the loosely organized fan groups and other web forums and online portals. Pirates like Xiang Li are middlemen—to use Xiang Li's own phrase—operating websites like CRACK99 to market and sell the cracked software to the retail market. As an added and important service, some middlemen—like Xiang Li—guide customers through the difficult process of installing the pirated software. Without this service, complex, industrial-grade software—even after being cracked— is often inoperable.

As his customers, we had seen Xiang Li perform this middleman role with skill and enthusiasm. We saw the same services rendered to Best and Wedderburn. Xiang Li was a busy businessman: between February 2008 and June 2011, Xiang Li and his customers exchanged more than twenty-five thousand e-mails relating to pirated software. In thousands of these e-mails, Xiang Li served the crucial function of guiding his customers through the installation and operation processes. He was a critical cog in the process.

The result is U.S. technology in the hands of adversaries like China. Whether or not Xiang Li was connected to the Chinese government, his acquisition of U.S. software helped fulfill China's strategic vision of technological parity with the United States. The thousands of software titles advertised on CRACK99—aerospace and aviation simulation and design, communications systems design, electromagnetic simulation, explosive simulation, intelligence analysis, precision tooling, oil field management, and manufacturing plant design—are now part of China's technology inventory.

The use to which China will put this stolen technology is anyone's guess. As the 3PLA indictment showed, the Chinese government is willing to utilize stolen trade secrets to benefit Chinese companies commercially, to the disadvantage of American businesses. As their hacking of U.S. military technology demonstrates, the Chinese are employing that as a method for upgrading their military capability at low cost. Whether the Chinese will use the stolen technologies—from hacked radar software for the F-35 stealth joint strike fighter to AGI's STK software—militarily against the United States is entirely up to the Chinese. But one thing is clear: America has lost control.

Xiang Li's case can be described with a number of superlatives: the most substantial—at over $100 million or $1 billion, depending on whether you count sales or inventory—software pirate ever convicted; the only Chinese software pirate lured from China for prosecution in the United States; the heaviest criminal copyright sentence ever imposed. For a government that loves metrics, these self-congratulatory descriptors made the case important. But beyond the backslapping, the most important result of the case was proving the concept that federal law enforcement should go to the play. Federal law enforcement has the tools to address the problem of software piracy, if it is only willing to use them. There is much more work to be done. Taking down Xiang Li and CRACK99 was a good start, but it didn't solve the problem. Given that the "national industrial policy goals in China encourage IP theft," it stands to reason that cyber pirates operating from China abound.

A necessary first step in addressing this problem is a rigorous national strategy on cyber piracy. By rigorous, I mean actionable, as opposed to white papers with the word "strategy" in the title. Law enforcement has an important role to play, but it cannot be expected to solve this problem alone; the military and the intelligence community must play their parts. Equally invested is the commercial sector, whose intellectual property is being stolen and distributed on the Internet. All stakeholders need to be involved in the solution. But they also need to be called to action.

Former members of the 9/11 Commission released a report in July 2014, on the tenth anniversary of their original report on the 9/11 attacks. The main purpose of the more recent report was to assess how much progress the United States had made in the last ten years in addressing the threat of terrorism. But they couldn't help but comment on the cyber threat:

Cyber readiness lags far behind the threat. The senior leaders with whom we spoke are uniformly alarmed by the cyber threat to the country. One former agency head said, "We are at September 10th levels in

*terms of cyber preparedness." American companies' most-sensitive pat-
ented technologies and intellectual property, U.S. universities' research
and development, and the nation's defense capabilities and critical
infrastructure, are all under cyber attack. . . . One lesson of the 9/11
story is that, as a nation, Americans did not awaken to the gravity of
the terrorist threat until it was too late. History may be repeating itself
in the cyber realm.*

The threat is manifest, and universally recognized. What is missing is will: the determination to accomplish a result even at great cost.
What is missing is the desire to go to the play.

A few months after returning from Saipan, I gave each of the
agents a vial of sand from Green Beach encased in a shadow box. I
told them how honored I was to work with such a noble and dedicated
team, and particularly in that sacred place. I noted that the United
States was not prepared for war in 1941. But that changed, and by
1942 the Marine Corps was taking the fight to the enemy, pushing
northward from Guadalcanal toward the Japanese homeland, including in 1944 the sovereign Japanese territory of Saipan.

The U.S. Marines went to the play. We can all learn something
from that.

Acknowledgments

I AM GRATEFUL to the following people:

Jenny, Elizabeth, Richard, and Rebecca, for your highly constructive criticism of previous drafts—and for making me so very proud for so long;

Mike Ronayne, Brendan Cullen, Alex Zuchman, and Ed McAndrew, for your fact-checking, and more importantly for your exemplary professionalism and dedication to duty;

Robert and Darius, for laboring courageously in anonymity;

John Malandra, for leaning forward;

Joe Motto, guardian angel;

Peter Kann and Bob Wittman, for encouraging me to publish this book;

Andrew Wylie and Jin Auh, for knowing what to do;

John Glusman, for making this book better than the one I gave you.

Thank you also to the many men and women with whom I served in the government for making me a better public servant. And thank you to all who serve still.

Notes

CHAPTER 1: PERFECT SURE

17 "A recent study reported": U.S. Department of Justice, "Attorney General Holder: Justice Dept. to Collect Data on Stops, Arrests as Part of Effort to Curb Racial Bias in Criminal Justice System," Justice News, April 28, 2014, at http://www.justice.gov/opa/pr/2014/April/14-ag-445.html. See also NAACP Criminal Justice Fact Sheet, at http://www.naacp.org/pages/criminal -justice-fact-sheet (accessed March 11, 2015): "Together, African American and Hispanics comprised 58% of all prisoners in 2008, even though African Americans and Hispanics make up approximately one quarter of the US population."

18 "The United States Attorney": *Berger v. United States*, 295 U.S. 78, 88 (1935).

21 spacecraft mission design and operations: Government Sentencing Memorandum, United States of America v. Xiang Li, Criminal Action No. 10-112-LPS, May 30, 2013 (citing AGI's STK marketing brochure), at http://www.ice .gov/doclib/news/releases/2013/130611wilmington.pdf.

21 "which sensor to task": Ibid. (citing AGI's STK "Dynamic Analysis Software" marketing brochure).

22 "Operate Effectively in Cyberspace and Space": U.S. Department of Defense, *Sustaining U.S. Global Leadership: Priorities for 21st Century Defense*, January 2012, p. 5, at http://www.defense.gov/news/defense_strategic_guidance.pdf.

CHAPTER 2: FAST FOOD

32 component that assists screenwriters: Federal Bureau of Investigation, "Working with the FBI: A Guide for Writers, Authors, and Producers," at http://

www.fbi.gov/news/stories/2008/october/a-guide-for-writers-authors-and-producers-1 (accessed March 11, 2015). See also Alana Goodman, "FBI Goes Hollywood by Showering Taxpayer Money on Conferences, Special TV Unit," *Washington Times*, April 12, 2013, at http://www.washingtontimes.com /news/2013/apr/12/fbi-goes-hollywood-showering-taxpayer-cash-confere/.

34 "For example, before 2001": Jed S. Rakoff, "The Financial Crisis: Why Have No High-Level Executives Been Prosecuted?," *New York Review of Books*, January 9, 2014, at http://www.nybooks.com/articles/archives/2014/jan/09/financial -crisis-why-no-executive-prosecutions/.

36 "seems clearly to contemplate": *Dowling v. United States*, 473 U.S. 207, 216 (1985).

37 "obtained the source material": Ibid., p. 218.

CHAPTER 3: DISCORDANT NOTE

50 "Telecom and Wireless": U.S. Securities and Exchange Commission, Form 10-K, Altera Corporation, December 31, 2011, at http://www.sec.gov/Archives /edgar/data/768251/000076825112000013/altera10k12312011.htm.

50 "which consist of field-programmable gate arrays": Ibid.

52 "It is now routine": Simon Singh, *The Code Book: The Science of Secrecy from Ancient Egypt to Quantum Cryptography* (New York: Anchor Books, 1999), p. 279.

58 "Foreign economic collection": Office of the National Counterintelligence Executive (ONCIX), *Foreign Spies Stealing US Economic Secrets in Cyber Space: Report to Congress on Foreign Economic Collection and Industrial Espionage, 2009–2011*, October 2011, p. i, at http://www.ncix.gov/publications/reports /fecie_all/Foreign_Economic_Collection_2011.pdf.

58 "Chinese actors": Ibid.

59 Jobs said: "Steve Jobs Tells the Blue Box Story," video, 1994, at http://www .youtube.com/watch?v=dxCNvNwl60s.

59 range of hacking techniques: See generally U.S. Department of Homeland Security, U.S. Computer Emergency Readiness Team, "Publications," at https://www.us-cert.gov/security-publications (accessed March 11, 2015).

61 "US corporations and cyber security specialists": ONCIX, *Foreign Spies Stealing US Economic Secrets in Cyber Space*, p. 5.

61 "vast majority": Mandiant Corporation, *M-Trends 2010: The Advanced Persistent Threat* (Alexandria, Va.: Mandiant Corporation, 2010), p. 2, at https://www.mandiant.com/resources/mandiant-reports/.

61 "Over the past five years": Ibid., p. 1.

62 "The scale, operation and logistics": Ibid., p. 2.

63 "Beijing's Project 863": ONCIX, *Foreign Spies Stealing US Economic Secrets in Cyber Space*, p. 8.

63 "advanced materials and manufacturing techniques": Ibid.

63 "One focus of China's 863 Program": Ibid.

64 "Aerospace/aeronautics": Ibid.

65 "The probable-cause standard": *Maryland v. Pringle*, 540 U.S. 366, 371 (2003) (quoting *Illinois v. Gates*, 462 U.S. 213, 231 (1983)).

66 "I know it when I see it": *Jacobellis v. Ohio*, 378 U.S. 184, 197 (1964).

CHAPTER 4: HACKER, CRACKER, SATELLITE TRACKER

73 shot down a weather satellite: "China Confirms Anti-Satellite Missile Test," *Guardian*, January 23, 2007, at http://www.theguardian.com/science/2007/jan/23/spaceexploration.china.

74 "On January 11, 2007": Shirley Kan, *China's Anti-Satellite Weapon Test*, CRS Report for Congress, April 23, 2007, at http://www.fas.org/sgp/crs/row/RS 22652.pdf.

74 "It was the first such destruction": Ibid.

75 "The longer-term implications": Ibid.

76 "In 2008, the U.S. Department of Defense": Deputy Secretary of Defense William J. Lynn III, "Defending a New Domain: The Pentagon's Cyberstrategy," *Foreign Affairs* (September/October 2010), at http://www.foreignaffairs.com/articles/66552/william-j-lynn-iii/defending-a-new-domain.

76 "Over the past ten years": Ibid.

77 "One of these combatant commands": U.S. Strategic Command, "Mission," at http://www.stratcom.mil/mission/ (accessed March 11, 2015).

77 "Cyber Command has three missions": Deputy Secretary of Defense William J. Lynn III, "Defending a New Domain: The Pentagon's Cyberstrategy," *Foreign Affairs* (September/October 2010), at http://www.foreignaffairs.com/articles/66552/william-j-lynn-iii/defending-a-new-domain.

78 "a variety of partners": Ibid.

79 Just the year before: Siobhan Gorman, August Cole, and Yochi Dreazen, "Computer Spies Breach Fighter-Jet Project," *Wall Street Journal*, April 21, 2009, at http://online.wsj.com/news/articles/SB124027491029837401?mg=reno64-wsj&url=http%3A%2F%2Fonline.wsj.com%2Farticle%2FSB124027491 029837401.html.html.

79 documents called "strategic plans": U.S. Department of Justice Archives, "Publications & Documents Archive," at http://www.justice.gov/archive/index-publications.htm (accessed March 11, 2015).

88 "ANSYS Simplorer": ANSYS, "Systems & Embedded Software," at http://www.ansys.com/Products/Simulation+Technology/Systems+&+Multiphysics/Multiphysics+Enabled+Products/ANSYS+Simplorer (accessed May 22, 2013).

88 "With Simplorer": Ibid.

CHAPTER 5: THAT GIANT SUCKING SOUND

94 integral part of the U.S. economy: U.S. Department of Commerce, *Intellectual Property and the U.S. Economy: Industries in Focus*, March 2012, p. vi, at http://www.uspto.gov/news/publications/IP_Report_March_2012.pdf.

94 Commerce Department has identified: Ibid., p. vii.

95 "Intellectual property accounts": "The Role of Intellectual Property in the Economy," in *Economic Report of the President* (Washington, D.C.: U.S. Government Printing Office, 2006), p. 219, at http://www.gpo.gov/fdsys/pkg/ERP-2006/pdf/ERP-2006-chapter10.pdf.

95 "Of that [$5 trillion]": Jim Garamone, "Cybercom Chief Details Cyberspace Defense," American Forces Press Service, September 23, 2010.

95 "The ongoing cyber-thefts": Keith B. Alexander, National Security Agency, "An Introduction by General Alexander," *Next Wave*, vol. 19, no. 4 (2012).

95 2013 report: Dennis C. Blair, Jon M. Huntsman Jr., Craig R. Barrett, et al., *The IP Commission Report: The Report of the Commission on the Theft of American Intellectual Property* (Seattle: National Bureau of Asian Research, 2013), p. 9.

95 In February 2014: Bureau of Labor Statistics, "The Employment Situation–February 2014," News Release, March 7, 2104, at http://www.bls.gov/news.release/archives/empsit_03072014.pdf.

96 "uncovered 1,800 cases": U.S. Senate Committee on Armed Services, *Inquiry into Counterfeit Electronic Parts in the Department of Defense Supply Chain*, 112th Cong., 2nd sess., Report 112-167, May 21, 2012, at http://www.gpo.gov/fdsys/pkg/CRPT-112srpt167/pdf/CRPT-112srpt167.pdf.

96 Seventy percent: Ibid.

96 "the direct costs to enterprises": John F. Gantz et al., "The Dangerous World of Counterfeit and Pirated Software: How Pirated Software Can Compromise the Cybersecurity of Consumers, Enterprises, and Nations . . . and the Resultant Costs in Time and Money," IDC, White Paper No. 239751, March 2013, pp. 3–4, at http://www.computerworld.com.pt/media/2013/03/IDC030513.pdf.

96 probability of encountering malware: Ibid.

96 "'Pirated software'": Ibid., p. 1.

97 approximately 70 percent: Blair et al., *IP Commission Report*, p. 5.

97 "What has been happening": Clarke quoted in Michael A. Riley and John Walcott, "China-Backed Hacking of 760 Companies Shows Cyber Cold War," *Bloomberg Businessweek*, December 22, 2011, at http://www.businessweek.com/news/2011-12-22/china-based-hacking-of-760-companies-shows-cyber-cold-war.html.

97 American Superconductor: Michael A. Riley and Ashlee Vance, "China Corporate Espionage Boom Knocks Wind out of U.S. Companies," *Bloomberg Businessweek*, March 15, 2012, at http://www.businessweek.com/news/2012-03-15/china-corporate-espionage-boom-knocks-wind-out-of-u-dot-s-dot-companies.

97 loss of more than $800 million: U.S. Department of Justice, Office of Public Affairs, "Sinovel Corporation and Three Individuals Charged in Wisconsin with Theft of Amsc Trade Secrets," Justice News, June 27, 2013, at http://www.justice.gov/opa/pr/2013/June/13-crm-730.html.

97 Chinese hack of iBAHN: Riley and Walcott, "China-Backed Hacking."

98 30 million times: Leo Hindery Jr., "China's Latest Target in Its Trade War against American Manufacturing: The U.S. Solar Industry," *Huffington Post*, March 6, 2012, at http://www.huffingtonpost.com/leo-hindery-jr/china-solar -panels-_b_1323568.html.

98 David Yen Lee: U.S. Attorney's Office, Northern District of Illinois, "Former Paint Manufacturing Chemist Sentenced to 15 Months in Prison for Stealing Trade Secrets Valued up to $20 Million," FBI Press Release, December 8, 2010, at http://www.fbi.gov/chicago/press-releases/2010 /cg120810-1.htm.

98 Chinese national Kexue Huang: U.S. Department of Justice, Office of Public Affairs, "Chinese National Sentenced to 87 Months in Prison for Economic Espionage and Theft of Trade Secrets," Justice News, December 11, 2011, at http://www.justice.gov/opa/pr/2011/December/11-crm-1696.html.

98 "the PRC government": U.S. Attorney's Office, Northern District of California, "Former DuPont Scientist Pleads Guilty to Economic Sabotage," FBI Press Release, March 2, 2012, at http://www.fbi.gov/sanfrancisco/press -releases/2012/former-dupont-scientist-pleads-guilty-to-economic-espionage.

98 Dongfan "Greg" Chung: U.S. Department of Justice, Office of Public Affairs, "Former Boeing Engineer Convicted of Economic Espionage in Theft of Space Shuttle Secrets for China," Justice News, July 16, 2009, at http:// www.justice.gov/opa/pr/2009/July/09-nsd-688.html.

99 "National industrial policy goals": Blair et al., *IP Commission Report*, p. 3.

99 Between 1820 and 1950: Ibid., p. 9; Angus Maddison, *The World Economy: A Millennial Perspective/Historical Statistics* (OECD, 2007).

100 "all forms of trade secrets": Office of the U.S. Trade Representative, *2013 Special 301 Report*, May 2013, pp. 13, 30–38, at http://www.ustr.gov/sites /default/files/05012013%202013%20Special%20301%20Report.pdf.

100 Between 50 and 80 percent: U.S. Customs and Border Protection, "Intellectual Property Rights: Fiscal Year 2012 Seizure Statistics," Office of International Trade, 0172-0113, January 17, 2013; Blair et al., *IP Commission Report*, p. 15.

100 "By legal as well as illegal means": Blair et al. *IP Commission Report*, p. 15 (citing Patrick Blain (presentation at the 2013 Geneva Motor Show OICA Press Conference, Geneva, March 6, 2013), p. 10, at http://oica.net /wpcontent/uploads/pc-oica-geneve-2013-v3b.pdf; the International Monetary Fund's 2011 "World Economic Outlook"; and the 2030 projection from the World Bank).

100 "The F-35 data theft": Bill Gertz, "Stolen F-35 Secrets Now Showing Up in China's Stealth Fighter," *Washington Free Beacon*, March 13, 2014, at http:// freebeacon.com/national-security/stolen-f-35-secrets-now-showing-up-in -chinas-stealth-fighter/.

101 "Chinese cyber spying": Bill Gertz, "Stolen F-35 Secrets Now Showing Up in China's Stealth Fighter," FoxNews, March 13, 2014, at http://www.foxnews

.com/politics/2014/03/13/stolen-f-35-secrets-now-showing-up-in-chinas
-stealth-fighter/.

CHAPTER 6: THE LAST WAR

113 book about that caper: John Shiffman, *Operation Shakespeare: The True Story of an Elite International Sting* (New York: Simon and Schuster, 2014).

135 "Foreign states and terrorist organizations": U.S. Department of Justice, "Justice Department and Partner Agencies Launch Counter-Proliferation Initiative," Press Release, October 11, 2007, at http://www.justice.gov/opa /pr/2007/October/07_nsd_806.html.

137 eve of winter: John Schiffman, "Shadow War: Treasure Trove," *Philly .com*, at http://www.philly.com/philly/news/special_packages/20100920_ StingChapter5.html (accessed March 11, 2015).

145 HSI annual reports: U.S. Customs and Border Protection and U.S. Immigration and Customs Enforcement, Department of Homeland Security, *Intellectual Property Rights: Fiscal Year 2010 Seizure Statistics—Final Report*, January 2011, at http://www.ice.gov/doclib/news/releases/2011/110316washington. pdf; U.S. Customs and Border Protection and U.S. Immigration and Customs Enforcement, Department of Homeland Security, *Intellectual Property Rights: Fiscal Year 2011 Seizure Statistics Prepared by CBP Office of International Trade*, at http://www.ice.gov/doclib/iprcenter/pdf/ipr-fy-2011-seizure -report.pdf (accessed March 11, 2015).

CHAPTER 7: THE NEXT WAR

148 "At the very outset": Danny Russel, "Resourcing the Rebalance toward the Asia-Pacific Region," White House Blog, April 12, 2013, at http://www .whitehouse.gov/blog/2013/04/12/resourcing-rebalance-toward-asia-pacific -region.

148 "Our new focus on this region": "Remarks by President Obama to the Australian Parliament," Parliament House, Canberra, Australia, November 17, 2007, at http://www.whitehouse.gov/the-press-office/2011/11/17/remarks -president-obama-australian-parliament.

148 "My guidance is clear": Ibid.

149 report from the cybersecurity firm: Mandiant, *Apt 1: Exposing One of China's Espionage Units*, Mandiant Center Intelligence Report, at http:// intelreport.mandiant.com/ (accessed March 11, 2015); David E. Sanger, David Barboza, and Nicole Perlroth, "Chinese Army Unit Is Seen as Tied to Hacking against U.S.," *New York Times*, February 19, 2013, at http://www .nytimes.com/2013/02/19/technology/chinas-army-is-seen-as-tied-to-hacking -against-us.html?pagewanted=all&_r=0.

149 "a series of related attacks": James T. Bennett, "The Mutter Backdoor: Operation Beebus with New Targets," *FireEye*, April 17, 2013, at http://www.fireeye

.com/blog/technical/malware-research/2013/04/the-mutter-backdoor -operation-beebus-with-new-targets.html.

150 "The DoD, and its contractor base": U.S. Department of Defense, Defense Science Board, *Task Force Report: Resilient Military Systems and the Advanced Cyber Threat*, January 2013, p. 3, at http://www.acq.osd.mil/dsb/reports /ResilientMilitarySystems.CyberThreat.pdf.

150 "Should the United States": Ibid., p. 5.

150 China and Russia: Ibid., p. 2.

151 "Degradation or severing of communication links": Ibid., p. 25.

151 "The cyber threat is serious": Ibid., p. 31.

152 "There is a huge future threat": Elaine Wilson, "Cyber Attacks Present 'Huge' Threat, Gates Says," DoD News, November 17, 2010, http://www.defense .gov/news/newsarticle.aspx?id=61729.

152 "most significant breach": Deputy Secretary of Defense William J. Lynn III, "Defending a New Domain: The Pentagon's Cyberstrategy," *Foreign Affairs* (September/October 2010), at http://www.foreignaffairs.com/articles/66552 /william-j-lynn-iii/defending-a-new-domain.

152 "the proliferation of dangerous technology": "CIA Director Leon E. Panetta Unveils Blueprint for Agency's Future," CIA, News & Information, April 26, 2010, at https://www.cia.gov/news-information/press-releases-statements /press-release-2010/director-panetta-unveils-blueprint-for-agency-future.html.

153 journalists from Bloomberg news: Michael Riley and Ben Elgin, "China's Cyberspies Outwit Model for Bond's Q," *Bloomberg*, May 2, 2013, at http://www .bloomberg.com/news/2013-05-01/china-cyberspies-outwit-u-s-stealing -military-secrets.html. See also Matthew J. Schwartz, "China Tied to 3-Year Hack of Defense Contractor," *InformationWeek Dark Reading*, May 2, 2013, at http://www.darkreading.com/risk-management/china-tied-to-3-year-hack-of -defense-contractor/d/d-id/1109795.

153 "We found traces": Riley and Elgin, "China's Cyberspies Outwit Model for Bond's Q."

153 "Among the victims": Ibid.

154 "God forbid": Ibid.

154 QinetiQ was awarded: Ibid.

154 "In 2012, numerous computer systems": Office of the Secretary of Defense, *Annual Report to Congress: Military and Security Developments Involving the People's Republic of China 2013* (Washington, D.C.: U.S. Department of Defense, May 2013), p. 36. See also Chapter 2, Section 2: "China's Cyber Activities," in *2013 Report to Congress of the U.S.-China Economic and Security Review Commission* (Washington, D.C.: U.S. Government Printing Office, 2013), p. 245, at http://origin.www.uscc.gov/Annual_Reports/2013 -annual-report-congress.

154 "full-spectrum global mobility solutions": U.S. Transportation Command, "About USTRANSCOM," at http://www.transcom.mil/about/whatIs.cfm (accessed March 11, 2015).

155 "The committee's inquiry identified": *Inquiry into Cyber Intrusions Affecting U.S. Transportation Command Contractors: Report of the Committee on Armed Services, United States Senate* (Washington, D.C.: U.S. Government Printing Office, 2014), p. i, at http://www.armed-services.senate.gov/download/sasc_cyberreport_09-17-14.

155 "Of the at least 20": Ibid.

155 "Chinese military analysts": Ibid., p. ii.

155 "Cyber espionage": James A. Lewis, "Factors Influencing the Advancement of China's Military Technology," testimony before the U.S.-China Economic and Security Review Commission, January 30, 2014.

156 "In these circumstances": George F. Keenan (under pseudonym "X"), "The Sources of Soviet Conduct," *Foreign Affairs* (July 1947), at http://www.foreignaffairs.com/articles/23331/x/the-sources-of-soviet-conduct.

157 "During the past three decades": U.S. Department of Defense, *Annual Report on Military Power of Iran*, April 2012, at http://www.fas.org/man/eprint/dod-iran.pdf.

157 "We assess Iran": James R. Clapper, "Statement for the Record: Worldwide Threat Assessment of the US Intelligence Community," Senate Select Committee on Intelligence, March 12, 2013, at http://www.dni.gov/index.php/newsroom/testimonies/203-congressional-testimonies-2014/1015-statement-for-the-record-worldwide-threat-assessment-of-the-us-intelligence-community-sasc.

158 publishes a brag sheet: U.S. Department of Justice, "Summary of Major U.S. Export Enforcement, Economic Espionage, Trade Secret and Embargo-Related Criminal Cases (January 2008 to the Present: Updated March 26, 2014)," March 2014, at http://www.pmddtc.state.gov/compliance/documents/OngoingExportCaseFactSheet.pdf.

159 thirty thousand arrests each year: Drug Enforcement Administration, Statistics & Facts, at http://www.justice.gov/dea/resource-center/statistics.shtml#arrests (accessed March 11, 2015).

160 "We believe": Mandiant, *APT1: Exposing One of China's Cyber Espionage Units*, Mandiant Intelligence Center Report, pp. 7–8, at http://intelreport.mandiant.com/.

161 "The co-conspirators used e-mail": 3PLA Indictment, paragraphs 11–12.

162 "While a Pennsylvania nuclear power plant": Ibid., paragraphs 2–3.

162 "For example, one": Ibid., paragraph 4.

163 3PLA stole: Ibid., paragraphs 6a, 19–24.

163 "hostnames and descriptions": Ibid., paragraphs 6c, 28–30.

164 "On at least four occasions": Ibid., paragraph 35.

164 "a huge victory for American workers": USW press release, January 30, 2012.

164 "China's predatory": USW statement.

164 "sensitive, non-public, and deliberative information": 3PLA Indictment, paragraphs 36–37; 6e.

165 "it would be a travesty": Ibid., paragraph 38.

165 another alleged victim of 3PLA: Ibid., paragraphs 6f, 40–42.

CHAPTER 8: ONWARD THROUGH THE FOG

172 "There's two issues": "Transcript: Gen. Martin Dempsey at Disrupting Defense," Atlantic Council, May 14, 2014, at http://www.atlanticcouncil.org /news/transcripts/transcript-gen-martin-dempsey-at-disrupting-defense.

172 "Given that cyberspace permeates": "White House Staff, Obama's Top Military Adviser Disagree on Cyber Security," *Inside Cybersecurity*, at http:// insidecybersecurity.com/Cyber-Daily-News/Daily-News/white-house-staff -obamas-top-military-adviser-disagree-on-cyber-strategy/menu-id-1075 .html?s=dn (accessed March 11, 2015).

173 On March 13, 2013: United States Attorney's Office, Western District of Washington, "United States Attorney Durkan Testifies before the House Judiciary Subcommittee regarding Cybercrime Prosecutions," News, March 13, 2013, at http://www.justice.gov/usao/waw/press/2013/March/cyber.html.

175 "In his 2013 State of the Union Address": U.S. Department of Justice, "Attorney General Eric Holder Speaks at the Press Conference Announcing U.S. Charges against Five Chinese Military Hackers for Cyber Espionage," Justice News, May 19, 2014, at http://www.justice.gov/iso/opa/ag/speeches/2014 /ag-speech-140519.html.

176 "American policy in this area": Dennis C. Blair, Jon M. Huntsman Jr., Craig R. Barrett, et al., *The IP Commission Report: The Report of the Commission on the Theft of American Intellectual Property* (Seattle: National Bureau of Asian Research, 2013), p. 10.

177 Supreme Court case about Elvis Presley: *Dowling v. United States*, 473 U.S. 207, 216 (1985).

178 "obtained the source material": Ibid., p. 218.

178 "the world's leading": Keysight Technologies, "Advanced Design System (ADS)," at http://www.home.agilent.com/en/pc-1297113/advanced-design -system-ads?&cc=US&lc=eng (accessed May 22, 2013).

179 "solutions for structural": Siemens, "NX for Simulation," at http://www.plm .automation.siemens.com/en_us/products/nx/for-simulation/ (accessed May 22, 2013).

179 "the ability to effectively collect": Hexagon Metrology, "Enterprise Metrology Solutions," at http://hexagonmetrology.us/products/software/pc-dmis -ems?gclid=CNXjz7vUmr8CFa4WMgoddG8AYw (accessed May 22, 2013).

179 GibbsCAM 2009: GibbsCAM, "What is GibbsCAM?" at http://www .gibbscam.com/solutions/what-gibbscam (accessed May 22, 2013).

179 "For example, turning, milling": U.S. Department of Commerce, *Critical Technology Assessment: Five Axis Simultaneous Control Machine Tools*, July 2009, p. 5, at https://www.bis.doc.gov/index.php/forms-documents/doc_ view/138-five-axis-simultaneous-control-machine-tools.

CHAPTER 9: PLEASANT SURPRISES

192 Viktor Bout: For more on Bout, see Douglas Farah and Stephen Braun, *Merchant of Death: Money, Guns, Planes, and the Man Who Makes War Possible* (New York: John Wiley, 2007).

192 "Between November 2007 and March 2008": U.S. Department of Justice, "International Arms Dealer Viktor Bout Convicted in New York of Terrorism Crimes," Justice News, November 2, 2011, at http://www.justice.gov/opa/pr/2011/November/11-ag-1442.html.

193 "One of the judges": Thomas Fuller, "Thailand Blocks Extradition of an Arms Dealing Suspect," *New York Times*, August 11, 2009, at http://www.nytimes.com/2009/08/12/world/asia/12bangkok.html?_r=0.

194 Spain sold the island: "Northern Mariana Islands," *Encyclopaedia Britannica*, at http://www.britannica.com/EBchecked/topic/419782/Northern-Mariana-Islands/273250/German-and-Japanese-control (accessed November 1, 2014).

197 "A lure involves": *United States Attorneys' Manual* (USAM), section 9-15.630.

CHAPTER 10: UNPLEASANT SURPRISES

209 origins of the case: *United States v. Bond*, 581 F.3d 128, 131-132 (3d Cir. 2009), *rev'd*, 131 S. Ct. 2355, 180 L. Ed. 2d 269 (2011); Jeremy Roebuck, "U.S. Supreme Court: Not Terrorism, Just a Love Triangle," *Philadelphia Inquirer*, June 4, 2004, at http://articles.philly.com/2014-06-04/news/50304534_1_clifford-bond-myrlinda-haynes-chemical-weapon.

209 Vowing revenge: Roebuck, "U.S. Supreme Court."

209 "surprising": *Bond v. United States*, 134 S.Ct. 2077, 2087 (2014).

209 charged Bond: Prosecutors also charged Carol Anne Bond with mail theft in violation of 18 U.S.C. § 1708. Ibid.

209 Chemical Weapons Convention Implementation Act: 18 U.S.C. § 229 et seq.

209 "verify the destruction": Organisation for the Prohibition of Chemical Weapons, *Brief History of the Treaty*, at http://www.opcw.org/news-publications/publications/history-of-the-chemical-weapons-convention/ (last accessed June 22, 2014).

209 Convention targets: Ibid.; see also Organisation for the Prohibition of Chemical Weapons, *Demilitarisation*, at http://www.opcw.org/our-work/demilitarisation/ (last accessed June 25, 2014).

209 "Bond's prosecution": *United States v. Bond*, 681 F.3d 149, 166 (3d Cir. 2012), *rev'd*, 134 S.Ct. 2077 (2014).

210 "reluctant to ignore": Ibid.

210 federal crime: David L. Hall and Ivana Greco, "Bond: Defining the Limits of Federal Police Power," *New York Law Journal*, January 12, 2015, at http://www.newyorklawjournal.com/in-focus/id=1202714332059/Bond-Defining-the-Limits-of-Federal-Police-Power?mcode=1202617377215&curindex=5.

211 "I believe this is": Kindlund quoted in Edward Wong, "Hacking U.S. Secrets, China Pushes for Drones," *New York Times*, September 20, 2013, at http://www.nytimes.com/2013/09/21/world/asia/hacking-us-secrets-china-pushes-for-drones.html.

211 "The military significance": U.S. Department of Defense, Defense Science Board, *Task Force Report: The Role of Autonomy in DoD Systems*, July 2012, p. 71, at http://www.acq.osd.mil/dsb/reports/AutonomyReport.pdf.

212 "In a worrisome trend": Ibid., p. 69.

212 "In this defense-dominated field": Ibid., p. 71.

212 Chinese plan on using: Eugene K. Chow, "What Would a U.S.-China War Look Like?," *Week*, January 1, 2014, at http://theweek.com/article/index/254400/what-would-a-us-china-war-look-like; Matt Schiavenza, "How a Tiny Island Chain Explains the China-Japan Dispute," *Atlantic*, December 4, 2013, at http://www.theatlantic.com/china/archive/2013/12/how-a-tiny-island-chain-explains-the-china-japan-dispute/281995/; Agence France-Presse, "Japan Scrambles Jets for Drone near Disputed Islands," *DefenseNews*, September 9, 2013, at http://www.defensenews.com/apps/pbcs.dll/article?AID=/201309091337/DEFREG03/309090019.

CHAPTER 11: DEAD OR ALIVE

227 "National industrial policy goals": Dennis C. Blair, Jon M. Huntsman Jr., Craig R. Barrett, et al., *The IP Commission Report: The Report of the Commission on the Theft of American Intellectual Property* (Seattle: National Bureau of Asian Research, 2013), p. 3.

241 "the culmination of many years": CST—Computer Simulation Technology, "CST Studio Suite," at https://www.cst.com/Products/CSTS2 (accessed May 22, 2013).

241 "the leading edge tool": Ibid.

241 "tool for the design": Ibid.

241 "has been developed": Ibid.

241 "allows engineers and designers": Government Sentencing Memorandum, United States of America v. Xiang Li, Criminal Action No. 10-112-LPS, May 30, 2013 (quoting ANSYS website), at http://www.ice.gov/doclib/news/releases/2013/130611wilmington.pdf.

241 National Institute of Standards and Technology: NIST Engineering Laboratory, "Questions and Answers about the NIST WTC 7 Investigation," September 19, 2011 (updated June 27, 2012), at http://www.nist.gov/el/disasterstudies/wtc/faqs_wtc7.cfm.

242 "the industry-standard simulation tool": Government Sentencing Memorandum, United States of America v. Xiang Li (quoting ANSYS website).

244 his guilty plea: United States Attorney's Office, District of Delaware, "Chinese Citizen Pleads Guilty to $100 Million Internet Software Piracy Con-

spiracy," News, January 8, 2013, at http://www.justice.gov/usao/de/news
/2013/01-08.html.

244 "This is the way": T. S. Eliot, *The Hollow Men* (1925).

CHAPTER 12: THE AMERICANS

246 the 9/11 attacks: *The 9/11 Commission Report*, pp. 157, 168, at http://www
.9-11commission.gov/report/911Report_Ch5.htm. See also *The 9/11 Commission Report*, pp. 226–27, 246–47, 273–75, and 347 (use of flight simulators).

251 "ANSYS Maxwell": ANSYS, "Systems & Embedded Software," at http://www
.ansys.com/Products/Simulation+Technology/Systems+&+Multiphysics
/Multiphysics+Enabled+Products/ANSYS+Maxwell (accessed May 22, 2013).

256 "infused with tones": Government's Sentencing Memorandum, United
States of America v. Best, Criminal Action No. 12-16-LPS.

257 "For info": Ibid.

259 "has been a leader": Ibid.

259 "use software only in accordance": Ibid.

260 "MPD will not tolerate": Ibid.

265 "power integrity, signal integrity": ANSYS, "ANSYS SIwave," at http://www
.ansys.com/Products/Simulation+Technology/Electronics/Signal+Integrity
/ANSYS+SIwave (accessed May 22, 2013).

268 "Huawei . . . provide[s]": *Investigative Report on the U.S. National Security
Issues Posed by Chinese Telecommunications Companies Huawei and ZTE*,
Permanent Select Committee on Intelligence, U.S. House of Representatives,
112th Cong., October 8, 2012, p. 3, at http://intelligence.house.gov/sites
/intelligence.house.gov/files/documents/Huawei-ZTE%20Investigative%20
Report%20%28FINAL%29.pdf.

269 "The capacity to maliciously modify": Ibid.

269 "The Committee also received": Ibid., p. 34.

269 "During an interview": *2013 Report to Congress of the U.S.-China Economic
and Security Review Commission*, 113th Cong., 1st Sess., November 2013, p.
250, at http://www.gpo.gov/fdsys/pkg/GPO-USCC-2013/html/GPO-USCC
-2013-1.htm.

271 We charged Wedderburn: United States Attorney's Office, District of Delaware, "Chinese Nationals Charged with Software Piracy and Exporting
Technology to China; American Customer Pleads Guilty to CopyRight
Infringement Conspiracy," News, April 18, 2012, at http://www.justice.gov
/usao/de/news/2012/Li%20Press%20Release.html.

CHAPTER 13: SLAYING THE DRAGON

275 sentencing of Wronald Scott Best: Office of the United States Intellectual Property Enforcement Coordinator, *Intellectual Property Spotlight*, March/April

2013, at http://www.whitehouse.gov/sites/default/files/omb/IPEC/spotlight /ipec_spotlight_mar_apr_2013.pdf; U.S. Immigration and Customs Enforcement, "Chief Scientist of Government Contractor Sentenced for Conspiring to Obtain Pirated Software from Chinese and Russian Cyber Criminals," Intellectual Property Rights, News Releases, March 18, 2013, at http://www .ice.gov/news/releases/1303/130318wilmington.htm.

275 "Innovation": Economics and Statistics Administration and the U.S. Patent and Trademark Office, U.S. Department of Commerce, *Intellectual Property and the U.S. Economy: Industries in Focus*, March 2012, at http://www.esa.doc .gov/sites/default/files/reports/documents/ipandtheuseconomyindustries infocus.pdf.

276 "currently accounts": National Intellectual Property Rights Coordination Center, *Intellectual Property Rights Violations: A Report on Threats to United States Interests at Home and Abroad*, November 2011, p. 18, at http://www .iprcenter.gov/reports/ipr-center-reports/IPR%20Center%20Threat%20Report %20and%20Survey.pdf/view.

276 Best fought back: Government Sentencing Memorandum, United States of America v. Best, Criminal Action No. 12-16-LPS.

277 gave Best one year: U.S. Immigration and Customs Enforcement, "Chief Scientist of Government Contractor Sentenced."

278 what Xiang Li's lawyer asked for: Sentencing Transcript at 14, United States of America v. Xiang Li, Criminal Action No. 10-112-LPS.

279 "I was learning about computer software": Government Sentencing Memorandum, United States of America v. Xiang Li, Criminal Action No. 10-112-LPS, May 30, 2013, at http://www.ice.gov/doclib/news/releases/2013/130611 wilmington.pdf.

279 "The culture of hacking in China": Edward Wong, "Hackers Find China Is Land of Opportunity," *New York Times*, May 22, 2013, at http://www.nytimes .com/2013/05/23/world/asia/in-china-hacking-has-widespread-acceptance .html?pagewanted=all&_r=1&. See also Ellen Nakashima, "Confidential Report Lists U.S. Weapons System Designs Compromised by Chinese Cyberspies," *Washington Post*, May 27, 2013, at http://www.washington post.com/world/national-security/confidential-report-lists-us-weapons -system-designs-compromised-by-chinese-cyberspies/2013/05/27/a42c3e1c -c2dd-11e2-8c3b-0b5e9247e8ca_story.html.

279 report estimating China's illegal software market: Business Software Alliance, *Shadow Market: 2011 BSA Global Software Piracy Study*, May 2012, p. 6, at http://portal.bas.org/globalpiracy2011/downloads/study_pdf/2011_BSA _Piracy_Study-Standard.pdf. However, the largest market for pirated software is the United States, with a commercial value of pirated software approaching $10 billion. Ibid., p. 6.

280 "You are illegally selling": Government Sentencing Memorandum, United States of America v. Xiang Li.

280 We let AGI do the talking: Ibid.

281 "I didn't [have]": Sentencing Transcript at 46, United States of America v. Xiang Li.

281 "Brendan can prove": Ibid.

282 "Mr. Li": Ibid., pp. 46–47.

282 "I believe everyone": Ibid., pp. 47–48.

282 "presents to this Court": Ibid., pp. 48–49.

282 "This is someone": Ibid., p. 54.

283 "the extensive amount of crime": Ibid., pp. 58–59.

283 "highly sophisticated": Ibid., pp. 57, 60.

283 "There is no doubt": Ibid., pp. 61–62.

283 twelve years in prison: United States Attorney's Office, District of Delaware, "Chinese Citizen Sentenced to 12 Years in Prison for Cyber-Theft and Piracy of Over $100 Million in Sensitive Software and Proprietary Data," News, June 11, 2013, at http://www.justice.gov/usao/de/news/2013/06-11.html.

287 "national industrial policy goals": Dennis C. Blair, Jon M. Huntsman Jr., Craig R. Barrett, et al., *The IP Commission Report: The Report of the Commission on the Theft of American Intellectual Property* (Seattle: National Bureau of Asian Research, 2013), p. 3.

287 "cyber readiness": Former 9/11 Commission Members, *Today's Rising Terrorist Threat and the Danger to the United States: Reflections on the Tenth Anniversary of The 9/11 Commission Report*, Bipartisan Policy Center, July 2014, p. 7, at http://bipartisanpolicy.org/wp-content/uploads/sites/default/files/files/%20BPC%209-11%20Commission.pdf.

About the Author

DAVID LOCKE HALL retired in 2013 from the U.S. Department of Justice after serving for twenty-three years as an Assistant United States Attorney. He received the Director's Award for Superior Performance, the DHS/ICE Excellence in Law Enforcement Award, the DHS/ICE International Achievement Award, among other commendations. He served in the U.S. Navy Reserve for thirty years as an intelligence officer, commanding three intelligence units and retiring at the rank of captain. He was awarded the Defense Meritorious Service Medal, Meritorious Service Medal, Joint Service Commendation Medal, and the Navy and Marine Corps Commendation Medal. He is married and has three children and two grandchildren.